SNIFFING THE COAST

An Acadian Voyage

SNIFFING THE COAST

An Acadian Voyage

Silver Donald Cameron

Macmillan Canada
Toronto

Canadian Cataloguing in Publication Data

Cameron, Silver Donald, date.
  Sniffing the coast: an Acadian voyage

ISBN 0-7715-9014-8

1. Saint Lawrence, Gulf of—Description and travel.
2. Sailing—Saint Lawrence, Gulf of.   I. Title

FC2004.C35 1993   917.1′096344   C93-094310-4
F1050.C35 1993

1   2   3   4   5   FP   97   96   95   94   93

Cover design by David Montle

Front and back cover photos by Silver Donald Cameron

Macmillan Canada wishes to thank the Canada Council and
the Ontario Ministry of Culture and Communications for
supporting its publishing program.

Macmillan Canada
A Division of Canada Publishing Corporation
Toronto, Ontario, Canada

Printed in Canada

*For Farley
and Claire*

*with admiration
and gratitude*

When one has good wine,
A graceful junk,
And a maiden's love,
Why envy the immortal gods?
                    —Li T'si Po (705–762 AD)

"Nice? It's the only *thing," said the Water Rat*
solemnly, as he leant forward for his stroke.
"Believe me, my young friend, there is nothing—
absolutely nothing—half so much worth doing as
simply messing about in boats. . . .
    "In or out of 'em, it doesn't matter. Nothing
seems really to matter, that's the charm of it.
Whether you get away, or whether you don't;
whether you arrive at your destination or whether
you reach somewhere else, or whether you never get
anywhere at all, you're always busy, and you never
do anything in particular; and when you've done it
there's always something else to do, and you can do
it if you like, but you'd much better not."
    —Kenneth Grahame, *The Wind in the Willows*

CONTENTS

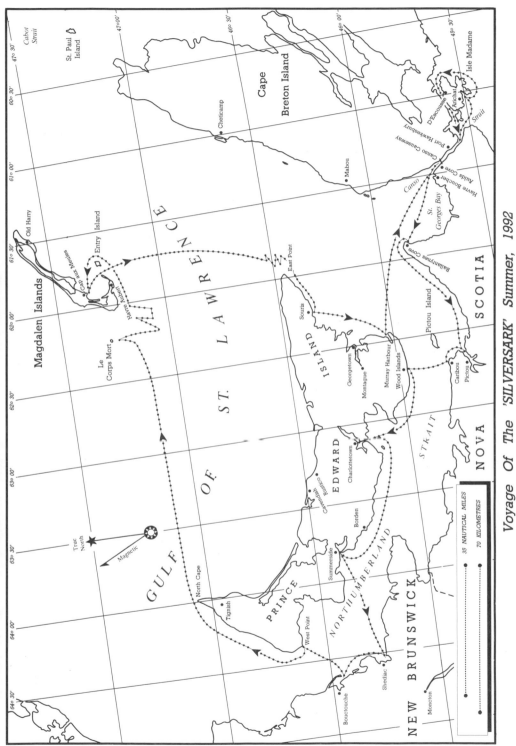

Voyage Of The 'SILVERSARK' Summer, 1992

Graham Mackay, LRIS, Summerside, PEI

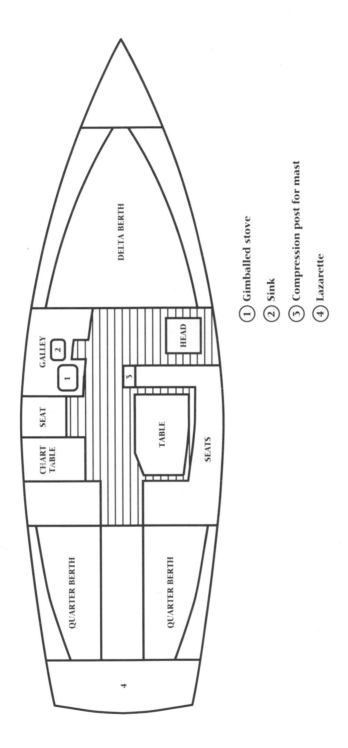

DELTA BERTH

GALLEY

SEAT

CHART TABLE

TABLE

SEATS

HEAD

QUARTER BERTH

QUARTER BERTH

1 Gimballed stove
2 Sink
3 Compression post for mast
4 Lazarette

**Accommodations Plan of *Silversark*/Modified
Bruce Roberts *Adventure 25***

BAT

AND

SEABAG

I groped my way on deck at six o'clock in the dingy morning, yawning and muzzy-headed, with a mug of coffee for each of us. The sea and the sky met in a smudge at the horizon, grey on grey. Dirty foam spilled down the face of the waves. The wind had eased. With only her two headsails set, *Silversark* was shuffling along at three knots, like an old man in carpet slippers.

"We're going to have to get the main on her," said Lulu, sipping her coffee. "Be careful. There's a bat in the sail somewhere."

"A *bat* in the sail?"

"It was flying around the boat at daybreak," said Lulu. "I guess it was looking for someplace to rest. There wasn't anywhere else for it to go."

1

I looked around. In the middle of the Gulf of St. Lawrence, halfway between western Prince Edward Island and the Magdalen Islands, *Silversark* was alone on the sullen water. The coast was not just hiding behind the mist: it was far behind us. The nearest land was forty miles away.

"I kept saying to it, *Get under the dinghy, you silly bat,*" said Lulu. "But it just kept flying around, and then eventually it crawled into the folds of the mainsail."

We drank our coffee. *Silversark* had made a dozen miles during Lulu's three-hour watch, but the wind had been steadily dropping. I put the mugs below. I cast off the ties on the mainsail and crept forward to the base of the mast. I reclipped my safety harness and hauled the big burgundy sail aloft.

Yanked from a sound sleep, the bat flew clear, fluttering like a self-propelled leaf in the wind and squeaking indignantly.

"I know how you feel," I muttered.

Back in the cockpit, I took the tiller. Lulu sat with me for a companionable moment, watching the bat swoop and circle and cling briefly to the mainsail. She yawned. Her shoulders were weary from three hours of steering, her eyes gritty from staring at the dimly lit compass on the main bulkhead. She yawned once more, then leaned over and kissed me fleetingly.

"God nat," she said, in one of the Danish phrases which have insinuated themselves into our family's language.

"Sov godt," I answered. *Sleep well.*

With one eye on the compass, I watched her through the open companionway hatch as she peeled off her safety harness, her floater jacket, her oilskin trousers, her sweater, her seaboots. Yawning again, she squirmed into a quarterberth and dropped into sleep like a stone.

I glanced up. The bat swooped behind the mainsail and landed on the leech, the trailing edge of the sail—a bright-eyed fragment of brown fur with leathery, humanoid fingers. In the slackening wind, the boat rolled to windward, relaxing the tension on the sail. It rolled back again, snapping the sail taut. The bat clung to her perch, tiny black hands clutching the smooth red Dacron. The boat rolled back and forth. The sail jerked once more, throwing the bat into the air.

She flew forward into the slot between the jib and the jumbo staysail. She fluttered up the mast and back to the leech of the mainsail. The sail flexed and snapped, flexed and snapped. The bat catapulted into the air.

"The dinghy," I said. "Go under the dinghy. Nothing's going to bother you there."

Once more she circled the boat, scanning the rigging, the sails, the hull. Then she swooped behind the sails and disappeared.

I stood up, squinted behind the sails and looked around the boat. No bat. She had simply vanished.

I sat down again, looked at the compass, hauled on the tiller to bring the compass card swinging back to 108 degrees magnetic. I scanned the horizon. Nothing but crumpled grey water and a ground-glass sky.

No bat. No Lulu. Not a living creature in sight but myself.

Suddenly I felt small and cold and lonely.

Every cruise has its defining moment, a freeze-frame which encapsulates the essence of the whole venture: a moment of delight, of terror, of insight or wonder. The moment lingers in memory, gaining lustre as it recedes in time. It is not necessarily typical of the cruise: it may even stand out for its distinctiveness. A two-week cruise in fog and driving rain may be defined forever by a single sunbaked afternoon with a pod of dolphins or a perfect landfall on a low, anonymous coast.

For years, Lulu and I had been visited by fantasies of offshore cruising—days and nights at sea capped by arrival at an exotic destination: Nassau, Lisbon, Suva. But it took eight and a half years to build the boat, and by then our son, Mark, was in school and we had other responsibilities. So we had trimmed our ambitions, cruising the waters of the Maritimes rather than the oceans of the world. For Nassau, read North Sydney; for Lisbon, Louisbourg.

It was not a terrible sacrifice: yachts come from all over the world to enjoy the beauty and character of this coast. This summer we were making a 600-mile voyage from our home on the Atlantic coast of Cape Breton through the Strait of Canso into the Gulf of St. Lawrence. We had traversed Northumberland Strait, touching the coasts of Nova Scotia, New Brunswick and Prince Edward Island, and then sailed down the west coast of the Island before jumping off for the Magdalen Islands, a crescent of red bluffs and sandbars in the middle of the Gulf. Later we would turn south to the eastern end of PEI and home. This was our longest passage ever: 143 miles non-stop from West Point, PEI, to Cap-aux-Meules in the Magdalens. When I came on watch, we had been 24 hours at sea, and we were still 40 miles short of the Magdalens, 50 miles short of Cap-aux-Meules.

I scanned the horizon again. Forty miles off or four hundred, the sea would be like this: wide, featureless, lonely. *The lonely sea and the sky.*

The notion of voyaging stretches back into the soft-focused reaches of a bookish child's vivid imagination. Perhaps it came from that wonderful writer Arthur Ransome, whose novels of youth and sailing I can still read with pleasure. Whatever its source, it seems always to have been there.

In 1949, when I was just entering junior high, I somehow acquired a bag made of khaki duck with a drawstring threaded through brass grommets, the sort of bag one might use to pack sails or a tent or a sleeping bag. I loved that bag, and throughout my school years, I carried loose-leaf binders and textbooks in it. When we travelled, it held my clothing. Eventually the bottom wore out, and my mother reinforced it from inside with a disc of blue denim from a pair of terminated jeans. Some people called it a school-bag, and my mother called it a dunnage bag. I usually called it a duffle bag, but I was affronted when someone else called it a gunny sack. I knew perfectly well that it was none of those things, but I was unwilling to speak its real name aloud.

It was my seabag.

Now this was very odd, because I had no real intention of doing anything so useful or interesting as going to sea; I was going to be a lawyer. Nor was there any salt water in my blood: both of my parents were educators, one of my grandfathers was a Manitoba farmer, and the other had been an accountant with the Canadian Pacific Railroad. True, we lived in Vancouver, but for many Vancouverites the city is only peripherally a port. From my little bedroom at the top of the house near Dunbar Street, you could just barely see the water. In 1945, when the freighter *Greenhill Park* exploded and burned at a downtown wharf, I saw the plume of smoke from my window, and on foggy nights I drifted off to sleep listening to the distant foghorns—*BEEEE-ohh! BEEEE—ohh!* But that was as close as we got to the harbour.

There was no harbour at South Beach, in Washington State, where we spent our summers. The shore was just a wide swath of sandbars below a crescent of bluffs which rose like a wedge from west to east. The beach was splendid, but it was completely exposed to the 15-mile fetch of the Strait of Georgia, and when the wind blew hard a big surf broke on the beach. The falling tide exposed a quarter-mile of sand—lovely to run on, superb for sand castles, but not much of a place for a sailboat.

Walter Largaud had a fishing boat there—a thirty-foot gill-netter with a flaring bow and a stern wheelhouse. I thought Largaud an old man, but he was probably in his fifties. Unusual though she was, his boat was the most graceful small fishing vessel I had ever seen. My father and I met Walter on the beach once, and my father complimented him on her.

"She has lovely lines," said my father, shading his eyes as he gazed out to where the boat tossed at her mooring. I cringed. My father was a professor of education, an indoor man who wore vests and watch-chains: what did he know about boats and "lines"? But he was quite right, and Walter Largaud smiled with satisfaction.

Largaud's farm was at the west end of the beach, where the sand and the bluffs disappeared and the beach became a steep bank of cobbles. East of the house, right on the cobbles, was a boneyard of boats a whole line-up of locally-built workboats which had outlived their usefulness: seine-boat skiffs, dories, gill-netters with stepped cabins, reef boats.

One small double-ended gill-netter on Largaud's beach was called *Gypsy*. She was weathered and dry and brittle-looking, probably rotten, but she was complete—engine, shaft, steering wheel, everything. She had wooden berths, primitive cupboards and an old stove in her snug fo'c'sle. Who needed more? Mired in the melodramas of youth, I dreamed of reviving her: caulking, painting, reconditioning the engine and taking her back to sea. She would be my home. Nobody else seemed to have any use for *Gypsy*—or, I thought, for me. Two rejects. Together we would show them. I used to climb aboard and stand in her wheelhouse, my eyes narrowed, the wooden spokes of *Gypsy*'s wheel in my hand, steering with a certain casual elegance earned through years of experience on the seven seas. Gazing landward from her wheelhouse, I steered her over the beach and the hayfields

beyond, wishing they had towed her up by the stern, with her
bow still pointing out to sea.

The only boat we ever owned was a ten-foot plywood rowboat
for which my father paid $40. It was a fine little boat, light and
strong and beautifully balanced, with plenty of freeboard, safe
even in strong winds and thundering surf. Once, when I was
about 12, I pulled her down off a log, and a broken branch on
another log punched a hole in her bottom. My father came to
inspect the damage. I was crying bitterly, sick with remorse.
How could I have done such a stupid thing?

"I love that boat more than anything in the world," I sobbed.
My father looked at me in astonishment. I had just paid 65 hard-
won dollars for a new Royal Enfield three-speed bike.

"More than your new bike?" he said.

"Way more," I said. "Way, *way* more."

"We'll get it fixed," he said quietly. He put an arm around my
shoulder and gave me a short, hard squeeze, and I suddenly
knew how much I loved him. He died two years later, and I
mourn him yet.

That rowboat was the crucial resource in my first business
ventures. I had a paper route, summers only, delivering the
Vancouver Sun all along the shore. We were in the United States,
but the cottagers were all from greater Vancouver: Point Roberts
remains the only place on earth where Americans are worried
about Canadian domination. My paper route included 15 or 20
cottages at Crystal Waters Beach, right on the shore beneath the
eastward bluffs. They could not be reached by road; the only
approach was down endless flights of stairs from the parking area
high above. Rather than riding my bike to the clifftop and then
trudging up and down those stairs, I rowed to Crystal Waters and
walked along the shore. Sometimes, at high tide, I could row
close enough to throw the rolled newspapers right up on the
porches without even beaching the skiff.

My friends and brothers and I also made money from the
fishery. During the season, the waters off the point were flecked
with purse seiners—big boats from Anacortes and Tacoma which
set pouches of net around schools of salmon, drew them tight
and then brailed the fish aboard with huge dip nets. When the
seiners anchored off the beach in the evenings—and sometimes
when they were fishing—we would row out and visit. The fisher-

men were robust, genial men, lounging on deck, drinking Rainier beer and smoking Lucky Strikes and asking whether we knew any girls "that'd like to rassle a bit on the seine pile."

The salmon they caught were running towards the Fraser River to spawn and couldn't be caught with a hook and line. In my innocence I once asked a fisherman why.

"Well, my friend, look at it this way," he said. "If you were on your way to get laid, would *you* stop for a sandwich?"

They always caught some "blackmouth," salmon too small for processing but plenty big enough for supper. If a boy rowed up beside a seiner and asked, most crews would give their blackmouth away. When we had ten or twelve fish, we would row ashore and sell them for a dollar or two each to cottagers and day-trippers from Vancouver. It was the ideal business: a ready market, no operating costs, pure profit.

But a ten-foot skiff does not make a seaman. Yet I had a seabag, and—secretly—I had oilskins and seaboots, too. It pleased me to think that my high school peers believed I was wearing gumboots and slickers just like theirs. It was the perfect disguise. They were landlubbers: I was a voyager—at least in imagination. Ortega y Gasset once said something to the effect that the novelist represents the truest model of human consciousness: just as the novelist imagines a reality and strives to embody it in the shape of a book, so the human individual imagines a reality and strives to embody it in the shape of a future life.

So now I sat, forty years later, in the snug cockpit of a red-sailed 27-foot cutter, like the one in Ransome's *We Didn't Mean To Go To Sea*. I was steering towards an archipelago of sandy islands still hidden below the horizon—islands which had captured my imagination years before, but which I had never seen. They were not tropic islands, admittedly. But perhaps the destination matters less than one thinks. When you arrive, after all, the adventure is over. The joy is in the journey.

And perhaps the seabag represented not a fantasy, but a promise. That morning, in the middle of the Gulf of St. Lawrence, the promise seemed fulfilled.

THE

BREAK

OF DON

The summer started badly. A miserable spring had followed a fierce winter. From late February to April, blizzards and gales pummelled the Maritimes. Cape Breton was tantalized by some golden days in May, only to be chilled and soaked by easterly winds and spilling rain throughout June. And now it was the worst July in living memory: rainy, blustery, downright cold.

The boat was ill-trimmed, overloaded and sluggish.

The putative skipper was savouring his nervous breakdown. He had worked hard for it, he had waited a long time for it and he was not going to surrender it without a struggle.

And there was something else. Sometimes the land itself seems determined to hold you, to keep you from going to sea. This was one of those seasons.

We had sent Mark off to visit friends and family in Denmark in late June, and we planned to sail immediately thereafter. But *Silversark* herself had been neglected for two years. Her brightwork needed varnish, her bottom needed paint, her leaky portlights had to be removed and rebedded, her battery replaced, her new dinghy completed.

She was on a trailer behind the house, down by the water, and the weather had been no help at all. We raced outside to paint and varnish whenever we saw a lull in the wind and rain and fog, but there were precious few lulls.

The financial climate was similarly chilly. Writers suffer from recessions along with everyone else. As the economy shrivels, publishers and broadcasters cut budgets. Advertising shrinks, magazines fold, governments and corporations postpone or cancel projects. Life becomes a wet, draining beat to windward against choppy seas and a foul tide. Unlike Central Guaranty Trust and the Reichmanns, we stayed afloat—but it was not a pleasure cruise. Then, when the economic weather broke in May and June, I found myself whirled away to unexpected assignments and out-of-town meetings—in Halifax, in Ottawa, in Toronto, in Halifax again. Work which had been pending for months suddenly became urgent.

The days flicked by, and the boat still rested on the beach. When we finally launched her on July 1, a howling gale held her pinned to the wharf for two days. We couldn't even step the mast.

We finally cast off in mid-afternoon on July 9 and sailed to an uninhabited cove in Haddock Harbour, six miles away. Far from exulting in shiphandling and navigation, I was depressed, jittery, exhausted. The weather was still cold and raw—more like May than July. The forecast called for an overnight gale from the southeast. We set the plow anchor and launched *Marksark*, the new dinghy. I rowed two hundred feet to windward, dragging the nylon anchor rode behind me, and dropped a second anchor. By the time we finished supper, my eyes were closing.

"Coffee?" asked Lulu.

"No, thanks," I said. "I'm going to bed."

I crept forward into the delta berth and slept for thirteen and a half hours.

The southeast gale did arrive, late in the evening. Far away, I heard and felt *Silversark* sheering and diving about her mooring—but it was Lulu who woke to the sound of the wind shrieking in the rigging, Lulu who pulled on her boots and went out to check the anchor rodes for chafe, Lulu who noted the bearings of points ashore to be sure the anchors weren't dragging.

I woke in mid-morning, still groggy and slow. The gale had blown itself out, and a brisk westerly was chasing banks of cloud across a high, broken sky.

"If we had left at first light, what would we have seen?" Lulu asked.

"What?"

"The break of Don."

We got underway at noon. The sky had cleared, but the wind was indecisive, puffing up and then fading away. Each time it slackened we looked at one another, asking whether we should change the working jib for the large and unfamiliar genoa, a recent acquisition designed to keep us moving in light winds. But whenever we decided to set the genny, the breeze piped up, the boat heeled and we quickly changed our minds.

The wind came in more firmly as we tacked out the western end of Lennox Passage, giving us a fast reach across the mouth of Inhabitants Bay and into the high, narrow corridor of Canso Strait. Then it died away altogether, and we did set the genny, delighting in the way it caught the gossamer remnant of the breeze and pulled the boat along. A big ketch came floating down towards us, flying the Stars and Stripes. On the transom we read *Bright Star*, Portsmouth.

Two years ago, on this same stretch of water, we had seen a deer swimming from Bear Head, on the Cape Breton side, towards the mainland, much to Mark's delight. Remembering that, we missed him very much: we had never sailed more than a day or so without him, and the boat suddenly felt empty.

"We better get that genny down," said Lulu, glancing forward. "Look at that sky!"

A heavy black curtain of cloud hung low over the water. I scampered forward, dropped the genoa and lashed it against the lifelines just as the first gusts came flying down the Strait. Suddenly *Silversark* was working hard to windward in an erratic rising wind. Under the mainsail and the jumbo, we tacked past Point Tupper's mothballed oil refinery, the power plant, the pulp mill. Beyond the gypsum dock, the waterfront of Port Hawkesbury appeared to starboard, and we quickly took stock. It was nearly five o'clock, and the next reasonable harbour was dead to windward, beyond the Canso Causeway. Time to quit.

A big ocean-going tug, *Point Viking*, was tied up on the face of Port Hawkesbury's government wharf. We tacked farther up the shore, lowered the jumbo and scooted downwind under the mainsail alone. Once abreast of the wharf, Lulu turned sharply, steering straight for the tug's stern, while I went to the bow with a dock line. At the last moment, I called "Port!" As Lulu swung *Silversark* up into the wind, I scrambled aboard the tug and tied the line. Lulu tossed me the stern line, sprang to the mast and lowered the sail. *Silversark* bobbed alongside, looking like a model boat beside the massive tug.

"Good afternoon," said a startled voice. A crewman had opened a wheelhouse door behind me. "You'd be better off over there," he said, pointing towards a more sheltered berth.

"We'll warp her over," I said.

"Give me your stern line," he said, and together we moved the little black cutter into the lee of the wharf.

We walked on the wharf, came back to the boat, had a drink and ate some chili.

"Coffee?" asked Lulu, as I cleared away the dishes.

"No, thanks," I said. "I'm going to bed."

"What, again? It's only eight-thirty."

I crept forward into the delta berth and fell asleep. The wind rose to near-gale force again, howling and shrieking across the wharf, coating our deck with sand and grit. At two-thirty Lulu woke and checked the mooring lines, then burrowed back under the blankets.

BRaaAA!

The evil roar drowned out the screeching of the wind. It was four-thirty. I dressed and climbed on the wharf. The racket was coming from the high-revving diesel in the pilot boat *Sharon Alexander*, moored directly behind us. I walked up the dock, past *Keyanow*, a graceful fibreglass ketch from Toronto, which was due to depart at daybreak for Bermuda and the Virgin Islands. A radar reflector on a fishing boat cast a shadow shaped like an arrowhead on the water, dark against the amber gleam from the street lights.

BRAAA!

Sharon Alexander moved out into the Strait, heading north to pick up a pilot from a bulk carrier loaded with aggregates and bound for Prince Edward Island. Despite the roaring wind I could hear her all the way to the Causeway, three miles away. I went back to bed and slept till nine-thirty.

We walked to the post office, two blocks away, to buy some stamps. The land still held us: I had a batch of bills to pay. Oddly enough, the sun was shining and the day was warm. *Keyanow* was gone, but a young woman was working on a steel pinky schooner, *Caper's Dream*, in a cradle on the beach.

In mid-recession—and seen from the waterfront—Port Hawkesbury looked whipped and beaten. At the head of the wharf, a sign nailed to the Strait of Canso Yacht Club advertised showers and charts, but *Keyanow*'s crew stayed at the wharf for several days and never saw the clubhouse open. Behind it lay the railway tracks—the CNR main line from Sydney to Truro—and the VIA Rail station. But there is no passenger rail service in Cape Breton now, and the station was abandoned, grass growing through the cracks on the platform.

A freight train hooted across the harbour near the bankrupt shipyard. The sound should have made me nostalgic; instead it made me angry. With VIA gone, CN proposed to sell the entire Truro-to-Sydney main line to a U.S. short-haul operator—a prelude, perhaps, to shutting it down altogether, like the vanished branch lines from Port Hawkesbury to St. Peter's and Inverness. But the main line helps sustain two paper-mills, a steel plant, several coal-mines and various smaller industries.

Granville Street, once Port Hawkesbury's main thoroughfare, has been supplanted by Reeves Street and Sydney Road, up the top of the hill on what was originally a by-pass. The town's businesses have moved into three shopping malls and a light industrial park, draining the life-blood from the old downtown. A three-year recession intensified the bleeding.

Now Granville Street looked like a ghost town. The gas pumps had been removed from Eddie Fougere's Irving station, and the building was boarded up. Weeds rioted in vacant lots. Empty storefronts stared blankly at the empty street. On a group of dilapidated buildings, once the home of the weekly *Scotia Sun*, a For Sale sign flapped in the breeze. Canso Realties, who had the listing, is owned by Jim Marchand, a dapper little Acadian from Louisdale, near D'Escousse.

"The trouble with Port Hawkesbury," Marchand once told me, "is this industrial boom-and-bust cycle. An industry starts up and you make a little money for a year or so, and then you lose money for the next three years. Then you have a good year, but you only make enough to keep you alive through the next downturn. You never get ahead.

"Antigonish is only 30 miles away, but it's completely different. They've got a university, and some government offices, and a stable farming community, and they make a little money every year. Well, a person can build a business that way. You can't do that here."

Two buildings bravely bucked Granville Street's decline: the Royal Bank and the law firm of Evans, MacIsaac, Macmillan— our own lawyers, now housed in a dignified new building designed by Mark's godfather, Halifax architect Syd Dumaresq. The bank is probably 20 years old, and its Universal Anonymous Modern design already looks vulgar and dated. Dumaresq's design, by contrast, derives from the indigenous architecture of the province. It looks as though it has been there for a century, and it will look just as good when it *has* been there for a century.

While I wrote cheques, Lulu wrote a letter to Mark, then in Copenhagen but bound for Jutland.

"Funny feeling," she said. "I've never been apart from him long enough to have to write him a letter."

It was mid-afternoon by the time we sailed out into the Strait, tacking up towards the Causeway in the cool, sunny afternoon. The night's strong westerly winds had lost their teeth, and the encircling shores gave us a pleasant beat in smooth water. By the time we reached the entrance to the lock, the wind was so light that Lulu simply pointed *Silversark* at a berth, and I stepped ashore with a line.

The bridge swung open, and two locksmen came to help with the lines. We walked along the canal wall with the lines, towing *Silversark* while Lulu stayed aboard to steer.

"Last sailboat we towed through was in hard shape," said one. "He got caught in a freak storm up north of PEI and capsized.

Rolled right over. It was late in the year—October, I think. After that his engine didn't work."

"He was sailing alone, " said his mate. "Lost everything. Lost his radio, and his diaries, and his log."

This story began to sound familiar.

"John," I said to Lulu. "It sounds like J.J. Vincent's buddy John. We heard something about that." I turned to the locksman. "Little fellow, almost frail-looking? Snowy white hair?"

"That's him. Said that was the end for him: he wasn't going sailing any more after that."

John Struchinsky was a retired Navy man, perhaps five feet three inches tall, slight, a bachelor with a faint European accent, courtly and reserved. He must have been well into his 60s, perhaps in his 70s, when we met him. His boat was a mature 25-foot wooden Vertue, a classic English design, and he had covered thousands of ocean miles with her, usually alone. I remember taking his lines at the D'Escousse wharf one summer morning.

"Welcome back," I said. "How are you?"

"Tired," he said. "It was a long trip from Halifax." He had just sailed 200 miles, non-stop and alone, in 55 hours. It was sad to think he had swallowed the anchor—and that it had been a desperate experience that had persuaded him to do so.

The lock gates closed behind us and opened in front of us. We towed the boat out along the seawall into the Gulf of St. Lawrence, raised the sails and cast off. The two locksmen stood on the wall for a long time, watching.

We sailed away smartly, heading for Havre Boucher, seven miles away. In the light head wind, it would take us three hours or more to get there. We might just make it in daylight.

But as we tacked back and forth between Cape Breton and the Guysborough County shore on the mainland, the wind slackened by almost imperceptible degrees. We didn't want to know about it. Each time the wind decreased, we told ourselves it was only a lull. It would come up again. We would make Havre Boucher soon after dark. Well, maybe an hour after dark. Welllll . . .

Two miles from the Causeway, just before sunset, the wind diminished to a western whisper. It was time to face reality.

"We're not going to make Havre Boucher," I said, looking glumly at the smooth water. "Let's go back to Auld's Cove."

"The wind might come up again," said Lulu tentatively, voicing her hopes rather than her judgement.

"We can't go to windward in this," I said. "We'll wind up spending the night becalmed out here. It's too deep to anchor and too narrow to drift. Neither one of us will get a decent night's sleep. Auld's Cove is downwind. We could turn around and tie up there."

"We've been sailing three days," she said, "and we're only half an hour's drive from home."

"It's been all westerly winds," I said. "Makes it slow going if you're heading west."

"We've got to get moving. We've got a long way to go."

"We won't get any farther by jilling around here all night."

The sails flapped lazily. The wind had eased again. *Silversark* swung her head even farther off the course.

"Oh, all right," said Lulu unhappily. She put the tiller up, turned the boat downwind and eased out the mainsail. I went forward and poled out the genoa with the boat-hook. With her two largest sails spread on either side, *Silversark* tiptoed down the Strait of Canso like a student ballerina holding out the hem of her skirt with her fingertips.

I took the helm while Lulu went below to start supper. The Strait narrows like a funnel as it approaches the Canso Causeway. We were on the mainland side, near the Cove Motel, with its dining room overlooking the Strait. Children were playing outside the motel, and a solitary traveller sat on a rock at the water's edge. Beyond the motel, the Trans-Canada Highway descends to the shore past service stations, diners, a lobster pound, a vegetable market. That string of roadside enterprises is Auld's Cove.

The apparent wind is always gentler when you sail before it, but this dying breeze had become exceptionally gentle. Lulu came back on deck and looked over the stern to see whether we were moving. We were not.

Silversark weighs three tons. Without an engine, in a calm, we have a simple choice: wait or row.

While the pressure cooker hissed, we rowed slowly in front of the motel, skirting the rocks, then turned into the short channel between the sandbars, which leads to the sturdy little wharf. Two men and a woman stood on the wharf, ready to take our lines.

"Quite an engine you got there," said one of the men.

"Cheap on gas," I said, grinning.

Small fishing boats, many of them deckless, clustered around the wharf. The two-month lobster season was just over, and traps were piled all over the wharf. The people were shy and helpful. One of the men wore a black Western shirt with white piping, slicked-down hair and long sideburns: Johnny Cash, but with the almost fierce diffidence I associate with Guysborough County people.

We towed *Silversark* in behind the dock, sheltered from any wind that might arise in the night.

The biggest thing in Auld's Cove is the Irving Big Stop, which caters to truckers: service station, restaurant, convenience store and truck wash all in one. The Big Stop's management is probably almost unaware that the wharf exists—but it actually provides much of what a cruising sailor needs. After supper I took a shower there: $4.75 for a washcloth, a huge fluffy towel, soap, a shaving kit and a clean tiled shower room. After three days aboard the boat, it seemed a bargain.

We went back to the boat. I slept for 11 hours.

Lulu stayed up, writing in her diary. Just before going to bed, she went on deck and saw that I had put out bow and stern lines, but no spring lines to hold the boat from ranging backwards and forwards.

"He's a lot better than he was, but still not top of the line yet," she wrote in her diary. "I'll have to still be on the watch until he's totally over this. I saw a *skate* while I was putting out springs. Beautiful night."

FATHER TERESA

AND THE

URGENT

CONVERSATION

We woke early, looked out at the Strait
and went back to bed. Under dirty grey clouds, the wind was
blowing briskly from the west, sending ranks of white-capped
grey waves rolling down on the Causeway. And the fog was
stealing in. We waited till mid-morning for the weather to clear,
and then headed out against the leftover chop, clawing our way
westward into the wind. It was slow, hard going.

The wind was still dropping—and *Silversark* needs plenty of
sail power to punch her way to windward in a chop. That meant a
sail change, a new procedure for us; until this summer we had
only the three working sails, all of them permanently in place.

Other boats have better systems and more experienced crews,
but I was slow and clumsy at sail changing and reluctant to do it
at all. It meant crouching on a narrow, plunging bow, rising and

falling ten or twelve feet in the waves while I hanked the new sail on the wire forestay below the old one and led its sheets back to the cockpit. Then I would pull down the old sail and unhank it, snap the halyard on the new sail and haul away. If I had done everything right, the sail would rise smoothly to the masthead— rightside up—with the sheets running fair to the cockpit. The genoa made an enormous difference. With it, *Silversark* would muscle her way steadily upwind; without it, we would butt and wallow and go nowhere.

So I hauled the sail bag to the bow and set the genoa. *Silversark* heeled over and started to sail, working her way out of the gradually widening funnel of the Strait. Slowly, yard by yard, like football players, we gained ground to the westward. First down, ten to go . . .

The wind came up: the genoa came down. The wind went down: the genoa went up. We found ourselves almost becalmed right under the round white tower of the North Canso light-house. A fiberglass sloop sailed through our lee and vanished out into St. George's Bay, the next body of water we had to cross.

"Probably motorsailing," I said, through gritted teeth.

Lulu cast a skeptical eye over *Silversark*'s rig.

"I don't know what's wrong with this boat. She just isn't moving."

Wind up, genny down. Wind down, genny up. Wind up . . .

"What's wrong with this bloody boat?" I snarled.

"That other fellow must be motorsailing," said Lulu.

We tacked out into the bay in the teeth of a rising westerly. The seas were piling up again, and I was on the bow for yet another sail change. *Silversark* was rolling heavily, going nowhere. Sail hanks jammed. I slipped on the slick Dacron sailcloth. I swore steadily and furiously.

"We'll be a year getting across this bloody bay," I snarled.

"Frig it. Let's go into Havre Boucher," said Lulu. "You're in no shape to—"

"*Don't go blaming it on me! There's nothing wrong with me!*"

"We're *going* into Havre Boucher."

Oh.

We eased the sails. *Silversark* took off, loping across the mouth of the Strait and into smooth water behind the low western point of the harbour. We dropped the mainsail, swung around the bow of a fishing boat, came smoothly alongside the face of the wharf, tied up, tidied up and called Ralph DeCoste, a partner of mine in a small software company.

Ralph arrived with a brace of small boys. Ralph is normally surrounded by children. He has six of his own, and they have cousins by the dozens. He is in his late 30s, a sandy-haired, genial man whose down-home cracker-barrel manner masks a shrewd, realistic mind and a droll sense of humour. We all climbed into the family mini-van and drove to his home in East Tracadie, one of the Acadian enclaves which dot the shore of the bay.

On a summer evening, East Tracadie—the east bank of the Tracadie River estuary—is an image of rural tranquillity. Hay-fields slope gently down to the winding channels and wooded islands. The DeCostes have a substantial garden, a big woodpile, a workshop in the barn, a pert little dory-like sailboat, which Ralph never has time to use, and a storey-and-a-half house full of computers, music and children.

Beyond their house, the Barrio Road winds through small farms and old houses till it ends at the shore of the bay. On the bluff, looking out to the unbroken horizon, is a wood-heated, oil-lit cabin. Ralph and Maria built it. It is their summer cottage. It is all of a mile from their home.

Ralph grew up in the house across the Barrio Road from his present home, and half the families on the road are brothers, cousins, aunts and uncles. His family is so meshed into his community that he probably finds it hard to tell where the one ends and the other begins. We sat on the sun-deck in the evening sunlight. While the kids played scrub baseball, we soaked up the good humour and sanity of the household while Sam, the baby of the family, crawled around beaming at everyone.

"I never saw a more cheerful baby," Lulu said.

"Can't read," said Ralph.

"What?"

"He can't read," said Ralph. "That's why he's cheerful. If he could read he'd know how desperate awful everything is, and he'd be just as miserable as the rest of us."

Ralph was having trouble with a government official who was "helping" us.

"I called that fella," Ralph reported. "I told him we didn't

think his behaviour was in accordance with Section 224 of the
How To Get Along in Life Act. He didn't seem unduly distressed
about it. Said he'd call me back later. I told him I'd be incon-
ceivably happy to converse with him again at absolutely any
moment of his choosing.

"But look, there's somethin' we got to consider about the way
we're tryin' to sell this software.

"You see this knuckle on my right hand, right where the little
finger joins the palm? See how much lower it is than the other
knuckles? Now that's something they call a boxer's break, and it
comes from hittin' things that don't yield, like people's heads.
Doing that ain't good for the joints in your hands.

"Know how I got that? One time I was trying to get a cow out
of the pasture, and the foolish thing wouldn't come. We went
through a lot of animated conversation and a fair bit of pushin'
and pullin', and I finally got a little exasperated and I hauled off
and slugged her in the face. Didn't faze her in the least. She
didn't even have the common decency to *blink*. Which isn't any
great wonder, because it turns out the place that I slugged her is
backed up by two inches of solid bone.

"I looked at my hand, and I knew right away it was broken,
and I said, Ralph, b'y, there's a lesson for you: *Don't be slugging
bloody cows.*

"Now are we ever gonna sell this software outside the Maritimes without puttin' a whole pile of cash into marketing? You
know, are we beatin' on a bloody cow?"

"Good question," I said.

"Great product," Ralph said. "But we need some investment.
We don't need any more boxer breaks."

We crept out of Havre Boucher on the faint promise of a breeze,
inching our way through the entrance like a big black snail and
on to the Cape Jack light buoy. We set a course for Cape George,
at the western limit of the bay.

In the middle of the bay, the breeze died.

Sometime I would love to explore St. George's Bay: its narrow
tidal rivers, its beaches, the pretty cathedral town of Antigonish.
Although Antigonish is actually on the mainland, its diocese
includes all of Cape Breton, and its Scottish Catholic university,

St. Francis Xavier, has always been a natural first stop for Cape Bretoners pursuing a higher education. One of its graduates, indeed, was at the helm of *Silversark*. Right now, however, I had no desire to explore the bay: I wanted to get to the westward. But the gods of the wind were otherwise engaged.

From where we lay immobilized on the water, I could just make out the wharf at Bayfield. If we were going to be stuck somewhere in this bay, it would have been much nicer to be stuck at the wharf at Bayfield, where we could walk up to visit Luke Batdorf and Teresa MacNeil. Luke is an occasional consultant, a community development activist, an investor and a passionate patron of the arts. Teresa heads the famous Extension Department of St. Francis Xavier University.

Teresa has been involved with co-operatives and adult education all her life, as extension fieldworker, educational television producer and professor of adult education. She grew up in the hamlet of Johnstown, Cape Breton, where her father was a farmer, bus driver and general storekeeper—a typical rural Maritimer, hammering together a livelihood from whatever scrap material came to hand. He and his wife, Elizabeth MacAdam, were also devout co-op supporters, and all their children, says Teresa, "have a tremendous need to be in some line of service. It's *in the bone.* Growing up in Johnstown, the co-op ethic was just the way you lived."

Johnstown's co-op ethic actually stemmed from the Extension Department, which Teresa now leads. Its first head, Monsignor Moses Coady, was a big, handsome, charismatic Cape Breton priest who chaired a Royal Commission on Fisheries in 1927. The commission's report on the appalling poverty of Nova Scotian fishermen led to the establishment of the Extension Department, with a mandate to organize the fishermen. Coady and his colleagues in what became known as the Antigonish Movement spent the rest of their lives forming "study clubs" in which communities asked themselves, as Coady put it, "What shall we study? What can we do?" Their answers produced a wave of credit unions and co-operative organizations throughout the Maritimes.

Many of Coady's co-ops have since faltered, folded or merged, but some have become local powerhouses. Bergengren Credit Union in Antigonish itself, population 5,200, has $63 million in

assets and 12,000 members—more members than Antigonish
County has residents. (The extras are students who reside
elsewhere, former residents who maintain their memberships,
and organizations.)

Teresa's knowledge and credibility took her in some surprising directions. In 1985, she chaired a blue-ribbon committee on
Cape Breton's economic prospects. When the committee recommended a super-agency to replace a confusing welter of development assistance programs, she became vice-chair of Enterprise
Cape Breton. The major agency on the island, however, was the
Cape Breton Development Corporation, or Devco. When Devco's chairman resigned, Teresa replaced him; in 1987, when the
president was fired, Teresa became interim president.

At the time, Devco had 3,500 employees and $182 million in
sales. Its coal mines made it the largest industrial organization
east of Montreal, and its Industrial Development Division was
involved with every aspect of the island's economic life—tourism
and agriculture, manufacturing and culture. Devco was, in
effect, the government of Cape Breton Island—and Teresa Mac-
Neil was the governor.

Devco eventually found new, full-time executives, and Teresa
turned her attention back to adult education—but in some new
and surprising forms. Recently, for example, she spearheaded a
quiet initiative called the Baddeck Symposium, which brought
together restless, successful people from across Atlantic
Canada—people in business, government, labour and education. Our region is confronting a series of linked crises. Everyone
is worrying and talking about our prospects and strategy: this is
what I came to call the Urgent Conversation, a discussion we
experienced everywhere on the voyage. Everyone can see the
problems, but we have few mechanisms through which to share
our thoughts. And so Teresa—like Coady—brought us together
to ask, "What shall we study? What can we do?"

At first glance, Luke Batdorf is an odd counterpoise to this
driven, impassioned community servant. He eschews public
life—so much so that he sometimes feels himself to be "Mr.
MacNeil." He might equally well be called "Father Teresa." He
soars through life like an osprey, scarcely moving his wings,
riding the economic and aesthetic updrafts, enjoying a wide and
spacious view of things. His Act is spectacularly Together.

A tall, broad-browed, smiling man of sixtysomething, Luke writes down his plans for his day before he gets out of bed. Every day, he listens to a piece of great music. Every week, he reads a novel, a book on history and a book on art. In the summer he swims and gardens. He has made his own wine for 40 years. In the fall he shoots a deer. From time to time he makes comfortable amounts of money as a consultant.

The MacNeil-Batdorf house has a sweeping view over Northumberland Strait. A leafy, passive-solar design, it is rich in paintings, prints, sculptures and *objets d'art* from around the world. Behind it is an extensive garden and a set of cages full of Luke's peacocks, quail and rare pheasants.

"A peacock's tail shimmering in the sun is a beautiful thing," says Luke. "And beauty is the spirit that keeps us living. The whole business of living is an art; it's important to magnify the pleasures of sound, sight and thought."

He was raised near Philadelphia, of a Pennsylvania Dutch family. He came to Nova Scotia in the 1950s as a Lutheran pastor serving a Lunenburg County congregation. Though he and his family lived on his parson's salary, he had the security of a small inheritance, which "has probably allowed me to be more venturesome in my personal choices." His choices eventually carried him entirely away from his clerical beginnings. The process began with literacy, when new federal regulations required that fishing skippers and mates obtain certificates.

"Those fishing masters were very intelligent, capable men, and often they had systems of personal hieroglyphics, which they'd developed over the years for professional uses," Luke remembers. "But they couldn't read or write enough to pass examinations, and they couldn't admit their illiteracy in public." So their 24-year-old pastor quietly began to tutor them individually.

That experience led to a B.Ed. degree at nearby Acadia University, and then to the creation of an adult residential educational centre called Catidian Place. It was overwhelmingly popular, but the parish couldn't afford to winterize it. Batdorf solved the problem by harnessing profits for social purposes. He established a charcoal-manufacturing business, which later merged with a hardwood sawmill; both were ultimately sold at a profit.

By 1967, education and local development had become Batdorf's main interests. Inheritance, he says, is one form of security; marketable skills and competence provide a much better one, and a much more broadly accessible one. He went to work for a federally funded job development organization, the Nova Scotia NewStart Corporation, supervising research and training projects in adult basic education, job training and entrepreneurship. Again and again, he found economic failure linked with illiteracy. But literacy, he finally decided, was not only the basic ability to read and write: it also meant the ability to plan, and the ability to evaluate.

"These are really three levels of literacy," he says, "and they're all trainable skills." So, when the NewStart operation wound down, he applied for a job teaching adult education at St. Francis Xavier University. He was interviewed by the department head, Dr. Teresa MacNeil. By now his marriage had ended. Dr. Teresa hired him—and then, in 1973, she married him.

He taught for 12 years. Fledgling entrepreneurs found their way to his office, seeking help with planning and development— a health food store, a restaurant, an automobile dealership, an art gallery. Occasionally he made small investments in the businesses himself.

"I've never lost a dime on an investment in one of these little businesses," he says. "Never. I once helped an ironmonger get started—he made those andirons in the fireplace—but after he'd been operating for a while he decided he really didn't want to continue. But he kept the business operating until he'd repaid every cent, with interest—and then he closed the doors.

"Those are very satisfying relationships. You develop a real bond when you work with people in the creation of a business."

Luke resigned from St. Francis Xavier in 1983, after an administrator refused to honour a predecessor's promise. Meanwhile, he and Teresa had built their dream house in Bayfield, a tiny community reliant on a small fish plant. When the plant closed in 1982, the community faced a crisis. Luke bought the plant at the bankruptcy sale and turned it around.

"A manager's major skills," he explains, "apply equally in a large corporation, a parish council or a kitchen. The fundamental skill of a manager is to make quality information come together at the right time to yield good decisions. The other major skill is evaluation, which ensures that you're operating in accordance with reality, that you aren't kidding yourself. All the other professional skills are less relevant than those. The critical thing is to get information and make it flow properly."

He sold the plant profitably in 1985, but it had made him think again about literacy. One innovation in the plant had been literacy training, which made a "phenomenal" difference to productivity, absenteeism and safety: illiterate workers, for example, don't read warning signs. Luke spent three years as president and chairman of Laubach Literacy of Canada, super-vising 7,000 volunteer tutors as well as a large publishing and distribution operation.

"That's a lot harder than managing a business," he says. "You use the same skills, but the management of people is much more complex. You're up against prima donnas and instant experts. There's a crisis factor in managing volunteers, and there's no way you can protect yourself against it. You're con-stantly remotivating people, but not with money."

Luke Batdorf's life is not about money—but he understands the symbolic and practical importance of money better than almost anyone else I know. He knows how to get it, how to use it to make good things happen, how to multiply it. But he also knows what to buy with it: beauty, understanding, freedom.

"An assured income leaves you freer to manoeuvre economi-cally in creative ways," he says, "and it certainly frees you up to be more sensitive to the spiritual and aesthetic dimensions of life. That's one of the reasons I favour a guaranteed annual income.

"In the end, money is a tool. It does spawn more money, but in a well-managed life that's not the reason you do the things you do. I'm not often conscious that the money is multiplying, but I'm pleased that it does. It should, after all. If it doesn't do that, you're not wielding the tool well."

At three-thirty, a breeze stole in from the east—a lovely little breeze, dead astern. With the tanbark mainsail far out to star-board and the big white genoa held out to port by the boat-hook, *Silversark* moved out at a trot, her wake gurgling as she gathered speed. The dark blue hump of Cape George grew larger. Now we could see the blocky white lighthouse high on its shoulder, and

as the afternoon waned into the evening we could see four or five
fishing boats around us converging on the tiny artificial harbour
below it.

I was still thinking about Luke and Teresa and the Urgent
Conversation. For two or three generations, our region has been
part of a shameful deal: a half-acknowledged agreement that if
the Maritimes would surrender any right to full participation in
the life of the nation, the federal government would pay us off
through make-work grants, equalization payments, unemployment insurance and military spending, to mention only the most
obvious. The Deal has lasted half a century or more.

The Maritimes once had a prosperous, self-confident world
trading and industrial culture, focused on the Intercolonial Railway and the myriad ports and rivers. That ended with the advent
of "national" institutions like the CNR and the St. Lawrence
Seaway, aimed like arrows at the heart of our prosperity. Banks
created in Nova Scotia—the Royal Bank, the Bank of Nova
Scotia—shifted their attention to Quebec, Ontario and the West.
Canada abandoned its merchant marine. The tariff legacy of the
"National Policy" obliged us to buy cars and refrigerators from
Ontario, not from New England or Germany. Our manufacturing industries withered or were bought out and closed. That cost
us money—and, even worse, it cost us power, people, technology
and self-esteem.

Our only remaining industries were based on natural
resources which could not be physically removed: the fishery, the
forests, the gypsum quarries, the coal mines. None of these was
protected by tariffs; we bought in a protected market but sold
against world competition. But Canada at least paid the region a
form of rent for our ruined economic prospects.

Now the resource industries themselves are in crisis. The cod
population has collapsed, recycling is hurting the paper-mills,
the bottom drops out of coal as the oil price slumps. And now
Canada is balking about paying the rent. Canada, we are told,
can no longer support the feckless free-loaders of the east coast.
New chill winds of international competition are blowing, trade
barriers are falling, social programs are threatened. The new
rhetoric of social progress boils down to *Root, hog, or die.* Diane
Francis, the clown princess of business journalism, sashays into
Nova Scotia and confides that we need to entice immigrant

entrepreneurs from Hong Kong to show us how it's done. Nobody laughs. Dear God, have we lost our sense of humour as well as our knowledge of history?

The Urgent Conversation in the Maritimes goes like this: if The Deal is dead, we'll have to do something else. *What are we going to do? And how will we do it?* What kind of people are we, anyway, and what are we good at? What can we make, or do, and for what market? What do we need to learn in order to do that?

All over the Maritimes, people are trying to discern the features of the future. Louisiana Pacific has built a mill in Port Hawkesbury to make a new wall-board of wood fibre and gypsum: that looks promising. Tourism helps, though the season is short. What about value-added food products, shipping potato puffs and cod *au gratin* rather than raw potatoes and fish? What about aquaculture, whisky, ocean technologies? What about painting and theatre, film and video? Rita MacNeil, John Allan Cameron, The Rankin Family: we already count music among our major exports, and the strength of our culture and quality of life should be major assets in an increasingly homogeneous world.

There may be completely new things to do. With our partners, Ralph DeCoste and I are marketing software with modest success. What about bio-engineering, telemarketing, aerospace? In the global village, with its nervous system of fibre optics and its micro-electronic ganglia, location should hardly matter: maybe we can do things that Maritimers could never have done before.

The Urgent Conversation eventually spawns a subversive notion. If Canada ceases to pay the piper, she has no further right to call the tune. As traders situated in the middle of the North Atlantic trade triangle, we were traditionally the most cosmopolitan of Canadian societies. We prospered under free trade before: why can't we do it again?

I have a hunch that the immortal Pogo said it perfectly: we are surrounded by insurmountable opportunities.

But we were much more ebullient and confident before our spirit was corroded by The Deal. To regain our self-reliance, we need a fresh outlook—Luke Batdorf's knowledge and confidence, Teresa MacNeil's commitment to community development and continuous learning. I am becoming more and more convinced that the prospects of Maritime prosperity are inextricably linked with information, self-esteem and knowledge—with education, broadly construed. That is why educators like Luke and Teresa are at the centre of the Urgent Conversation.

There is a strange irony here, for education seemed to be part of my past, not part of my future; I resigned a position as a tenured professor 20 years ago in favour of a freelance writer's uncertain life. It had been a good life, and I felt no special desire to reshape it again. But maybe it was time, somehow, to paint it a different colour. Maybe it was time to write a book about education.

Maybe I was doing that already.

By now *Silversark* was beating into a firm westerly wind, and the sun was dropping behind Cape George. It would be dark when we made Ballantyne's Cove, but the harbour had a light on the end of the breakwater, and I had sailed into it once before.

"Good grief, what's that?" Lulu asked, pointing to the tip of the cape. Something chunky and black, bristling with spikes and poles, was coming fast along the shore.

"It looks like a bloody porcupine on the water," I said.

The Porcupine disappeared against the shore, black on black. We beat on into a solid breeze, dodging fishing buoys and tacking close under the dark red bluffs, then reaching in past the breakwater with the mainsail alone. Under the wharf lights a group of men was unloading fish from a blocky fibreglass boat, black hull with a black house, spiky with booms, aerials, gallows frame: The Porcupine, actually named *Frankie and Katie*. Lulu swung *Silversark* into the wharf and I jumped ashore with the mooring lines.

The men finished unloading, and the black boat wanted to move ahead, making space for another boat still to come. We could hear the other boat outside the harbour, its big GM diesel roaring in the darkness. With the men on the wharf, we warped *Silversark* forward. They accepted our offer of a beer. They were fish buyers from Lismore, on the other side of the cape, and they had made a long day of it already.

The last boat, *Timothy Dawn*, charged around the end of the breakwater. The buyers scrambled off our boat, rigged their tackle again and began winching fish ashore—grey plastic hand crates, each bearing 150 to 175 pounds of grey sole, flounder, hake and cod. A young man with a thick black moustache seemed to be in charge of the boat.

When we fell asleep, they were still unloading. Lazy bloody Maritimers. Why couldn't they work for a living, instead of hanging around a wharf in the middle of the night?

FISH,

FLESH

AND FOWL

Ballantyne's Cove was settled by a Scottish soldier named Ballantyne after the War of 1812. He had served in the defence of Kingston, Ontario, and a grateful sovereign gave him a green and lovely piece of hilly shoreline, swathed in hardwood and close to the fishing grounds. We learned this from Harold Ballantyne, his descendant, an angular, balding fisherman who came over to introduce himself the morning after our arrival. Harold was the first son after a succession of daughters, who always referred to the new baby as "Him." That later evolved into the diminutive "Himmie," the name by which Ballantyne is still known.

The cove sees a good many yachts in the course of a summer, says Himmie; it is the only tolerable harbour for miles in either direction. Like many small harbours, it was created by dumping huge piles of rock to form a breakwater, building a road along the breakwater and then constructing a quay wall on the inside of the road. It is a busy and well-equipped fishing centre, rimmed with gear sheds and with power and light on the wharf. It has a stand-alone chemical toilet for the fishermen's use, and the fish-and-chip stand at the head of the wharf may be the best in the Maritimes. No wonder yachtsmen like it.

We sailed late, at eleven-twenty in the morning, sliding out to Cape George on a friendly little westerly. Half an hour later we passed the sea buoy at the tip of the Cape and sailed on into the open water where St. George's Bay meets Northumberland Strait. Himmie had told us that the strong tidal streams of the Strait can create a nasty chop here, when they meet the eddies and swirls from the bay, but today the water was a deep blue, and the seas were modest and amiable. And the wind was fading. At twelve-thirty we raised the genoa. *Silversark* ambled on. By two o'clock the wind had vanished, and the sea was almost flat. Far off to the east we heard a familiar sound: Puh-*phoo!* Swivelling quickly, we caught a glimpse of a browsing whale.

Where would the wind eventually come from, and how strong would it be? Murray Harbour, Prince Edward Island, lay about 18 miles away to the northwest. Pictou, Nova Scotia, was nearly 30 miles to the west. If we could average four knots, we could just make one or the other in daylight—but we had no hope of doing four knots without a solid, steady wind. We checked the forecast: moderate southwest winds today, northwest winds of 25 to 30 knots after midnight. All we could do was wait and see. We got our books and sat reading in the cockpit. It was a pleasant place to be, on the smooth, undulant sea in the milky golden sunlight of a hazy summer afternoon.

"Don't you have some phone calls to make?" Lulu asked, looking up from her book. "And we could call Mark."

We could? We could. I hadn't absorbed the fact of the Novatel cellular phone in the chart table: it was just too improbable. I brought it on deck and made a couple of calls. One colleague was out of his office, but expected back momentarily.

"Well, he can't normally reach me because we don't normally have the phone turned on," I told his secretary. "We can't afford the electricity. But if he comes back in the next few minutes, he can try my cellular number."

I hung up.

"Want to try Mark?" said Lulu.

"Why not?"

She picked up the phone and dialled Denmark. The phone rang in Padborg, a small town in Jutland near the German border.

"Dag, det er Inger," said the voice of the well-loved friend with whom Mark was staying just then.

"Det er Lulu," said Lulu happily, switching to Danish.

"Lu*L U!*" cried Inger, and the two of them were off. Mark was a very cultured young man, said Inger. They had been having interesting philosophical and political discussions. Different expressions passed over Lulu's face like fast clouds across the sun, revealing vindication, astonishment and infinite maternal pride.

Then Mark came on the line. Philosophical? Political? With parents, he communicates like . . . well, like a teenager.

"How are you?"

"Good."

"Having a good time?"

"Oh, yeah."

"See Terkel?"

"Uh-huh."

"How was that?"

"Fine."

"We miss you."

"Yeah. Me too."

"We just saw a whale."

"Oh, cool!"

Then something triggered the topic of radio-controlled model cars, Mark's current evangelical enthusiasm.

"Mom, I met this guy, he's got this incredible RC car, it's a PDQ-10 with a 20-dingaling whangbanger, and an *awesome* 240 push-pull input-output, double knobble-bobble 12-klick tires and a Gerschtunkelbunk speed control, and man, you should see that thing take off, it's just *awesome*! And . . . "*

After she hung up, Lulu reported the conversation to me.

"He had a really good time in Copenhagen. Katrina and her boyfriend took him to visit the Technical University—"

Woodle-oodle-oodle oodle! Woodle-oodle-oodle oodle!

---

* Mark insists that this is not actually what he said.

What was that weird sound? Where—

The telephone! Out here in the middle of Northumberland Strait, *the telephone was ringing.*

I picked it up, but I was laughing too hard to speak.

"Aren't you ashamed of yourself?" asked the voice on the other end.

We put the phone away, read our books, fooled with the sails, tried to catch the fragments of breeze that drifted by. As the hours went by, the time-speed-distance equation grew ever more depressing: to reach a port in daylight we would have to average 5 knots, 5.5, 5.7, 6.1 . . .

By suppertime it was clear that we could reach a harbour in daylight only if an unpredicted favourable wind freed us to sail at speeds which would support water-skiing. With one exception.

Ballantyne's Cove.

And the wind, when it came, was northwest and rising—a terrible wind for either of our alternative destinations. It was still a dozen miles or more to Murray Harbour, and only two hours of light remained. But it was a fine wind for going back.

"I think we'd better go back to Ballantyne's," I said.

"What?"

"I think we'd better go back to Ballantyne's. This is the beginning of that heavy wind. We're going to wind up crashing around here at night, trying to sail up to a low coast against big seas. If we *had* to do it, we'd do it. But we don't have to."

"Go back!" Lulu said. "Did I hear you say *go back?*"

"Let's just go into Ballantyne's and get a good night's sleep and try again—"

"@#$#@$%!!!" said Lulu. "&*&%$#!!!"

"Well, true, but—"

"&*&!!! %$#!!!"

"But, Lulu—"

"@#&)(&%$!!!"

The problem with marrying a lion-hearted woman is that she can't turn it off. She's a lion all the time. Retreat is anathema, an unthinkable personal affront. Guns to the right of her, guns to the left of her . . .

Ultimately, however, Lulu is lion-hearted but not foolish. And she recognizes a chicken-hearted man when she sees one. *Silversark* romped off towards Ballantyne's Cove on a reach, sails broad

off, bow wave foaming. It had taken us eight hours to get out
there; it took two hours to get back. We tacked up to the breakwater in a moody, puffy wind and bumped the wharf as we
landed.

Timothy Dawn was in before us, and her crew—three lusty
young lads from Cape Breton—joined us for an attack on a bottle
of Cape Breton's own Smuggler's Cove rum. The skipper, Kevin
Fraser, was 22, the father of a daughter, and he already had a good
reputation in Ballantyne's Cove. Industrious, capable, decisive,
he was working his crew and his boat hard and making good
catches. He was from Cheticamp; his crewmen, Blair Timmons
and Kenneth Roach, were from neighbouring Pleasant Bay.

Kevin *had* to work hard: his father had backed him for the
purchase of his boat and gear, and the two of them were on the
hook for more than $100,000. He was delighted with the Cape
George fishing grounds. In the northern Gulf, where he normally
fished, he set his gear far out, in a hundred fathoms of water or
more. In these shallow southern waters, he was filling his Danish
seine rig just three miles from shore, and in 30 or 40 feet.

Hearing this, Lulu and I felt the first twinges of a growing
summer-long disquiet about the living salt-water world. *Timothy
Dawn* was just one boat, in one small port, but she was bringing
in three or four tons of fish every working day—and had to, if
Kevin were to survive; he had to cover the cost of food, fuel,
maintenance, depreciation and interest before there would be
even a nickel for his crew, himself, his lady and their daughter. A
$100,000 investment is a heavy burden on men, families, boats
and equipment.

It also puts an unendurable pressure on the resource itself.
With electronic navigation and fish-finding, power winches and
synthetic nets, our ability to locate, pursue and kill fish now far
exceeds the capacity of the fish to reproduce. The result is over-
fishing, stock collapse and savage reductions in quotas. The
crisis had already confronted Newfoundland, but it had touched
the Gulf lightly. In the fall of 1992, the fierce reality of deep
quota cuts would come home to the Gulf, as well, and I would
suddenly remember this self-assured, entrepreneurial young
man and hope he could survive it.

For all three of them, fishing was not just a job: it was a
liberation. Kenny Roach, by his own account, had been a trou-

bled kid who dropped out early, drifting to Toronto and doing menial jobs and various drugs before migrating home again, like a bruised animal. Now, at 28, he was living with a "wonderful girl," making decent money, doing work he enjoyed, straightening out his life. Like his mates, he was optimistic. His future would hold plenty of problems, but nothing that ingenuity, cunning and hard work couldn't resolve.

The three of them were massively indifferent to the broader topics of science, politics, art, international affairs, the world of concepts and ideas. In the prime of their physical lives, the crew of *Timothy Dawn* were working hard, playing hard, laughing and drinking and fathering children. They made me feel like the Yeats of *Sailing to Byzantium*, watching

> . . . The young
> In one another's arms, birds in the trees
> —Those dying generations—at their song,
> The salmon-falls, the mackerel crowded seas,
> Fish, flesh, or fowl, commend all summer long
> Whatever is begotten, born, and dies.
> Caught in that sensual music, all neglect
> Monuments of unageing intellect.

We had intended to sail on towards Byzantium the next morning, but even in Ballantyne's Cove, sheltered by the bulk of the Cape, the northwest gale was howling in the rigging. We slept late and spent the day restowing, tidying and devising small improvements, like a way to lash *Marksark* more solidly to the deck. No boat is ever really finished, and improvements are a major pleasure of life afloat: patiently analyzing problems, devising solutions and executing them with the tools and materials on hand. There is always another small problem to be solved, another incremental advance to be gained—something that will slightly improve the boat's safety, speed, appearance or convenience. A devoted skipper practises something like *kaizen*, the attainment of quality in Japanese industry by constant minor improvement. And loves every minute of it.

Just at dusk another sailboat came chugging into the cove on her outboard motor—a dainty, charming gaff cutter with a glorious wooden transom in a herring-bone pattern, towing a rowboat almost as long herself. The two boys aboard were Dr. Paul Price,

FRCS(C), a young ophthalmologist from Antigonish, with a friend named Ian MacGillivray. And we had met the boat a couple of years earlier, in the St. Peter's Canal. At that time she belonged to a lanky, laconic Newfoundlander named Frank Best and his wife, Susan. Paul poured an authoritative shot of rum and suggested we visit Frank: Ian had a car on the wharf, Frank lived nearby, and he and Susan were now three years into a ten-year boat-building project.

Ian roared over the twisting shore road in the black night, turned off on a dirt side-road and shot into a driveway in the woods.

"Look!"

"What's that?"

"An owl!"

It was indeed an owl—the very picture of interrupted dignity, glaring at us with round comic-book eyes while its talons clutched a furry something which might have been a rabbit. As we watched, it lumbered into the air on big slow wings, as ungainly and archaic as an old biplane.

Frank and Susan created their house organically, bit by bit, taking their time, letting it accrete around them: octagonal rooms, towers, balconies, decks, elaborate inlaid wood floors, stained glass, a huge stone fireplace. But nobody was in the house, so we started down a path through the woods, past a duck pond, towards a distant light. Two figures emerged from the shadows: Frank Best and a neighbour named Don Cranford. Susan, said Frank, had given birth to a baby girl in Halifax the previous day. This called for a drink—it was one of those evenings in which much less momentous events could have called for a drink—but first we went to Frank's shop, a cavernous building tucked in among the spruce trees.

The hull of the big boat was almost complete, still upside-down, sweeping up from the stern towards the rafters and flowing down again at the bow. It was a Roberts 44 ketch, designed by *Silversark*'s designer. With its upthrust keel, it looked like a fin-backed spruce-clad whale. The first impression is always like that: something vast, sleek, alien to the right angles and plane surfaces of normal carpentry, something with a shape as sinuous and organic as that of a mink or a salmon, something more like a sculpture than a construction project. The second impression has to do with the meticulous fitting of the wood, the care and effort which has already gone into creating the effect of an almost living creature.

Frank Best has the mystical casualness which characterizes the essential Atlantic Canadian character, particularly in Newfoundlanders: their minds are on some internal fixities, not on their physical surroundings. I asked Frank how old he was—I wondered how old he would be in seven years, when the boat might be launched—and he eventually conceded he was 43, but the point did not matter to him, and he gave the faint impression that anyone interested in such minor issues must have a second-rate cosmological outlook.

We ducked underneath the hull, into a space like the inside of a narrow, extruded bell. Frank was building by the same principles we had used: heavy laminated frames to define the shape, with the skin of the planking sprung over them. He was about to cover the exterior with fiberglass before rolling her upright and building the interior.

I looked at Lulu, and Lulu looked at me.

"I'm homesick."

"Me too."

Our hands itched for the tools, and our minds for the puzzles. It all came flooding back: the camaraderie of the shop, the banter, the learning, the well-earned weariness, the joy of watching that lovely, big-bellied, tapering presence slowly take shape under your hands. When we were building *Silversark*, we occasionally worked all night on long jobs like epoxy-coating the hull. By the time we were done it would be dawn, and the birds would be showering us with song as we walked back to the house in the rose-and-silver glow that comes before the sunrise, tired and happy and very much in love.

The others were standing at the shop door, ready to leave.

"Come on, Don," said Lulu softly.

"Let's build another one," I said.

LA

GRANDE BAIE

DE

SAINT-LAURENT

We sailed at seven-thirty on a playful northwest breeze, which carried us in less than an hour into Northumberland Strait. The day was more like autumn than summer—but then most of the days had been tolerably warm only when the wind was still, and we had grudgingly become accustomed to heavy wool watch caps, layers of sweaters, ski gloves and wool socks. Most Maritime summers include long stretches of warm, sunny weather broken by transient low-pressure systems: a week or ten days of blue sky and blue water interrupted briefly by rain and cloud, and then another chapter of high summer mixed with low overcast. I normally wear my insulated Mustang anti-exposure coveralls for fall sailing, but this summer I had worn them regularly. It was now the middle of July, and we had yet to sail in shorts.

We were not alone: everywhere east of the Rockies, the summer was cold and wet. Crops were late ripening, and the tourist trade had taken a beating. The problem, said the meteorologists, was El Niño, a vast errant eddy in the Pacific Ocean which had parked a ridge of high pressure on the Rockies, funnelling arctic air to the rest of the continent. In addition, the eruption of Mount Pinatubo in the Philippines had belched a veil of sulphur, ash and dust into the stratosphere, blocking the sunlight. At least we were not shivering alone.

Bundled up warmly, we beat out into the Strait. The northwest wind would do for Pictou, so we tacked over and laid a course down the coast.

The wind grew lighter and lighter. *Silversark* sailed slower and slower. By eleven-thirty we were still close enough to Cape George to identify houses on the shore. We were utterly becalmed. Again.

What a summer. Becalmed! In Northumberland Strait, at midday, in the middle of July!

In a typical Maritime summer day, the dawn comes on slowly, in pink and gold; sometimes the hour after sunrise is the only hour of sunlight, with a grey uniform overcast ruling the sky thereafter. Sunny or grey, the dawn is usually calm. A westerly breeze fills in slowly during the morning. During the afternoon it blows strongly; by suppertime it is dying away, and by dark it has retired for the night. If you like gentle sailing, go out in the morning. For a boisterous ride, wait until after lunch.

This summer had shown a new and distressing pattern. The breeze blew in the morning, carrying you smartly out of the harbour. Then it died at midday, reviving in the afternoon and blowing strongly after dark. The pattern was perfectly calculated to ensure that you could not reach your destination in daylight.

It is not particularly difficult to enter a new port after dark, shaping your course by light buoys, range lights and lighthouses; in fact it is an exciting and satisfying challenge. But daylight certainly makes it easier to gather additional information from other landmarks, the movement of other vessels, the shape of the waves, the colour of the water. And you want light to moderate winds—strong enough to give you control of your course, but not so strong as to send you careening through dark fleets of anchored boats.

My countdown calculations began again, unbidden. Ten hours of daylight, 30 nautical miles to Pictou. Three knots, average, to arrive in daylight. Possible, with good steady sailing.

Ah, well. We had come to see and enjoy the Gulf of St. Lawrence: we were in the Gulf: what more did we want? At that moment, the Gulf did not look very big, with the coast of Nova Scotia slanting away to the west, the low pencil line of the PEI coast to the north, the Cape Breton hills smoky blue on the eastern horizon. But we were in Northumberland Strait, a small corner of a vast inland sea. At 91,500 square miles, the Gulf is about the size of the Persian Gulf—bigger than the Aegean Sea, far bigger than the Adriatic. In *Coasting*, Jonathan Raban finds himself at a point in the Irish Sea where he can actually see the coast on every side, all the ancient kingdoms of Britain: Ireland, Scotland, England, Wales and the Isle of Man. No such experience is possible in the Gulf proper, which is more than twice the size of the Irish Sea. The Gulf's main body is about 230 miles from east to west, 325 miles from north to south. At a steady five knots, it would take *Silversark* nearly three days to cross from Nova Scotia to the North Shore of Quebec. Sailing south the same distance would take us halfway to Bermuda.

The Gulf sea floor is divided into two main regions. The Laurentian Channel, a trench 1,500 feet deep, sweeps along the North Shore of Quebec, through Cabot Strait and out to sea beyond Newfoundland. South of the Laurentian Channel, within the broad embayment between the Gaspé Peninsula and the coast of Cape Breton, lies a shelf called the Magdalen Shallows. Here the sea floor is almost flat, and the water is generally less than 200 feet deep. Prince Edward Island and the Magdalens stand on the floor of the Magdalen Shallows like haystacks on a prairie field.

This shallow water is constantly replenished by the great outflow of fresh water from the St. Lawrence River, and it freezes easily. In mid-winter, at the Canso Causeway, the open Atlantic water to the south throws up rolling banks of "sea smoke," the exhalation of the water's warmth into the clean cold air; to the north, in the Gulf, a field of ice stretches white and level from the causeway to the horizon.

By the same token, the Gulf warms up quickly in the summer, and its shallows are a pasture for plankton—microscopic floating algae invisible to the naked eye, subdivided into thousands of species of diatoms, chrysophytes, dinoflagellates and cocco-lithophores. Plankton are the fundamental components of the marine food web; sooner or later, they feed everything that lives in and from the ocean—clams, mink, whales, eagles, the Grand Captain of the Mi'kmaq nation and the Silver Stick in Waiting to the Queen of England. Since the first Europeans arrived, the Gulf fishery has been a major industry—though we may finally be plundering it beyond recovery.

We could see the plunder going on around us, fishing boats tiny and indistinct in the misty distance, crisp and large nearer at hand, trawling and seining back and forth. Lulu picked up the binoculars and identified *Timothy Dawn* in the middle distance, west and north of us. As we slowly rolled on the gently swelling water, *Timothy Dawn* came closer, steaming in a wide circle, her crewmen waving as they passed nearby, her industrious diesel rapping aggressively in the still air.

The chief problem of the Gulf fishery was always its distance from the European market compared with Newfoundland. The solution was to establish headquarters seaward of the Strait of Canso to assemble the catch from many little fishing operations around the Gulf. In 1654, the French Crown granted the entire region to Nicolas Denys, who set up headquarters at St. Peter's, Cape Breton. His outposts were on the New Brunswick coast at Miscou, Nipisiguit (now Bathurst) and possibly on the Miramichi.

More than a century later, Channel Island traders repeated the process, basing themselves in Arichat and maintaining a ring of posts around the Gulf, notably in Gaspé itself. Arichat is just six miles from our home in D'Escousse, and our house is built on land originally granted to a Jersey trader named Gruchy. Local places and families still bear Jersey names like Janvrin, Leves-conte, Mauger, LeBrun, Bourinot.

The people of the Channel Islands—there are still only 120,000 of them—are clearly a remarkable breed. They are great farmers; their tiny islands produced three distinctive breeds of domestic cattle (Jersey, Guernsey, Alderney), and they still export fruit, flowers and vegetables. They have been adept trad-ers for centuries. In Elizabethan times, more than 1,000 of them were involved in knitting, chiefly for export, and knit sweaters are still known as "jerseys" in England and "guernseys" in Newfoundland. The de Carteret family, whose name graces a Halifax street, once owned the swatch of North America which is still known as New Jersey. And the Jerseymen have given a distinct flavour to the entire Gulf coast, where some of the companies they founded still operate—like Robin, Jones and Whitman, in Cheticamp.

The Islanders were and are French-speaking subjects of the Duchy of Normandy, whose incumbent has, since 1066, also been the monarch of England. (That's why the islands are a tax haven today.) The fall of Louisbourg in 1760 left French-speaking populations in Cape Breton and Quebec living under British rule, a situation tailor-made for Channel Islanders. For more than a century, Jerseymen dominated the commercial life of the Gulf, bringing European manufactures in, carrying salt fish out and sometimes trading the fish in the Caribbean for rum and sugar, which they later sold in Europe.

Sailing up Northumberland Strait, we were following in the wake of French and Jersey sailors, retracing their path through a waterborne society organically connected by the waters of the Gulf. The great inland sea of the Gulf did not divide the people who lived on its islands and along its shores: it linked them. A fishing captain from the Magdalens might find his catch on the coast of Quebec, his market in Pictou, Nova Scotia, his new vessel in a New Brunswick shipyard and his bride in Cheticamp, Cape Breton. Highways, airlines and television have eroded, but not eradicated, those traditional links.

Indeed, the logic of the Gulf's marine society was once recognized politically by an innovation which may lead to some future amusement. Around 1653, the government of France created a *Province de la Grande Baie de St. Laurent*, notes Mark Haines, a devoted amateur historian in Guysborough County. The new province took in all the Gulf coast from the Isthmus of Chignecto, between today's Nova Scotia and New Brunswick, to Canso, Nova Scotia. It was a properly constituted jurisdiction; its governor was Nicolas Denys.

Just a year later, in 1654, the British captured Acadia; in 1670 they gave it back to the French; in 1690 and 1710 they recaptured it; and in 1713, under the Treaty of Utrecht, they forced the

French to give up, forever, "all Nova Scotia or Acadie with its ancient boundaries."

But what were the ancient boundaries of Acadia? Nobody knew, and an international commission was appointed to decide. The commission inaugurated a venerable Canadian tradition. It abducted and absorbed the issue as completely and permanently as a black hole absorbs light: it sat for 60 years and never reached a conclusion.

In the meantime, Acadia—including a great stretch of the adjoining continental land mass—became Nova Scotia. The continental territory was split off in 1784 and became New Brunswick, and both colonies became part of Canada in 1867. In all these transactions, the terrain covered by Denys's *Province de la Grande Baie de St. Laurent* was assumed to be part of Acadia— but Mark Haines can find no record that the province was ever extinguished or legally conveyed to the British. So the coast down which we sailed may still be a French colonial province.

I am eager to get a speeding ticket in New Glasgow or Antigonish. I will fight it on the grounds that the court has no jurisdiction, since the alleged offence did not take place in Canada, and Canadian laws do not apply in the *Province de la Grande Baie de Saint-Laurent.*

The sails flapped. *Silversark* turned lazily around.

Wind. Wind!

And the sun had come out.

The forecast had proposed a southerly, but these vagrant puffs were coming from the east—a perfect breeze for Pictou. We spread our sails wide. The wake began to gurgle. The wind steadied and strengthened, and the seas began heaping up behind us. *Timothy Dawn* fell astern, and the coast slipped past: Malignant Cove, Arisaig, Moidart, Lismore. Rolling and swinging, *Silversark* hustled towards Pictou.

Lulu went below for a rest, and I took the helm. Far away and dead ahead, something burned on the water, putting up a heavy plume of smoke. It looked like a dredge or an oil rig on fire. I gazed at it through the binoculars, but I couldn't make it out. When Lulu came on deck, I pointed it out. It had been there for half an hour or more, and—

Wait a minute. I snatched up the binoculars and looked again.

The smoke was belching from the Scott Paper mill at Abercrombie Point, just across the harbour from the town of Pictou.

I had a phone call to make. I went below, turned on the Avante and dialled an editor's number.

"So where are you?" said the editor.

I glanced up at the Loran read-out.

"45 15 05 North, 62 15 03 West," I said.

"Oh, off Lismore," he said. "I've got a map in front of me."

I went back on deck. *Silversark* was boiling along.

"We've never had better sailing," said Lulu. "This is lovely. We'll be in Pictou by dark."

"If we're getting there that fast, I'd better have a look at the chart and the pilot book."

I went below again. Outside Pictou is a black and white fairway buoy with a long white flash and a short one: the Morse Code letter A. At that buoy, you're positioned to enter the channel, which is marked with red buoys to the right, green ones to the left. Most have coloured flashing lights. There's a lighthouse on the beach at the harbour mouth: leave that to port. And there are range lights: one mounted low on the lighthouse, the other high on a tower in the town. When you have the two in line, your course leads right to the harbour entrance.

Once inside the harbour, where would we tie up? There was a marina, but the entrance was too narrow to tackle at night, under sail, and there wouldn't be much room to manoeuver inside. We wanted to moor right in the town, but what facilities might there be at the Royal William Yacht Club, on the opposite shore? Or what about one of the three or four wharves right in the town?

I needed some advice from a local sailor—aha!

I would call them on the phone.

The yacht club had no facilities, and no sailors present in the club bar. The bartender gave me the name of an experienced local skipper, Cam Garrett, but he wasn't home. A call to the marina confirmed that their entrance was too narrow. They suggested I go to the town marina at Pier A.

But the chart showed Pier A as a ruin, with a pile of rocks with only one foot of water over them right at the end. The *Sailing Directions for the Gulf and River St. Lawrence* described the wharf as being "in a state of disrepair."

No, said the marina manager. The town had taken over Pier A

and was in the process of converting it to a very nice downtown marina. We'd find it very comfortable.

Very well. Make it so. But shoal water lay beyond Pier A, and I had no chart, no description of how the new marina was actually laid out. By the time we sailed up the harbour it would certainly be dark. Hmm.

We ate a snack in the cockpit. By the time we reached Pictou Road, the open anchorage outside the harbour, the wind was fading with the daylight. The lighthouse flashed, and the winking red and green lights of the channel buoys came on, one after another. But we saw no sign of the Morse A light on the fairway buoy.

I found the range lights, and we steered till we had them in line: a red light, well inland, pulsing above the lighthouse. We sailed briskly towards the shore in the dusk, nursing the remnants of the breeze.

"Don," said Lulu, "what's that red flasher away over to port? Right in along the shore? Shouldn't it be to starboard?"

"You'd think so," I said. "But we've got that range, so we must be in the channel." Other lights and marks didn't seem to be showing up in the right places, either. But you don't abandon something as solid and reliable as a range easily.

We sailed for 20 minutes when *another* red flashing light emerged from behind a hill to starboard, back in the town. In a flash, all the perplexities vanished. The new one was the rear range light; we were *not* on the range. Somehow, we had badly overshot the entrance. The red buoy *should* be to starboard; the Morse A was somewhere far behind us, off the port quarter. I shot below and scanned the chart. No dangers in the immediate vicinity. We tacked to the southeast, brought the lights in line and jogged in slowly towards the entrance.

As we bobbed past the lighthouse, the breeze died entirely, leaving us drifting aimlessly through a thick white scum on the water, like dirty soapsuds. We got out the oars and rowed slowly through the carpet of crud.

"Is this guck from Scott Paper?" Lulu asked.

"Presumably. Looks pretty horrible, doesn't it?"

"Gross."

A small breeze filled the sails, and we shipped the oars. Pictou is a spacious harbour, and the town is home to 4,400 souls. The sky above it glowed with light from signs, houses, cars and street lights. The shoreline was deep in shadow.

We sailed along the ends of the wharves, peering into the darkness—past the shipyard and the long quay wall in front of the old railway station, past the looming bulk of Pier C. A fishing boat was tied inside Pier B. We dropped everything but the jumbo and sailed in alongside her. I took the lines ashore.

It was midnight. We could lie there quite comfortably, but not in the strong southeast winds forecast for tomorrow. We furled the sails loosely and walked along the old railroad right-of-way to Pier A. Even in the dark we could see it was new and unfinished, but excellent: a square basin with a solid wharf on one side and a green flashing light at the entrance, with boats all along the wall. We walked out on the wharf. Tucked into the corner was a large power cruiser. There was no gangway down to the floating dock. We heard music. A man came out of the cruiser.

"No problem," he said. "You just moor down here and you climb over the top of my boat to get out.

We walked back to Pier B, made sail and cast off, tacking up the dark harbour till we were abreast of the green flasher. Lulu steered for the light. I dropped the sails. As we slid past the end of the floating dock, I jumped. We swung the boat around and made her fast, furled the sails and went below. It was two o'clock in the morning.

ENCOUNTERS

WITH THE

WATER RAT

Coming on deck in the grey morning, we found the southeast wind beginning to whistle—but *Silversark* was perfectly protected inside the uncompleted marina. We walked down the floating dock, looking at speedboats and runabouts, a couple of motor cruisers and a sizeable sloop from Toronto named *Footloose*. Crossing the deck of a motorboat, we jumped over to *Footloose*. I swarmed up the wharf and turned to give Lulu a hand. She came flying up the pilings.

"Careful, dear—ooh, watch out for splinters!" said a frail, grandmotherly-looking woman in old clothes.

"How are things in Cape Breton?" said a quiet, reedy voice in my ear. Turning to face the speaker, I suddenly became the Mole from *The Wind in the Willows*, seeing for the first time:

A little brown face, with whiskers.
A grave round face, with a twinkle in its eye.
Small neat ears and thick silky hair.
It was the Water Rat!

If there was ever a creature of the waterfront, it was the grey-haired elderly man who faced me in his Greek fisherman's cap and pea jacket. The Water Rat, the beloved Water Rat, who spent his whole life "just messing about in boats."

"Um—ah—things are fine in Cape Breton," I said, disoriented. After all, it *was* my first trip out of Mole End.

"We haven't been down to Cape Breton this year," said the frail grandmother. "We're getting too old."

"We were down 11 times in 13 years," said the Water Rat.

"Where's your boat?" I asked.

"Right there," said the Water Rat. I looked down over the other side of the wharf. *Skua* was a battleship-grey wooden 30-footer with a high, stepped pilothouse and a tall, narrow shed, which looked like an outhouse, in the cockpit. A husky rowboat was pulled up on the stern. *Skua* was a makeshift motorsailer, with a rough-and-ready gaff ketch rig—heavy canvas, sapling spars, yellow polypropylene.

"We met you before," said the Water Rat. "In D'Escousse. You bumped us in the night with your schooner."

"I did?" But when he said it, I remembered it, a moment I would rather forget: a dark night, a late arrival home, a momentary lapse in attention . . .

"Didn't do no harm," said his wife. "You were very nice about it, apologized for waking us up and everything."

"As well I might," I said. "You going to be here for a while? I'd like to get together later on."

"Oh, yeah," said the Water Rat. "Any time."

Pictou Harbour is the shared estuary of three rivers, and though Pictou is the oldest of the towns along the rivers, it has been eclipsed during most of the 20th century. Trenton and New Glasgow produce everything from electrical power and rail cars to electronic parking meters. Stellarton and Westville are coal-mining towns; Plymouth, where 26 miners had recently died in the Westray mine, is for all practical purposes part of Stellarton. Stellarton is also the home and headquarters of the Sobey clan, whose supermarkets utterly dominate the retail food business in the Maritimes. There is also a Scott Paper mill on Pictou Harbour, and a large Michelin Tire plant at nearby Granton.

The five towns are sometimes called the Five Towns, and when Nova Scotians talk about "Pictou County," they generally mean the industrial centres, not the whole county. Taken together, the towns constitute the third-largest industrial cluster in Nova Scotia, after Halifax-Dartmouth and the Sydney area. But Pictou has always been a port, not an industrial town and, as industry flourished and shipping declined, Pictou fell behind.

But Pictou was looking good. At the head of the wharf we found ourselves on the main street beside the DeCoste Entertainment Centre, the town's performing arts auditorium. Directly across from us was a row of substantial stone town houses, which could have been airlifted from Scotland. We aimed our cameras at them, and a short, wiry man stopped beside us. He was wearing a blue-and-white striped T-shirt. Without any preamble, he said:

"They were built about 1830. That first one was a store, and the second one was a ship chandler. I renovated the one on the end. It had been a tavern, a jail and a brothel at various times. There's a Judas door in the top floor so you can see who's coming up the stairs and hide the evidence of the card game or put the rum away or whatever.

"At one time there was another stone house in that gap where that garden is now. There's another one farther up the street, the Consulate Inn and Restaurant. It's called that because it used to *be* the American consulate at one time, back in the age of sail, when there was a lot of shipping going out of here."

"Thank you," I said.

"They're great, aren't they?" he said. "See you."

Scotland, Scotland. Elsewhere in Pictou we found red-brick commercial buildings, which might have been stolen from Dumfries, low stone cottages transplanted from the Hebrides. The names on the businesses are MacDonald, Chisholm, MacLean, Mackay. You can eat at the Braeside Inn, drink at the Highland Tavern, curl at the New Caledonian Curling Club. The Hector National Exhibit Centre, on the edge of town, displays all the Scottish tartans along with pictures and artifacts of Scottish culture both here and in what many a Scot still calls "the Old Country."

Right across the marina from *Silversark*'s berth, a replica of the ship *Hector* was under construction. The original *Hector* was the first ship to bring emigrants directly from Scotland to Nova Scotia; she is thus a kind of Canadian *Mayflower*. She arrived in Pictou on September 15, 1773, carrying 200 Gaelic-speaking Highlanders, chiefly from Wester Ross, Cromarty and Sutherland.

I wanted to have a closer look at the *Hector* before we left. It has been said that no ship is truly ugly, but the *Hector* comes close. Stubby, bluff-bowed and pot-bellied, she has all the grace of an oil drum, and she probably sailed like one. She took 11 weeks to waddle across the Atlantic, and she was so rotten that people could tear pieces of wood out of her sides with their bare hands. On her return to Europe she was scrapped.

But within 50 years her passengers and their successors had created a durable Scottish town with a powerful intellectual life. As a monument in a mid-town square declares, the *Hector* passengers were the "vanguard of that army of Scots whose intellectual ideals, moral works and material achievements have contributed greatly to the good government and upbuilding of Canada."

All that and modesty, too. Well, as our parish priest's bumper sticker explains, *It's Hard To Be Humble When You're Scottish.*

A block up Water Street is the square modern building which houses Grohmann Knives. I had lost a marlinspike from my holster of sailing tools, and Lulu had lost a knife. As their flyer notes, Grohmann Knives is "a small family business with a big reputation." Their knives are sold world-wide; their most famous model is the Canadian Outdoor Knife, otherwise known as the D.H. Russell Belt Knife.

The company was established in 1956 by Rudolph Grohmann, a German master knife maker who set up business in his garage, with his daughter and son-in-law as his first work-force. The company now employs 17 people. Their showroom is full of glorious knives—chef's knives, carving knives, boning knives, fillet knives, tomato knives, paring knives, butcher knives, cleavers, scimitars, lobster crackers, jack-knives, hunting knives, sailing knives, sharpening steels, marlinspikes. You can buy them with handles of rosewood, oak or polypropylene, either singly or in presentation sets. They have won 25 international awards, plus a Canadian Excellence of Design Award, and they have even been exhibited at the Museum of Modern Art in New York. None of their knives fit Lulu's sheath, but their marlinspike fit mine.

Despite the reputation of Scots for cupidity, there were no banking machines in Pictou. Fortunately, I knew John Meier at the DeCoste Centre. While Lulu browsed in the gift shops, I visited John, cashed a cheque and picked up a couple of tickets to *Nova Scotia Songbook*, the Centre's current offering. The Centre is a pleasant building, with long glassed galleries surrounding a cavernous central theatre. If Pictou is doing rather well at the moment, the DeCoste Centre may be the reason.

Before the DeCoste Centre was opened, people in the upriver towns simply saw no reason ever to go to Pictou. After it was opened, it became Pictou County's normal venue for shows and concerts—and once you have decided to go to Pictou for a show, you may well be interested in adding a good dinner and making a night of it, or stopping at some pleasant café for a snack and an Irish coffee afterwards. So the Centre started a virtuous circle which strengthened local pride and gradually developed a market for new restaurants, boutiques and inns.

The *Hector* project builds on that momentum, and so does the new municipal marina, set right in the heart of the town. When it is finished, the marina will have showers, a coin laundry, finger piers and berths for dozens of yachts. A Scottish pub will stand on one side of the basin, next to a 75-room hotel and a row of shops and offices. The person charged with bringing this plan to fruition is Graham Holman of the Pictou Waterfront Development Corporation. When someone told me that the little building at the head of the wharf contained showers and laundry facilities—and had been used the previous summer—I called him.

He came down to the marina later on, a cheerful tanned man full of quiet optimism. The little building had been cleaned out, and showers were available. He gave us the key and asked us to offer it to other visiting yachts which might come along during our stay. Another one was already there—a sloop from Caraquet,

New Brunswick. Graham was facing a pleasant problem: the marina was not open for business, but business was coming anyway.

He gave me a Ship Hector T-shirt to commemorate the first visit of a Cape Breton yacht to the new facility, and later he toured me through the Hector Heritage Quay and the *Hector* reconstruction. The Interpretation Centre, the largest post-and-beam structure east of Ontario, contains displays, artifacts and dioramas—life-sized, three-dimensional recreations of scenes from Scotland and from the voyage itself. The *Hector* passengers nearly ran out of food and water, while smallpox and dysentery killed 18 children. While the visitor hears the sounds of wind, wave and the creaking fabric of the ship, a mother tends a dying child and exhausted adults sleep in rough berths nearby.

A wooden catwalk from the third floor of the Interpretation Centre leads out over the shipyard, giving a panoramic view of the *Hector* under construction, looking like an array of huge, unstrung lyres. Her reconstruction will take three or four years; it has been seeded by government, but eventually it will be funded by the Hector Foundation, which will have to raise money for its continuance. A fine little gift shop stands next door, run by Don Mackay, whom I had known years before at the University of New Brunswick. The site also includes a complete, functional blacksmith shop—Graham's father's shop, carefully moved here from Mosher River, on the Eastern Shore.

"The Hector project needed a blacksmith shop, so I contributed it to the project," Graham said. "That stall over there is where my father used to shoe horses. See those ropes hanging from the rafters, right next to it? That was my swing when I was a child."

The *Hector* project is a tasteful presentation of an important historical episode, and Graham is rightly proud of it. The finished development will give Pictou a core of facilities and attractions which should please visitors very much. Largely because of the DeCoste Centre and the Hector Heritage Quay, Pictou is probably the fastest-developing town in the province: 16 new businesses started there in 1992, for instance, in the depths of a fierce and prolonged recession.

Until Graham Holman's workmen installed an aluminum gangway between the wharf and the floating dock, we had to clamber ashore across the motor cruiser and *Footloose*, and the southeast gale that first day pushed the cruiser far enough from the wharf to rub against *Footloose*. We adjusted the lines to keep *Footloose* farther away. On our next trip we met her owner, told him what we had done and suggested he look at the lines to be sure they were tied to his satisfaction. Roly Andrews was a tall, fit-looking man with thinning sandy hair, a Pictou native semi-retired from an engineering consultancy in Toronto. He and his crews had brought the boat all the way down Lake Ontario and the St. Lawrence, motoring through a thousand windless miles and splashing through blasts of wind as they crossed the Gulf.

Now he was planning a day sail on Sunday with some friends: would we like to come? We would. As a completely self-taught sailor, I rarely lose a chance to see the different—often better— ways that others do things. A Bruce Farr design, *Footloose* was bound to be fast. She had given Roly his share of successes in club races in Toronto. He would be a good model.

Meanwhile, I had heard that a man named Doug MacNeil was building a Bruce Roberts boat in Pictou. I found him not far from the Hector Heritage Quay, in a one-time service garage on the waterfront. The boat was a 31-footer made of C-Flex— flexible rods of fiberglass held in a mesh, capable of being shaped to the complex curves of a boat's hull and held there by the resin. I had never seen C-Flex used before.

Doug MacNeil's boat is only four feet longer than *Silversark*, but she is a far bigger vessel, deep-bellied and broad. Her hull had been primed in flat grey, and it was complete down to the propeller and rudder. I called out. A muffled voice answered from far above me, deep inside the boat. I climbed a ladder. The deck was complete, and the deckhouse was finished. Doug Mac-Neil was inside, a wiry little man in his sixties, with bright eyes and a wide, slow smile.

His engine was installed and much of the interior in place. He was panelling the bulkheads in V-joint veneer. He had made an astonishing number of his own metal parts, including the propeller shaft, the sea-cocks, the cabinet latches, all meticulously crafted.

"How long have you been working at this project?" I asked.

"Thirteen years."

"Thirteen *years*! We took eight and a half, and that was plenty."

"Well, it takes a long time, working two or three hours at a time," Doug said apologetically. "I can't afford the oil to heat the shop in the winter, and the insurance won't let me heat it with wood. So I can only work in the warm weather. During the winter I make little bits and pieces in the basement."

Doug is retired, and he has plenty of time for boat building— time enough to do a superlative job. What, one wonders, is all that time worth? He smiled.

"I've often wondered what she was worth. I know if I could get two dollars an hour for all the time I've put into her, she'd be worth a lot of money."

"Well," I said, "come down and see *Silversark*. She's solid proof that these things do eventually get done."

But he wasn't doing it to get it done. He was working for the sense of accomplishment, the joy of the thing itself. Character, says E.F. Schumacher, is formed primarily by work, "and work, properly conducted in conditions of human dignity and freedom, blesses those who do it and equally their products."

We had gone for dinner with friends, and we were late for the theatre. Slipping in quietly, we took a table near the back of the theatre, which was laid out cabaret-style. It is a cavernous space, like a warehouse, with the exposed structural members typical of modern gyms and auditoriums, but the layout of the seating, the colours and fabrics on the walls, made it warm and interesting all the same.

I had seen *Nova Scotia Songbook* before, in an earlier production in Cape Breton, where it was created. Essentially, it is an evening of the famous Nova Scotian songs—"Farewell to Nova Scotia," "Song for the Mira," "Sea People" and many others: musical comedy without the comedy, except in the form of farcical skits. Lacking the tension of a story line and the bite of a satire, the *Songbook* becomes a pleasant, harmless evening—but it, too, is being carried by the rising tide of Cape Breton culture, and the show was about to make a tour of Japan.

When the lights came up at intermission, a couple at a distant table waved us over to them: Rod and Robin MacLennan.

At an age somewhat north of 50, Rod is, quite literally, the ultimate Boy Scout. His idea of fun is to take a bunch of Scouts hiking across the Cape Breton Highlands into a deserted cove and to camp there with them until the food runs out. He was just back from Pond Inlet, in the Northwest Territories, where he and some companions had made a trip to the edge of the Arctic ice. He is rangy, energetic, classically handsome. He is a graduate of Dalhousie, Dartmouth, the Harvard Business School and (almost) the University of Wisconsin graduate school. He follows a vast range of subjects: the arts, business, politics, higher education, the outdoors, history, Volvos and milk. Milk? Yes, milk.

When you talk to Rod about China, he has memories of China. When you talk to him about the Gulf of St. Lawrence, he remembers what Cartier had to say about it. He chaired a provincial Royal Commission on Post-Secondary Education. If he were not so transparently genial and open-hearted, he would be terrifying.

He runs a small charitable foundation for the performing arts specifically in Colchester County and Cape Breton. The foundation honours his Truro-born father and his Glace Bay-born mother, and it supported Centre Bras d'Or, a Cape Breton arts organization, when I was its executive director. As we spoke, it was funding one of the Barra MacNeils to study music in Europe.

After the show we went to the MacLennans' summer home in Caribou River, which was built in the 1830s.

"My father bought it years ago," Rod said. "It's the old Cape Cod style; it has the central chimney with three fireplaces on the one chimney. In the wintertime, the old lady who lived here used to have her groceries delivered to the end of the driveway, and then haul them in on a sled."

He knows about milk because he is senior vice-president of Scotsburn Dairyfoods, one of Nova Scotia's two major dairy companies. We asked why it was so hard to find UHT milk, which is pasteurized at ultra-high temperatures and stays fresh for months at room temperature until opened. Since we have no refrigeration on the boat, we use a lot of UHT. In Nova Scotia it comes only in 2% form, though it tastes like whole milk to me.

"Two-percent milk now has a larger market share than whole milk," Rod said. "Except in Cape Breton. Nobody really knows why, but we think it may be because Cape Bretoners drink a lot of tea, and they like the taste of whole milk in their tea. Those things have a real impact. Tim Horton's coffee may be so successful because they always use 18% cream.

"UHT milk is more acceptable in Europe, where they don't mind the slightly cooked taste. Canadians and Scandinavians are used to fresh whole milk, and they don't accept UHT as readily. But it's been a great success with chocolate milk and milk shakes and other products where the flavour masks the cooked taste."

We ended up talking about the pivotal role of Nova Scotia's universities in the province's future. If the new economy is based on knowledge and information, the universities are vital resources. In a poor province with a population smaller than that of Vancouver, 14 universities have to work smart if they themselves are to be excellent, let alone help the community towards excellence.

The Urgent Conversation again.

The MacLennans dropped us back to the boat. In the afterglow of our visit, it occurred to me that Rod was an example of the kind of person I would want our universities to produce: professionally skilled, insatiably curious, deeply rooted in this haunting little province and yet a citizen of the world.

I found myself similarly fond of the Water Rat, who represents the origins of cruising—idiosyncratic, self-sufficient, craggily independent. In the early classics of cruising literature, eager voyagers go to sea in whatever vessels come to hand. The pioneers of cruising bought fishing smacks, pilot cutters, big dories, ship's lifeboats and similar cheap makeshifts, and converted them as best they could. Some built their own boats, often unskilfully. Once afloat, they sailed off—across the bay or around the world. The accommodations were rudimentary, the boats often leaked either through the hull or through the decks or both, and the navigational equipment ranged from impromptu to primitive. But most of the voyagers dodged the various obstacles thrown at them by man and nature in a world much less homogeneous than ours; they got home safely, and they had fascinating experiences along the way.

Cruising has since become another illustration of Cameron's Travel Axiom: The Easier It Is To Get Somewhere, The Less Reason There Is To Go There. (Think about it. Hawaii must have been lovely, once. Singapore used to be exotic.) Sleek fiberglass boats now crowd the endless marinas along the coasts of the developed world. Many of them are used rarely, some not at all—and when they do travel, they frequently travel in packs.

The Water Rat harks back to the independent and innocent spirit of that earlier day. His name is Tony Eastman. After a lifetime at sea, he is spending his retirement cruising the coasts of the Gulf and Cape Breton with his wife Bertha. The boat is Tony's passion, not Bertha's. She enjoys it, but she does no sailing, no steering, no navigating. She just keeps house, ashore and at sea. She wouldn't know what to do if anything happened to Tony.

Tony sailed first on his father's freight schooner on the Bras d'Or Lakes, carrying heavy wooden pit props for the coal mines. After some years in the Navy, he ended his career aboard oceanographic research vessels. He spent 11 summers in Ungava Bay and the eastern Arctic doing survey work.

Skua was a survey launch, declared surplus by the Department of Fisheries and Oceans—a solid, seakindly old wooden boat. She remains simple, functional, unfussy. The cockpit structure which looks like an outhouse *is* an outhouse, with a built-in shower. The cockpit is rimmed with bottles, cans, lines and gear, all lashed away tidily under the narrow side decks. Tony steers from a high, open shelter pierced by the unmuffled, uninsulated exhaust pipe from the Mustang 289 engine.

"Manual transmission," says Tony. "Works all right, but it's got no low gear. Jams sometimes when you try to put her into reverse. Then you have to jig with it. Have to drop the anchor sometimes till you get it fixed."

The interior is simple and clean—freshly painted, freshly scrubbed. Two plain plywood benches serve as seats and sleeping berths. A few functional cabinets complement a cast-iron stove, a big brass barometer screwed to a bulkhead and a piece of

board fixed between two beams with Tony's screwdrivers and
chisels thrusting down through it. A small TV sits on a forward
shelf.

"Twelve volt, that TV," Tony explains. "Runs off a deep-cycle
battery. I charge the battery with a little Honda generator. I run it
for an hour every other day, that's all it needs."

By today's fiberglass and teak standards, *Skua* is spartan
indeed. But Tony is grateful to have her.

"I grew up in North Sydney," he says. "When I left, people
were abandoning their houses. They couldn't find work and they
couldn't keep their houses up, couldn't pay the taxes. Everybody
was more or less in the same boat. They couldn't sell their
houses, nobody wanted to buy. So they were just walking away
and leaving the houses."

And now, in his late seventies, Tony spends his summers
wandering the coast on a pleasure boat with his wife, and his
winters in a snug home in Pictou. When he compares his boy-
hood and his retirement, he feels rich. When I went looking for
them next morning, Tony and Bertha were gone. Someone said
they had left early, heading for Lismore.

The greatest Pictonian of all time was a pawky Presbyterian
minister named Thomas McCulloch, who arrived in Pictou with
his wife and three children in November, 1803. By the time he
died in 1843, he had precipitated democratic government in
Nova Scotia, inaugurated three notable educational institutions,
distinguished himself as a scientist and lecturer and—in the
opinion of no less an authority than Northrop Frye—founded
Canadian humour.

In Scotland, McCulloch's parents' generation had included
the most brilliant intellectual circle in Europe. Robert Burns had
just died, and Walter Scott was publishing his earliest poems; he
would dominate European literature for a generation. In Edinburgh, the men who met as the Oyster Club included the philos-
opher David Hume; the architect Robert Adam; the chemist
Joseph Black, the discoverer of carbon dioxide; James Watt, the
inventor of the steam engine; Adam Smith, the founder of economics; Adam Ferguson, the founder of sociology; and James
Hutton, the founder of geology. Benjamin Franklin sat in on

some of their discussions and called them "a set of as truly great men . . . as have ever appeared in any Age or Country."

From the Scottish Enlightenment, as it became known, McCulloch absorbed the conviction that learning should lead not to a narrow pedantry, but to a broad and humane understanding of moral problems, the natural world and contemporary society. Distressed at Pictou's lack of educational opportunities, he resolved to start a school, and ultimately a college to train Presbyterian ministers and to provide a liberal education for young men preparing for the professions.

Pictou Academy began in McCulloch's home. At various times McCulloch himself taught logic, moral philosophy, chemistry, mathematics, political economy, Greek, Latin, Hebrew, theology and natural history. He was well-enough known as a naturalist to attract the attention of John James Audubon, who stopped by to visit him in 1833. Audubon found in McCulloch's collection "a dozen specimens of birds which I longed for and said so," so McCulloch gave them to him.

McCulloch soon established a Divinity Hall in the Academy, and in 1824 he sent three students to the University of Glasgow to be examined for the Master of Arts degree. They all passed handsomely, and Divinity Hall became a seminary, which eventually evolved into Pine Hill Divinity Hall, now part of the Atlantic School of Theology.

Pictou Academy never gained degree-granting status, and its financial situation was always precarious. Nova Scotia's elected Assembly repeatedly passed bills to support it, but the Council—appointed and mainly Anglican—frequently vetoed them. Eventually the issue became one of democratic and constitutional principle. Who was to control the affairs of Nova Scotia, the electorate or the elite? Joseph Howe became convinced of the rightness of McCulloch's cause, and went on to revolutionize the entire system of British colonial governance by winning responsible government for Nova Scotia. He used to say that he had learned its principles from a man in Pictou.

Though he wrote many polemics and a couple of stilted novels, McCulloch's literary reputation rests on one book, *The Stepsure Letters*, published serially in the *Acadian Recorder* of Halifax beginning in December, 1821, and reissued in 1960 as part of the New Canadian Library. Moulded by shrewd observation,

scathing irony and surprisingly coarse humour, the *Letters* make
a dry, entertaining book. When two evangelists recall what terrible sinners they used to be, another character nods "a cordial
assent." Elsewhere McCulloch's hero remarks that "amidst the
infirmities of age, it is a great comfort to old folks, that, whatever
destruction time works in their memory, they never find it affecting their judgment."

Meanwhile the Earl of Dalhousie, the Scottish Lieutenant-
Governor of Nova Scotia, had concluded that the province
needed a non-sectarian college modelled on the University of
Edinburgh—exactly what McCulloch had dreamed of creating
in Pictou. The cornerstone of Dalhousie College was laid in
1820, but the idea faced bitter opposition, and by 1838
Dalhousie had not opened its doors. When McCulloch opened
the letter inviting him to serve as its founding principal, he
smiled and said, "The Lord hath delivered the enemy into my
hands." By the time he died, five years later, "godless
Dalhousie" was on its way to becoming what it is today, the
leading university in the Maritimes.

And though McCulloch's beloved Pictou Academy never
became a degree-granting college, it produced an extraordinary
roll call of alumni: two provincial premiers, two lieutenant-
governors, four judges, 300 ministers, innumerable doctors and
lawyers and professors—and eight university presidents, of
whom the most famous was one of McCulloch's own students,
the celebrated geologist Sir William Dawson, principal of
McGill University and president of the Royal Society.

In the Maritimes' Urgent Conversation about The Deal and the
future, McCulloch should be an important example. Alas, he is
not. We went to his house, set among shrubs and flowers on a
gentle hillside overlooking the West River. McCulloch built it in
1806, using bricks imported on speculation by a local merchant.
When the importer found himself unable to sell the bricks, he
gave them to the minister. After McCulloch built the house, the
merchant sent him a bill for the bricks.

It is a snug little house, now part of the Nova Scotia Museum,
and we found some interesting pictures of early Pictou on the
walls, as well as a selection of old leather-bound books from

McCulloch's library in a glass-fronted bookcase. Some of the woodwork had been done by McCulloch's brother George, a cabinetmaker, and the plaster trim had been provided by an adept parishioner. In the dining room we saw a small round table that probably belonged to McCulloch: it was donated by Rod MacLennan's family, who had bought it from McCulloch's descendants.

But McCulloch was not there. The guide had little sense of his importance, scarcely noted that he was the first principal of Atlantic Canada's premier university, did not even mention that he was among the few Canadian writers of his era whose work is still read and studied. In the end, I found the McCulloch House not inspiring, but depressing. It is not easy to make McCulloch seem dull, but somehow the museum had managed it.

I found myself with a nagging uneasiness about the *Hector* project, and as I tried to describe it Graham Holman and I slipped into the Urgent Conversation. For the *Hector* project, like many other historic and quasi-historic tourist attractions, conveys an ambiguous and perhaps harmful message. If the achievements of the dead are *all* that we can show to visitors, then we are also implying that the living are less capable and less interesting than the giants of the past. That is the wrong message, both for the visitor and for ourselves. We should be standing on the shoulders of those giants and seeing farther, not crouching in their shadow and seeing less. The *Hector* was a worn-out Dutch trader which happened to be available when an emigrant ship was needed. The passengers mattered, but the ship did not. Is it the ship that we want to rebuild? Or is it the passengers, with all their courage, perseverance and self-confidence?

If I were a Pictonian, I said, I would look to McCulloch more than the *Hector* for strength and insight. The future of the Maritimes depends on knowledge, creativity, imagination, scientific curiosity. Those are McCulloch's themes, and they lie near the heart of the Urgent Conversation. If McCulloch were alive he would be passionately involved in the discussion.

If we are going to engage in ancestor worship, let us at least worship the right ancestors. And let us focus our minds on what is really important about them.

THE CLASS

OF '42

We boarded *Footloose* at one o'clock on a Sunday afternoon. The weather, as usual, was unsettled—windows of sunlight chased by slabs of cloud, the wind coming and going fitfully. Roly and Carol Andrews had two other couples aboard: Cam and Dimmie Garrett, John and Jean Wayling. As we motored out of the marina, Roly offered me the helm. He went forward and raised the mainsail. *Footloose* took off, sprinting down the harbour. Roly unfurled the big genoa, a gold-coloured semi-transparent racing sail made of Kevlar. *Footloose* speeded up. In a breeze of no more than 15 knots, she was travelling at six knots. Lulu and I looked at each other wide-eyed, with the same thought: compared to this boat, our beloved little *Silversark* was a torpid snail.

Cam Garrett was the skipper I had tried to phone for advice as we approached Pictou. As we passed the Royal William Yacht Club opposite the town, he pointed out his boat, a small wooden sloop with a pop-top, like a Volkswagen camper: underway, the deck stays down and the cabin is cramped—but at anchor part of the deck lifts up, giving full standing headroom.

The yacht club lacks a proper wharf, slip, moorings, guest facilities and almost everything else pertaining to boats; it survives as an agreeable bar. Its name commemorates the first ship ever to make a transatlantic passage entirely under power. The steamer *Royal William* departed Pictou on August 18, 1833, and arrived in the River Thames twenty days later. The Americans claim her feat was anticipated by the steamer *Savannah*, which crossed in 1819; the British usually cite the *Sirius* and *Great Western*. But the *Savannah*'s detractors note that she sailed most of the way, while the British ships made their crossings five years after the *Royal William*.

Pictou Harbour was busy that afternoon. Now Lulu had the helm, and *Footloose* was weaving through the crowd of sloops, speedboats, motor cruisers and ex-fishing boats. We sliced past the long beach at the lighthouse and out into Pictou Road, the boat full of happy chatter, Roly and Lulu enjoying the sailing.

I listened. These were obviously old, close friends, and they had all been out the previous night with a larger group of familiar people. They talked about who had married whom, and where someone was living, and what someone else had been doing lately. One of them remembered chiselling her initials into a rock near Merigomish long ago, and catching hell for losing the chisel. She had gone back to look at the initials the other day, and they were still there.

Carol Andrews set out trays of snacks—cheese and lobster on crackers, vegetables and dips, a bowl of sugared strawberries. Very civilized: so unlike the home life of our own dear ship.

And who were they? I knew Roly was an engineer, and Dimmie seemed to be a teacher. John and Jean had lived in India, but were now snowbirds, migrating between Nova Scotia and Florida.

I gave up and asked John.

"Oh!" said John. "We're all here for the reunion of the class of '42." One partner in each couple was a member of the 1942 graduating class at the New Glasgow high school. Last night had been their 50th-anniversary reunion.

"I think everyone should go below," Roly said suddenly. "Carol, would you pass up my oilskins, please?"

"I need some too, please," said Lulu, still at the wheel.

Everyone looked up: a squall was sweeping off the land towards us, a low dark cloud trailing thick curtains of rain. People scrambled below while Lulu and Roly pulled on foul-weather gear. The land and the other boats vanished as the rain hit. It was a wall of water: torrents of rain thundering on the deck, sheets of water pouring off the bottoms of the sails. The waves vanished, beaten flat by the rain; the surface of the sea bubbled up into a carpet of glass marbles. It seemed impossible that rain could ever be heavier than this. There simply wasn't enough room left between the drops for any more water. Lulu and Roly stood in the cockpit, Lulu holding the big destroyer-style wheel, both of them grinning as rain streamed off their oilskins.

The squall eased and moved off. The sun came out again. We went back on deck, mopping off the cockpit seats and taking up comfortable positions. Carol served Nanaimo bars, cookies and cake, tea and coffee. Lulu's food allergies put most of the food off limits, but she had attained a certain status from braving the rain. While she continued to steer, others in the party took turns impaling strawberries on long silver forks and delivering them into her mouth.

The class of '42. They were all nearing 70, and occasionally some comment revealed it: Jean had heart problems, for instance, and one of John's hip joints was made of plastic. But I had been watching them move about the boat, taking in dock lines and fenders, casting off sail ties, hoisting sails. They all looked trim, fit, robust. They were all experienced sailors, cat-like and sure-footed on deck. Roly dropped in and out of the conversation from time to time, part of his attention always directed towards the boat and the sailing, making small adjustments to the course, trimming the sails to keep her moving, directing the helm to steer a little off the direct downwind course in order to keep both sails full and drawing.

A reunion makes people look backward, but the class of '42 seemed to view the past with amusement and the future with enthusiasm.

The Waylings had been missionaries in India—"establishing trade schools," John said quickly, heading off the inevitable image of religious imperialism, "trying to give people something useful they could take back to their villages instead of just drifting into the cities." Back in Canada, he spent 12 years in parish work, ending up in a downtown Toronto church before moving to the Canadian Mental Health Association. Jean worked in communications with the Social Planning Council, the St. Lawrence Centre and the City of Toronto. Retiring at 55, they had spent their meagre savings on a Morgan 34 in Florida. They spent ten winters sailing the Bahamas and ten summers operating a bed-and-breakfast in Jimtown, on St. George's Bay. Their health problems two years earlier had induced them to sell the boat to a daughter and her husband. They had bought a small retirement home on the IntraCoastal Waterway in Florida. They hadn't sailed since, and they had obviously missed it: when John took the wheel, he beamed with pleasure.

Off Merigomish *Footloose* sailed through another heavy rain squall, then emerged again into the sunlight. The talk turned to the sermon delivered that morning at Trinity United Church in New Glasgow by the Reverend Dr. Peter Paris—a member of the class of '52, which was also holding a reunion.

"Did he give it to them?" demanded John. "About race? Really lay it on the line?"

Yes, he was assured, Peter Paris had laid it on the line. An internationally recognized scholar and teacher, Paris went from New Glasgow to Acadia University for degrees in arts and divinity, and then to the University of Chicago for his master's and doctorate. He taught at Howard and Vanderbilt universities and lectured throughout North America and Africa. He is now professor of Christian ethics at Princeton Theological Seminary.

And Peter Paris remembers very well what it was like to grow up as a black kid in Pictou County. In those days, Nova Scotia was a northern Dixie: in New Glasgow, blacks lived in a district called Nigger Hill, without town water or sewer. The main landlord, John recalls, charged exorbitant rents; he was the mayor, a devout Baptist. Blacks were obliged to sit in the balcony at the movie theatre and were closely followed by suspicious clerks whenever they entered a store. They were not served in restaurants, either. When the director of the Coady International Institute at St. Francis Xavier University stopped at a New Glasgow restaurant with some visiting African dignitaries, the waiter created a minor international incident by offering to serve the academic, but not his black guests.

"I am so *ashamed* about that!" cried John Wayling. "*We* could have stopped that. We could have picketed those theatres and restaurants ourselves, even at eighteen. But it never even *occurred* to us!"

We should all be ashamed. The report of the inquiry into Donald Marshall's 11-year false imprisonment for murder makes it very clear—if anyone doubted it—that racism in Nova Scotia is still widespread, deeply rooted and systemic. The report confirmed that the province's 11,000 natives and 13,000 blacks are unequally treated in almost every area of life: in housing, in employment, in education and throughout the justice system.

And Pictou County is still as bad as any place in the province. In recent years there have been several brawls between blacks and whites in Halifax, notably at the racially mixed high school in suburban Cole Harbour, but perhaps the most sickening incident occurred at the Stellarton campus of the Nova Scotia Community College, only four of whose 350 students are black. In January, 1990, six white students beat one of those blacks, punching him and beating his head against a steel door. He was held by two others while 100 more looked on. When one of the white students was suspended and charged with assault, fifty students walked out in protest.

The black student's name was Jeremy Paris. His father, Henderson Paris, is the youngest in a family of ten. The oldest is Dr. Peter Paris, the distinguished theologian.

Yet racism, as an issue, is hardly visible on Nova Scotia's political radar screen. It is not much talked about in polite company—a piece of evidence as revealing as any. John Wayling was once invited to preach at Trinity, too, and like Peter Paris, he laid it on the line about racism. He was never invited back.

But indignation is not John Wayling's natural *métier*. We will all live to fight racism another day, but at this moment we are still together, six old friends and two new ones, enjoying one another's company as we sail back into Pictou Harbour through flurries of small boats. The old town lies on its steep, low hills, bathed in streams of golden sunlight. The water sparkles; the wind drives *Footloose* quickly up the harbour.

And then, clutching the steering wheel, soaking up the pleasures of sailing and friendship, John Wayling says a wonderful thing.

"You know," he says, grinning happily, "life doesn't get much better than this, does it?"

I look at him, startled. Is this a peak moment, what the time-management theorists call a "flow experience," when one is so immersed in the moment that one loses track of self? Maybe so, and I bet John Wayling has had more than his share of such experiences. This man, with his generous gratitude, fully inhabits the passing moments which make up a lifetime. It is a rare gift, that capacity for appreciation, that ability to savour the moment rather than living forever in the future.

Life doesn't get much better than this.

I look at Lulu—and yes, she heard it, too.

John Wayling's voice will echo through our lives for a long, long time.

We sailed regretfully from Pictou at two forty-five the next afternoon, after a morning spent repairing the stove and doing last-minute errands. We had a crew: Dave Bateman, a close friend from the earliest days of our marriage, my one-time diving buddy. He now runs a small drafting and design business in New Glasgow, and we have seen very little of him in recent years. Why is so much of a lifetime taken up with necessities, so little reserved for the people we really enjoy?

We were sailing only to Caribou, five or six miles away—just an easy afternoon's sail. The trip began under a grey sky, the wind blowing puffy and fickle straight off the town. We set the main and jumbo, close-reaching down the harbour. When we lived in Louisbourg, Dave was not a sailor, but he had done some cruising since he moved to New Glasgow. He seemed as happy as John Wayling to have the helm, so we left him there.

The wind dropped outside the harbour, and we set the genoa, coaxing the boat forward. We passed the first outside buoy. At the second buoy we would turn up the Strait for Caribou. But just as we reached it, the wind disappeared. The light turned pearly. The land became indistinct.

"Fog?" I said. "Fog? There's no fog in Northumberland Strait in July."

"This year there is," said Dave. "What a summer."

"That buoy's getting farther away," said Lulu.

"Lot of current out here," said Dave.

The fog closed down firmly. The buoy disappeared. We hoisted the radar reflector into the rigging to ensure that *Silversark* would show up brightly on ships' radars. It looked like a big white fender.

"Odd-looking radar reflector," Dave said.

"It's supposed to be honeycombed with aluminum right angles inside," I said. "If a radar beam comes anywhere near, it should reflect it. They say it's a lot more effective than one of those little folding jobbies."

"Be nice to know for sure, though, wouldn't it?" Lulu said.

"At times like this it would."

I went below and checked our position on the Loran. Naturally we were drifting steadily eastward. The gods of wind and current simply did not want us going west this summer.

"You ever think about installing an engine?" asked Dave.

"All the time."

"I've got a friend who's got a couple of little diesels."

"Give me his number."

It started to rain—lightly at first, then more heavily. Before long it was another downpour. Dave is a short, powerful man; in a floater jacket and shorts, he sat grinning in the streaming rain, looking like a weight-lifter in the shower after a good work-out. There was still no wind.

We decided that our situation as sailors was like our situation as small businessmen. After two years of recession, the economy was like a foggy, windless sea. You could no longer see your destination, and no matter how skilful and determined you might be, you couldn't possibly catch the wind if there wasn't any wind to catch. When the whole economy was becalmed, you stayed alert, working hard to catch every vagrant puff, but the result might very well be that you simply kept losing ground.

I like sailing as a metaphor for business; it fits far better than the military analogies which often prevail. Our metaphors shape our attitudes: our attitudes shape our actions. If business is war, then the company is an army—hierarchical and rigid, with divisions and tactics, officers and recruits. Generals make major decisions, majors make minor decisions, and nobody else decides anything at all. There are companies in which managers actually refer to workers as "mutts" and "grunts"—the American GI's own term for himself.

But companies which function like armies—ponderous, imprecise, inflexible—are being slaughtered in the fluid, fragmented nineties, like Braddock's tightly formed battalions being cut to ribbons by French and Indian guerrillas firing from behind the trees. If we want better organizations, says management critic Tom Peters, we need richer metaphors—from sports, cooking, photography, orchestral music, education.

Or from sailing, which—to me—business greatly resembles. Companies like Four Seasons, Microsoft and Magna International navigate steadily forward through fair weather and storms, tacking and shortening sail in adverse winds, working patiently through calms, spreading clouds of canvas to a favourable breeze. The work unit at McDonald's is a "crew." The successful business, like the successful voyage, requires decisiveness and knowledge, enough self-confidence to hold your course even when you can't really see where you're going, a sound vessel, reliable charts and a capable, disciplined crew.

Silversark had all that, of course, but we were in a nautical recession: we were losing ground all the same. Dave looked over the side and snorted.

"Even the jellyfish are passing us," he said.

"Don't talk about it." We had been drifting for two hours.

"I think—"

We all felt it. A breath of wind—from the east, too.

"Shh! Don't say anything!"

We boomed the sails out. *Silversark* began to move—but very, very slowly. Dave glanced over the side.

"That's good, we're passing the jellyfish now," he said. And then, a moment later, "I can see the buoy."

"You can?"

"Yep. Right up there, a little off the port bow."

Lulu and I gazed into the grey murk. We couldn't see a thing.

"It's there," said Dave calmly. We sailed on, and a few minutes later the buoy emerged from the fog—the same buoy we had seen two full hours before. It was seven twenty-five.

"Land over there," Dave said, pointing ahead and to port. "Doctor's Island, I guess."

Lulu and I looked at each other.

"You can see land over there?" I said.

"Yeah. Right there."

I couldn't see anything but fog.

"From now on," I said, "any time we're going to sail in fog, I want you aboard."

"Lot of wildlife on that island," Dave said. "Somebody was going to put a big RV campsite on it, but the Nature Conservancy bought it."

We passed the buoy and set a course for the Caribou Harbour entrance. The wind was almost dead behind us. The current seemed to be helping us. The fog thickened and thinned, but Lulu and I still saw nothing. Halfway up the forestay, coming and going behind the jib, the sun hung like a pale silver disk in the flat white sky. It was quite eerie, and very beautiful: a world turned ground-glass grey, and glowing softly.

But we could hear a diesel engine drumming somewhere off to starboard, and up ahead were big car ferries, shuttling back and forth to Wood Islands, PEI. We did not want to dispute the narrow channel into Caribou with one of those. I called Northumberland Ferries on the VHF.

"*Silversark*, this is *Prince Nova*. Go ahead."

"We're an engineless sailing vessel heading for Caribou, and we don't want to get in your way in the channel. What's the schedule for ferry traffic in and out of Caribou?"

"We'll be sailing at eight-fifteen, and the *Lord Selkirk* will be coming in at eight forty-five." *Each one will be five minutes in the channel,* I thought, *so that's a 20-minute window between them. May the wind hold.*

"Where are you now, *Silversark*?"

"About two miles east of the fairway buoy, and doing three knots. So we might get to the buoy about the same time."

"Well, we'll be watching for you. Over and out."

We left the radio on, which we don't normally do: with no engine and no generator, we have only a finite amount of battery power. But if *Prince Nova* had anything more to say to us, we wanted to hear it. Suddenly the radio crackled.

"Calling the sailboat that was talking to *Prince Nova*, over."

"This is *Silversark*, go ahead."

"This is *Fleur de Lis*. I been wondering what that target was on the radar. I think I'm a little outside of you, heading east."

"You got a fair-sized diesel engine?"

"Yep."

"We can hear you off to starboard. Are we painting a good target on your radar?"

"Pretty bright, yeah."

"That's good to know. So that radar reflector works."

"Works just fine. Have a good trip. *Fleur de Lis* out."

Voices in the air, and nothing in sight.

We sailed on, willing our eyesight to pierce the fog.

"I can see the buoy," said Dave. "Dead ahead."

Eagle Eye Bateman. The buoy appeared, a smudgy charcoal outline on grey paper. I glanced at my watch: eight-ten. Ten minutes, probably, till *Prince Nova* would reach the buoy. We were going to arrive almost at the same time. I called *Prince Nova* and told her we had the buoy in sight.

The minutes crept by. The buoy grew larger, its edges more distinct. It became red, not grey. We heard engines in the distance, faint at first, then growing louder.

The buoy was 200 yards away. The engines were drumming.

"Look!"

A low, straight black form took shape in the fog, moving steadily towards us. It was—it was *just the hull* of the ferry. The superstructure was hidden in the fog: the air was clear for just six feet above the water. We watched, fascinated, as the narrow shape came towards us, grew longer, and blotted out the buoy. *Prince Nova* was turning away from us. The black shape narrowed again, then vanished. The radio crackled.

"*Silversark*, this is *Prince Nova*. All clear. We had you on the radar all the time."

"Thanks, *Prince Nova*. We show up well on your radar?"

"Clear as a bell. You'll have a nice sail in—there's no fog in the channel."

We turned at the buoy, and the thick fog went away. Suddenly our eyes were switched back on. We were already inside Caribou Harbour, a wide, low swath of water. I noted the big lighthouse on Gull Point, and the rows of cottages which stretched along the beach. This shore is less than two hours' drive from Halifax. The shoreline is sandy, the water is warm, and Haligonians in summer plumage are frequently sighted.

But the fog had left just a faint hint of haze over the low wooded hills, the sandbars and the islands. Diffused in the moist air, the setting sun cast gold dust over sharp black outlines. Every feature of the landscape looked breathless, bewitched, symbolic. It was an Alex Colville painting: images of ordinary things presented with extraordinary resonance.

The wind had stiffened just slightly, and the current was with us. We were flying past the channel buoys. We tacked up to the ferry slip, sailed past the fishermen's berths, chose a spot, turned and sailed in, rounding up beside the tugboat *George Bay*, which in turn was moored to a dredge.

It was nine-fifteen. It had taken us six and a half hours to cover about the same number of miles.

"Great day," said Dave.

We had no particular reason to be in Caribou; it was just a pretty harbour a bit closer to Charlottetown than Pictou. But the next day's breeze was strong and adverse; rather than struggle against it, we spent the day on boat chores. We borrowed Dave's truck to fetch our car; we would have to go to Halifax in a couple of days to do some shopping, research a magazine story, deliver a speech and, above all, pick up Mark at the airport. If we left the car in Caribou, we could sail to PEI and take the ferry back. Meanwhile, trying to lighten the boat, we loaded excess gear into the car, plugged minor deck leaks and made various small repairs.

"Silver Donald!"

A man on the dredge was calling and waving. It was Bruce Prout, a Westerner who had settled in L'Ardoise, not far from our home. He was not a happy wanderer just then; within seconds, we were back in the Urgent Conversation.

The federal Department of Public Works once had 18 dredges working in the Maritimes. Cutbacks and privatization had eliminated 16, and this one was in her last season. She was going to Newfoundland to give employment to displaced cod fishermen, so the entire crew would be laid off.

"They've offered us severance, but it amounts to a lay-off,"

Bruce said. "After 20 years established down here, I'll probably have to go back out West. I don't want to, but what can I do?"

He went back to work, and I walked up to the ferry terminal to make a phone call. I found myself thinking of the terrible depressions of the Maritime past: the Water Rat and his youth in North Sydney; farms and businesses abandoned during the 1950s and 1960s when the rest of North America was booming, the people emigrating to the Boston States, Upper Canada, the West. There were 1,492 people in our own village in the 1871 census; a century later there were just 228. Nothing remained of the forge, the lobster factories, the sawmill, the sail loft, the waterfront warehouses. Even the shorefront road on which they were located had been washed away by the sea.

Alex Colville once told me that Maritimers are wary of change because they do not share the "fatuous optimism" which grows as one moves west. Maritimers know that change may very well be for the worse. This ground is soaked with the blood of the French, English and Mi'kmaq people who fought for nearly 300 years to gain possession of it. The sea floor is littered with the bones of brigantines and submarines, fishermen and able seamen, Irish emigrants and French aristocrats. The Atlantic memory includes starvation, cannibalism, extinction, slavery, near-serfdom for fishermen and woodcutters. I know people in their 40s whose only meat during the winters of their childhood came from squirrels their fathers shot. "Ethnic cleansing" is what the British were doing to the Acadians in 1755.

That dark and bloody history makes us closer to Europe than to California in our outlook, and it gives the urgency to the Urgent Conversation. Hunger and despair are not things we imagine: they are things we remember. As the fishery, the mines and the mills close down, the federal government and its agencies cut everything that can be cut—lighthouses, military bases, post offices, railways, the CBC, even the dredges.

What are we going to do? And how are we going to do it?

That evening in Caribou, we set out to look for Gary Cameron.

Gary was Lulu's instructor when she studied for her 100-ton Master Mariner's Certificate. She passed the examinations handsomely, but was refused the certificate on the grounds that she did not have sufficient sea time *in fishing boats,* a requirement never mentioned when she enrolled. Yes, it did sound plainly sexist, and yes, the Human Rights Commission did take an interest; in the end, she received a letter saying that she had met all the requirements except for the sea time. And no, the government of Canada does not issue a Yacht Master's certificate, which is really what she wanted.

None of that had anything to do with Gary. We found his home on the Otter Road—named not for an animal, but for a family. It was a new house of traditional character. To one side, in a clearing in the woods, was the frame of a low, broad building: Gary's half-built gear shed. At the end of the driveway, beside the house, stood an enormous fiberglass fishing boat named *Sharran Ann.* We shouted. Gary answered from down in the bilge, where he was installing a new transducer. He emerged and took us to the house for coffee. His wife and children had gone shopping.

Like most Northumberland Strait fishermen, Gary depends primarily on lobster, augmented by other species at different times of the year. It had not been a good lobster season; he had taken 12,000 pounds this year as opposed to 17,000 last year and 23,000 the year before. But the lobster fishery has been tightly regulated for a generation, and the stocks seem to be in a natural cycle; lobster, unlike cod, is not likely to collapse. When we saw him, Gary was gearing up for tuna, which he fishes both in Northumberland Strait and in the Atlantic, off Shelburne. Like so much in a fisherman's life, tuna is a gamble

"You could catch a few fish, or none at all," Gary explained, "and I've seen the price as low as two dollars a pound and as high as seventeen. Then in late August we'll go for herring. There's a good quantity of herring to be caught, but there's no price for 'em." He had already been out for scallops, the first fishery of the year.

"As soon as the ice opens up, we're out there." He got out some photographs: *Sharran Ann* among the ice pans with her scallop rig on the stern. Gary laughed.

"With these fiberglass boats you don't worry much about ice," he said. "I've run right up on an ice pan and fallen off. You wouldn't try that with a wooden boat."

We told him we had been looking for him at the Caribou wharf, and he shook his head. He had a husky trailer for the boat, and when he wasn't fishing he took the boat home. It was handier to work on, and a ferry wharf is "the worst for fishermen."

"They want it kept clean, so they don't want gear sheds and equipment lying around. No gear sheds down there, did you notice? That's why I'm building the shed up here." He laughed again. "You got to look good for the tourists when they want to take pictures, but God forbid you should look like you're working there."

In the morning we were glad of the ferry terminal. We bought coffee and filled our thermos; I shaved in their washroom, and we sailed at seven-fifteen on a solid southwesterly, which carried us out of the channel just ahead of *Prince Nova*. I set a course for Point Prim, 23 miles away to the northwest at the entrance to Hillsborough Bay. From there it would be another ten miles into Charlottetown.

An hour later we were well offshore, watching the ferries plowing back and forth between Caribou and Wood Islands. We were making good progress northward across the Strait, but we were not very far westward. The breeze had become indecisive, and as it gradually waned we found ourselves closer and closer to the ferry lanes, and then to the east of them. Despite the forecast, the steady southwesterly was gone. We were drifting back towards Pictou Island, and the motion was dreadful. Without the steadying wind in her sails, *Silversark* rolled, pitched and bucked aimlessly, while the boom slatted, the sails flapped, the rigging creaked. The first time I was seriously becalmed was in these waters, nearly 20 years ago in *Hirondelle*, just across the Strait. I thought the noise and the motion would drive me mad.

"Can we anchor?" Lulu asked.

"Anchor? Here? There must be 50 feet of water here."

"Well, how long is the anchor cable? Two hundred feet?"

"It wouldn't hold very well."

"It doesn't have to. It just has to stop us from drifting."

True enough. I lowered the light Danforth anchor over the bow. It went down, down, down. If it goes any farther, I thought, it's going to come up with a wet and angry Hong Kong businessman hooked by the seat of his well-tailored pants.

The anchor caught, and *Silversark* swung quickly around, pointing her nose to the west, the anchor cable vibrating in a current much stronger than I had suspected. If we hadn't moored, we would have been carried backwards for miles.

Thanks, Lulu.

"Think nothing of it," said Lulu. "The currents around here are something else, aren't they?"

"I'd forgotten that," I said. "I've tacked back and forth out here for a whole afternoon and come about each time right in front of the same farmhouse. Sailing hard and getting nowhere."

"I don't think I want to do another trip like this without an engine," said Lulu.

Calms and strong currents: the worst possible combination for an engineless sailboat. I remembered the engines I'd had in *Hirondelle*: Stinky Sam, an old gas-powered make-and-break, and Sweet Sue, a four-cylinder 65 horsepower Volvo Penta diesel. In fact, it had been in this very body of water that Stinky Sam had made his last voyage with me, and it was near Pictou Island that Sweet Sue had done her very best to drown us. I had vowed never to have another engine—and yet now I found myself thinking fondly of a brutally simple one-cylinder Lister diesel that would fit nicely into *Silversark* . . .

"Maybe it's time for Mister Lister," I said.

THE

PROFILE OF

AFRICA

Your forehead is on a deck beam, your bum is in the air, and your belly rests on a fuel tank. Your left hand holds the engine water intake hose down into the bilge, pumping out the water which rushes in around your right hand. The stuffing box has come adrift, and you're slowing the torrent around the propeller shaft by grasping the spinning metal in your right hand, so that the side of your little finger makes a rough and ready seal. You let in just enough water to keep the engine cool, while your wife steers for the nearest land, eight miles away.

In this position, you have a rare opportunity for meditation.

One of the thoughts that flicks repeatedly through your mind is this: *I'm glad the new boat doesn't have a goddam engine.*

The year was 1980, and we were delivering *Hirondelle*, with her new owners, Lorenzo and Alvin Haché, to Bathurst, New Brunswick. When we left the Canso Canal, we found ourselves bucking a stiff northwesterly. Lulu and I would have sailed anyway, but the Hachés were hurrying. We motored all day, across St. George's Bay and up into Northumberland Strait. Near Pictou Island, Alvin—who had never been to sea before— noted a steady stream of water pouring overboard through a fitting in the boat's side.

The electric bilge pump was running continuously. I tore off the engine box and the floorboards. Water was already lapping at the transmission, surging in the bilge. The stuffing box had come loose, and the sea was pouring in around the propeller shaft.

Lulu steered for the distant shore of Nova Scotia. We started hand pumping, but still the water gained. I remembered a tip from W.S. Kals's indispensable *Practical Boating*. I shut off the engine water intake, cut the intake hose and stuck it into the water in the bilge. Now Sweet Sue herself was pumping water overboard, and we were gaining on the leak.

Lorenzo took over in the bilge while I reviewed the chart and tried to decide where to beach her. The nearest harbour was Merigomish. It had a narrow, twisting channel and strong currents, but never mind. Meanwhile, Alvin was in misery. He tried to inflate his borrowed rubber dinghy. It wouldn't inflate. His distress grew more profound.

The engine started racing: the blasted throttle control cable, always a problem, had slipped again. I tried to rig a temporary control. In the process I hit the kill button, and the engine stopped. So did Lorenzo's heart. I switched to the other fuel tank, to keep air out of the injectors, and restarted Sweet Sue and Lorenzo's heart. I rigged up a temporary throttle control with a bit of string.

Lorenzo discovered he could control the leak by holding his hand loosely around the spinning shaft. He was a surgeon, and his hand was just a foot from a rusty coupling, which would quickly have mangled it. But we could stop hand pumping. I took bearings and gave Lulu a new course, asked Lorenzo to double-check my navigation and relieved him in the bilge.

Your forehead is on a deck beam, your bum is in the air, and your belly rests on a fuel tank . . .

We made it, of course. I scrambled out of the bilge just as *Hirondelle* touched the shore. We bumped once on the way in— the tide was dead low, it was dark, and the channel was unlit— and slid gently onto a shelving beach right beside a wharf. At the head of the wharf was a large house full of people with oakum and extra line and other devices for repairing a stuffing box. We plugged the leak, positioned the schooner to dry out and went to the house for coffee and home-made rolls and jam and good talk. Always try to be shipwrecked near the Everett Baudoux family.

As we walked back to the wharf, I turned to Lorenzo.

"You know," I said, "this whole thing gives rise to some interesting reflections for those people who think that having an engine in a sailboat is a *safety* feature."

"Oh, I don't know," said Lorenzo earnestly. "I think if you have a good installation . . . "

His sense of humour was waterlogged. But then I wasn't really joking. *Hirondelle*'s engines were sometimes a convenience, let- ting me sleep in my own bed rather than bobbing about on a windless ocean or permitting me to motor through a canal rather than trudging along the towpath with the dock lines. But they never saved me from a disaster, and they often came close to causing one.

Engines are the devil's own work: given half a chance, they will burn, maim, bankrupt or drown you. Filth, stink and noise; explosive fuels and holes through the hull; intricate parts which corrode in salt air; baroque servicing arrangements; precious days of a short sailing season lost while waiting for parts; slower sailing because of propeller drag; overconfidence born of the notion that "we can always motor out of here"—and all this at a cost which would pay for a year's cruising in the tropics.

Engines do have a place in a sailboat's equipment: at the bottom of the harbour, sunk in the mud, attached to a nice piece of half-inch chain, they make excellent moorings.

On the other hand, here we sat, anchored in mid-Strait, trapped like a tadpole in a bottle. The ferries churned across our bow, back and forth between Caribou and Wood Islands. I imagined their passengers—retired couples from Omaha, young families from Scarborough, *Anne of Green Gables* fans from Kyoto, bus tours from Boston—lining the rail and asking one another, *What is that little boat doing, just sitting there?*

"Fishing. See the line running off the pointy end?"

"Maybe there's nobody aboard. Maybe they're all drowned."

"Diving. I bet they're divers."

"Poaching lobsters, eh?"

"Do you think they're lost, Elmer?"

"Probably some guy canoodling with his secretary."

"Do you think they're in trouble? Should we do something?"

"What would we do? Swim over there and knock on the door?"

"Maybe they just stopped for lunch."

Twenty minutes later, another ferry would pass by. *Mommy, what is that little boat doing, just sitting there?*

"Just waiting for its mommy, like a good little boat."

Mister Lister, where are you?

Eventually, of course, a breeze does spring up. At one-fifteen, the ghost of an easterly lazily lifted the flag. Wing and wing, we crept west and north again. At three-thirty the wind strengthened slightly and switched into the west. We found ourselves slowly closing the shore of PEI. At five-thirty, we were just off Indian Rocks, slightly west of Wood Islands. The day was gone, and even Point Prim was still 14 miles away. We altered course for Wood Islands, bobbing slowly shoreward on a tantalizingly light wind.

I had tied up in Wood Islands once before—in 1974, on *Hirondelle*. We had sailed all day against light winds and strong currents, and finally I had started Stinky Sam. Sam was an Atlantic Double Four, a brutish two-cylinder affair from the early days of the Industrial Revolution. To start him, you took an oil can filled with raw gasoline, opened the engine box, closed the petcock under the little brass cups perched atop each cylinder and filled the cups with gas. You then opened the petcock, let the gas run into the cylinders and closed the petcock. This was a nice juggling trick in a tumbling sea, producing ample spillage and a boat full of explosive vapours.

Next you seized a couple of big handles on the flywheel—Sam's original handles were six-inch carriage bolts—and "threw her over." Then you threw her over again. And again. At length, with luck, one of the two massive cylinders experienced an explosion, encouraging the other one. With a sound like a spastic jackhammer, the engine started—and you *jumped* away. Those protruding bolts on the spinning flywheel broke many a leg and mangled many an arm when make-and-break engines were standard on the fishing boats along the coast.

Stinky Sam had no neutral, no clutch, no transmission; he started at full speed, and in gear. To back up, you cut the ignition: just before the engine died, you snapped it back on. Sam would backfire violently, shaking the boat, and then the whole contraption—engine, shaft, propeller, everything—would simply run backwards. If you didn't exactly catch the rhythm with the ignition switch, he might very well go forward again, or die altogether. This factor introduced an exciting element of chance into harbour maneuvers, and yielded an unusual degree of privacy: other sailors tended to keep well away.

But sometimes Sam did start in forward, moving the boat off at a good speed. By the time you recovered from your astonishment—it *started*, by God!—and raced from the engine room to the tiller, *Hirondelle* would be in her Cyrano mode, using her bowsprit like a rapier, making rapid feints and lunges at other boats with it. On one occasion she came within a hair of impaling the Lunenburg museum schooner *Theresa E. Connors*.

The night we motored into Wood Islands, the crew included two friends, John and Darla Rousseau, and Margo Lamont, the lady in my life. One cylinder cut out just after I doused the sails. We discovered that it would fire if we pushed hard on a pin which controlled the ignition points. But someone had to crouch in the engine box, pushing on the pin with a stick of firewood.

The entrance to Wood Islands is a narrow cut with steel sheathing on both sides. Entering the harbour is like sailing down a hallway. In that confined space, the reverberations from the engine were astounding. The helmsman couldn't hear the bow lookout. We reached the wharf with Darla crouched in the engine room, Margo at the bow and me standing on the cabin roof, relaying Margo's instructions to John, who was at the tiller.

Yes, I remembered Wood Islands.

The wind had faded almost to nothing, and the current was carrying *Silversark* crabwise past the entrance to Wood Islands.

"We're going to have to row," said Lulu.

"@@#$%&," I said. "No."

"Yes," said Lulu. "Wait a bit if you want to, but we're going to have to row."

Why is that little woman always right? And why can I never make a stylish and dignified entrance into Wood Islands?

We lowered the genny, leaving only the mainsail set. I raised the main boom high enough to clear my head, then rowed. *Lord Selkirk* was plowing towards us from Caribou.

"We're going to get in that little entrance at the same time as that damn ferry," I panted.

"He's a long way out," said Lulu.

"Yes, but we're moving *very* slowly."

I rowed. Lulu picked up the VHF, called *Lord Selkirk* and explained our predicament. I rowed. It was getting embarrassing, constantly calling the ferries to warn them that we were disabled by calms and currents. Lulu took the helm. I rowed.

Just before we reached the entrance, *Lord Selkirk* bustled past our bow. Rowing hard, I pulled *Silversark* into the steel-clad entrance channel. People stared down from the deck of the ferry, now secured in her berth. I rowed. Out of the current, *Silversark* was scooting right along. My God, I was getting good with those oars—

"Don," said Lulu quietly, "we're sailing."

I stopped rowing. The baggy, shapeless mainsail had caught a little breeze—dead astern—in the entrance channel itself. *Silversark* was making a bubbling wake. I stowed the oars.

"I'm going to round up inside that little basin beside the ferry slip," Lulu called. "This side of that white sloop." She steered around the stern of the ferry into the quiet water of the basin and put the helm down. *Silversark* came around with her nose in the wind and coasted to a stop beside the quay. Four or five people were standing by.

"Bill Fitch," said the man who took the bow line. "From Moncton. We met a few years ago. Nice to see you again. This is Henri LeBlond, from Quebec."

Wood Islands is a ferry terminal, a basin for fishing boats and little else. We spent the evening with Henri, the Fitches and John and Darla Rousseau, who live four or five miles away. Having sailed Northumberland Strait for years, Bill and Linda Fitch are accustomed to its tidal currents and sandy harbours. As they pointed out, you're very likely to go aground in these waters, but not very likely to do any damage. They lent us Dale and Avis Gray's *Northumberland Strait Cruising Notes*, a strange little book which mixes useful facts and aerial photographs with rather bizarre observations on nature and society.

> Do not be alarmed if, on your departure from Wood
> Islands, a school of porpoises joins you for at least
> part of the day. This is their way of inviting you to
> return again when you can linger for a while and
> enjoy some of nature's treats.

We intended to moor *Silversark* in Wood Islands while we picked up Mark in Halifax. Early in the morning we rowed our little ship deep into the "bullpen," the perfectly protected compound where the fishing fleet lies, and committed her to the care of Kip Smith, a sometime CBC broadcaster who operates Crabby's Sea Foods.

On the ferry, we crossed the Strait in 95 minutes. It had taken us more than 14 hours to meander across on *Silversark*. By early afternoon we were in Halifax, picking up UHT milk, rub rails for *Marksark*, shock cord, a battery for the depth sounder, new seaboots for Mark's growing feet.

I had been thinking about racism: about John Wayling's sense of shame and about Dr. Carrie Best, one of New Glasgow's black leaders, looking into a CBC camera and saying, "I am a person created in the image of God." In Halifax I had to research a story about the razing of a black village on the shores of Halifax Harbour and the relocation of its people nearly 30 years before. We would spend the next day with 1,000 people, mostly black, at the annual picnic of the Africville Genealogy Society, which preserves the collective memories of Africville, a community which now exists only in the minds of those who care about it. How would a middle-aged white man be received? How would white people *deserve* to be received?

Racism is a Canadian problem, not a narrowly Nova Scotian one. The police shoot and kill black youths in Toronto and Montreal, and aboriginals in Winnipeg. British Columbia's reception of Asians does us no credit. Everywhere in Canada, the jails are full of native people. Racism has a longer history in Nova Scotia because Nova Scotia has a longer history.

A black seaman named Mathieu da Costa wintered at Champlain's Port Royal settlement in 1605 and 1606, and in 1767 black Nova Scotians outnumbered the Scots: in a population of 13,374, almost all Acadians, there were 104 blacks and just 52 Scots. About 3,500 Black Loyalists came to Nova Scotia after the American Revolution—1,200 were sufficiently discouraged that they moved on to Sierra Leone in 1792—and a group of Jamaican blacks, the Maroons, arrived four years later, though most of them soon emigrated to Sierra Leone, as well. Another 2,000 black refugees came to Nova Scotia during the War of 1812. From the start they were treated badly—accommodated in military prisons, given the worst land, denied basic services, ostracized and ignored.

We will not get away with this forever. In the ghastly summer of 1992, people all over the world were killing one another over colour, religion, language, politics. Bosnia, Somalia, Georgia, Ireland, Liberia, Azerbaijan, Pakistan, Sri Lanka, Los Angeles, Kurdistan, South Africa—the datelines changed, but not the images: the stones and batons, the bullets, the flames, the screaming wounded, the crumpled dead. Turn on a TV any time, and the stench of hatred floated into the room.

But we are one human family, on one small planet. If you prick us, we bleed; if you tickle us, we laugh; if you poison us, we die. We have a right, all of us, to seek our own destinies in our own ways, respecting the same right in others. We have a right to be judged not by our language, our gods or our skin, but by the content of our character.

People are dying, everywhere, because we have not absorbed those simple truths. If in our second century Canadians could build a society which lived by those truths, we might become, in Hugh MacLennan's incandescent phrase, "a nation precious to humanity."

That would be a citizenship worth having.

A small road winds down from Barrington Street under the Murray Mackay Bridge and ends at Seaview Park, where Africville once stood. Railway tracks and a highway run above it; the broad surface of Bedford Basin, Halifax's inner harbour, lies before it. All along the base of the hill are campers, vans, motor homes, tents. You are not normally allowed to camp in a city park, but for one summer weekend each year that rule is suspended at Seaview Park. Most of Africville's families still live in metropolitan Halifax, but others have moved to Boston, Montreal, Toronto and beyond. This picnic is the ninth annual reunion of a community of the heart.

The picnics began, in a sense, in 1958, when two 10-year-olds, Brenda Steed and Debbie Dixon, pricked their fingers and became blood sisters. Their friendship with each other and with Linda Mantley survived the relocation, and whenever the three got together, they found themselves talking about life "out home"—swimming, fishing and playing ball in the summer, skating and playing hockey on the frozen ponds in the winter, always nurtured by a close web of friends, neighbours, church and family. When the families of Africville began to drift apart after the relocation, the three women incorporated the Africville Genealogy Society, intended to "preserve the past, care for the present and prepare for the future," according to Irvine Carvery, the Society's current president.

It was a brilliant invention, focusing attention not on the site and the artifacts, but on Africville's surviving reality: its people and their relationships. The Society holds various social functions during the year and administers an educational trust fund based on the compensation the community received for its church. But its biggest event by far is the July weekend—a Friday night dance, followed by a day of children's games, puppeteers, music, a beer garden and much socializing.

I spent a day and a half at the picnic, wandering around and talking with people. I met Brenda Steed, who I took to be a young woman but who turns out to have grown children. And I met Dr. Ruth Brown Johnson, Africville's much-honoured unofficial archivist and historian, an activist and an elder, a great-granddaughter of one of the men who originally bought the Africville site in 1848.

"There were houses up there—and there—and there," she said, pointing up the steep hill. "There were three sets of railway tracks in between the houses. You can imagine the fun we had sliding in the wintertime! We'd put the heaviest kid on the first

sleigh, and tie the sleighs together. When we went across the
tracks, the sparks went flying everywhere!" She remembered
the baptisms: full immersion of whole groups of children in the
waters of Bedford Basin. If it happened to be December, the
elders "just chopped a hole in the ice, and in you went."

And she remembered the music.

"There was not a home in Africville that didn't have a piano or
an organ," she said. Ruth and her sisters all studied at the
Halifax Conservatory, and another Africville girl became the
organist at the largest black church in Chicago. The Baptist
congregation was famous for its singing, and for the Easter sunrise services, which began before dawn and went on into the
middle of the day. Duke Ellington always visited Africville when
he came to Halifax; the "sophisticated lady" for whom he wrote
one of his greatest tunes was Mildred Dixon, his second wife, the
daughter of an Africville family who had emigrated to Boston.

Africville did not seem like a slum to its own people, who
included stonemasons and coopers, railway porters, deep-sea
divers and stevedores, and it was no more impoverished than
many a rural village. But Africville differed in two ways: it was
within the Halifax city limits, and its people were mostly—
though not entirely—black. In the 1960s, that made the community a target for "slum clearance" and "urban renewal."

The savage irony is that the worst features of Africville were
created and sustained by the very society which then deplored
them. As early as 1858, the city established its sewage disposal
pits near the village. Through the years, Africville residents
repeatedly requested such basic city services as water, sewer,
electricity, policing, building permits, garbage collection and
paved roads. The requests were ignored. The city fathers always
took the view that the Africville site would eventually be required
for industry, and that residential use of the land should not be
encouraged. "There is no record," says Dalhousie University
sociologist Dr. Donald Clairmont, "of any concern for the health
and safety of the Africville residents."

Over the years, the city approved the construction of a bone-
meal fertilizer plant, a cotton factory, a rolling mill, a slaughter-
house and a coal-handling terminal. To service these industries,
three sets of railway tracks were laid right through the middle of
Africville. The area later received an Infectious Diseases Hospi-

tal, a Trachoma Hospital and a stone-crushing plant. In the 1950s, the city moved the municipal dump to a site just 100 metres from Africville. Have things changed? Today Metro Halifax is looking for a new dump site, and its first choice is Preston, a large black community near Dartmouth.

In 1992, the Africville picnic had two special occasions. One was the launching of a handsome illustrated book, *The Spirit of Africville*, edited by the Africville Genealogy Society. The book, like the acclaimed National Film Board documentary, *Remember Africville*, is an outgrowth of *Africville: A Spirit that Lives On*, a collection of Africville photos, artifacts and memorabilia, which has been touring galleries and museums across Canada since its initial presentation at the Mount St. Vincent University Gallery in Halifax, in 1989.

The second major event at the 1992 picnic was a sod-turning ceremony for the replica of Seaview African United Baptist Church. Established in 1849, the church was Africville's only real institution—village council, police force and social centre all in one. If one moment epitomizes the death of Africville, it is the night the church was bulldozed.

The sod-turning was a moving affair: a knot of people in the bushes on the stony hillside, a few words from each of the elders about what the church meant to them, some prayers punctuated with murmurs of "Yes, brother! Say it, say it! Amen!" The annual picnic of 1993 will be a major reunion of Africville families from across the continent, centred on the dedication of the rebuilt church as a permanent home for the travelling exhibit.

That same weekend, the first International Gospel Festival was taking place in Halifax. Like Celtic music or polka, gospel music has an international appeal to a narrow audience, with genuine stars who may or may not be known to outsiders. But Haligonians know them now: electrifying performers like Cissy Houston, Dutch Robinson and the incomparable Odetta. The superb Saturday night concert at Africville featured Lorraine Classen and Soweto Groove, a troupe of South African singers and dancers now living in Montreal. In the audience, black and white stood side by side in the seaside night, laughing together at the antics of small children, singing along, swaying to complicated rhythms rooted in the cultures of Africa. Like the rest of the picnic, it was a casual, happy affair: black Halifax "at home" to the rest of the city.

"There were always people here from the other black communities around—Preston, Hammonds Plains, Beechville," said Carrie Toussaint, who was raised on the stories of Africville even though her family had moved out before she was born, "but this year there are so many others that it hardly seems like our picnic any more. But they're all having a good time together, and that's what it's all about."

Irvine Carvery believes the people of Africville are entitled to compensation for several deaths that resulted from the dump, as well as for the relocation. Beyond that, he dreams of going back. The site is beautiful, the park is underutilized. Why not build a mixture of public, private and co-op housing, and invite Africville's people to return? Just this winter, the authorities agreed to reopen the file on compensation and, says Irvine, a new Africville on the old site is "definitely on the negotiating agenda."

We *are* improving, though still too slowly. In the summer of 1991, a black man was denied admission to a Halifax bar; the resulting racial brawl on Gottingen Street involved 150 people and was nationally reported as a riot. A couple of weeks later, however, 1,000 people—black *and* white, from a metropolitan population of 250,000—marched through the downtown streets chanting

> Hey, hey! Ho, ho!
> Racist bars have got to go!
>
> Halifax-Dartmouth, have you heard?
> This is not Johannesburg!

Blacks and natives are at last assuming positions of importance in Nova Scotia—as teachers, lawyers, musicians, civil servants, actors, broadcasters, politicians, film makers, poets. The black artists are important beyond their numbers, for they give us a direct view of the soul behind the skin, the person created in the image of God. Give the last word to Maxine Tynes, a powerful, flamboyant poet from Dartmouth:

> we wear our skin like a fine fabric
> we people of colour
> brown, black, tan coffeecoffee cream ebony

beautiful, strong, exotic in profile
flowering lips
silhouette obsidian planes, curves, structure
like a many-shaded mosaic
we wear our skin like a flag
we share our colour like a blanket
we cast our skin like a shadow
we wear our skin like a map
chart my beginning by my profile
chart my beginning by my colour
read the map of my heritage in
my face
my skin
the dark flash of eye
the profile of Africa.

THE ADVENT

OF THE

EVIL MAGICIAN

Mark charged out of International Arrivals, his Tilley hat pushed back on his forehead, his long legs eating up the floor, beaming and laughing and throwing his arms around us both.

"It was *awesome!* Give me a hug. Jorgen sends his love, and Fie, and Birgitte—give me a hug, I need a hug. You should see Torben's car! I'm so happy to be back! I met a girl from Australia on the plane. I need another hug! It's so good to see my parents! But it was *awesome . . .* "

We drove back to Wood Islands, Mark talking and hugging non-stop. While we had shivered, the Danes had sweltered. Mark had visited Lulu's closest friends from her seven years in Denmark, and his birth father, Torben Beyer. Jorgen Bjerregaard, who writes for the Copenhagen newspaper *Politiken*, had sent a gorgeous book on the Vikings. Between the lines, we sensed a tangled story of a 14-year-old boy navigating the unfamiliar waters of relationships with girls.

Awesome, clearly.

Meanwhile, Lieutenant Commander Lloyd Bourinot had persuaded himself that we needed an engine, at least for *Marksark*. (Once a printer and publisher, Lloyd is now a training officer in the naval reserve. The flavour of our long and sordid friendship is captured in a single oft-quoted line: "Bourinot, you have [BELCH] rendered me drunk.") He offered a tiny outboard, just right for the new dinghy. We picked it up and took it to Wood Islands.

Silversark was just as we had left her, but we had a new neighbour: a big Beaver Construction dredge on the outer wharf with two portable toilets on the stern, one labelled WOMEN and the other LADIES. We loaded our gear aboard *Silversark* and settled in for the night. When the oil lamps were blown out, Lulu and I were startled by a voice in the darkness.

"Listen, guys, no sex on this boat while I'm aboard."

"What?"

"I don't want to hear any funny noises from up in that double berth."

"Who are you, the Pope?" I said. "Or my mother? Telling married people how to conduct their sex lives."

"If I can't do it, you can't do it."

"Humph! Good night."

This is not the world I grew up in, I reflected. No doubt our parents made love—here we are, after all—but they obtained their conjugal satisfactions in conditions of secrecy beyond the wildest fantasies of John Le Carré. We lived in ordinary houses, not soundproof cells: I don't know how they did it.

How do people manage these things on small boats? The parameters of a boat like *Silversark* require that three or four people masticate, defecate, urinate, eructate, flatulate and fornicate in a space smaller than a bourgeois bathroom. I suspect that the forced intimacy of a small boat has absolutely prevented more than one shy person from cruising at all.

One searches the cruising literature for strategies—but in vain. Cruising literature may be the last stronghold of Victorian restraint. With rare exceptions, couples and families sail around the world without squabbling, without jealousy, without terror, without sex. They make no bad smells or vulgar sounds, and only their upper lips are stiff.

We are not such models of disembodied propriety. But what were we to do? Bow to the wishes of the young tyrant in the quarterberth and suspend our normal inclinations—or flout the expressed wishes of a commendably forthright young man who must be finding it difficult enough to navigate puberty responsibly?

The morality is all in the phrasing.

"Look," I whispered to Lulu. "Think of it this way. We're on fire with passion. Assume you're married to an evil magician. If he catches us, he'll turn you into a kitchen blender and me into a purée. But we can't keep apart; whatever the risk, we have to know the ecstasy of one another's arms. You're irresistible: one look at you and all my firm resolutions turn to Jell-O. We'll make our trysts, but we mustn't get caught. *Our lives depend on it.*"

"Okay," said Lulu. "When do we start?"

"Now," I said. "By going quietly to sleep. God nat."

"Sov godt."

"What are you guys whispering about?" said Mark, suspiciously.

"Sailing out of this little cranny in the morning," I lied. "God nat."

"Sov godt."

The subterfuges would probably add some extra spice to our love life, I thought sleepily. Mark might find himself being sent on errands at odd times, and he could be surprised to find us so accommodating when he wanted to stay ashore overnight with a new friend. And then I found myself wondering how we *would* sail out of this little cranny in the morning, and whether we would leave Wood Islands as awkwardly as we had entered.

If your mind switches that easily from sex to sailing, I thought, maybe you'll find it disconcertingly easy to control your libido. You're getting old.

And then the sunlight was streaming in the porthole, and it was morning. A steady southwesterly was blowing—not an ideal wind for Charlottetown, but a very acceptable one.

We surprised ourselves with a picture-perfect departure, demonstrating that unity of crew and vessel which marks seasoned cruisers—a quality I had often seen, but hardly expected to attain. Yet here we were, making sail inside the confined basin and reaching to the narrow entrance. We took two tacks down the outside face of the wharf and another under the stern of the waiting ferry, then bore off between the steel-clad quays. We departed at nine twenty-seven, the ferry at nine-forty. Before the ferry cast off, we were out in the Strait.

And that was the end of the good sailing. The wind faded, we set the genny, and the wind died. By eleven-fifteen we were anchored in mid-Strait again, almost in the wretched ferry lanes. The motion was worse than before: both Lulu and Mark were seasick. I tried to read and make notes while we pitched and rolled.

"I can't believe it!" Lulu groaned. "Not again!"

"We knew there were going to be times like this."

"Euu," Mark moaned.

"But not *every day!*"

"Well, it's *not* every day."

"I watched you pulling that anchor up the other day when there wasn't enough wind to sail up to it, and I thought, He's going to have a heart attack and *die*, and then where will we be?"

"*Euu*," said Mark.

"I'm not going to have a heart attack!"

"I'm just telling you, that's *it!*" snapped Lulu. "This is the last long cruise in this goddam boat without an engine!"

"*Euu*," Mark moaned. "Look out, I'm going to be sick . . ."

We built *Silversark* with long cruises in mind—and for long-distance cruising an engine is almost irrelevant. On a month-long ocean crossing, a day or two of calm is of no real consequence. A century ago, Nova Scotia's own Joshua Slocum circled the world alone, the first man ever to do so, in an engine-less oyster smack. Dozens of voyagers followed him; in the 1970s Lin and Larry Pardy made an engineless circumnavigation in the 24-foot *Seraffyn*. Even Albert Einstein sailed a boat without an engine. One really wants an engine chiefly at the beginning of the voyage, and the end: leaving a harbour, or entering one. On an offshore voyage, these are rare occasions.

But this was not an offshore voyage, alas. We lay at anchor for three hours before a hint of westerly breeze wafted past. No good for Charlottetown, but at least it would get us somewhere else.

And then the anchor windlass kept binding. I couldn't get the anchor up no matter how I sweated, cursed and strained. Perhaps I *was* going to have a heart attack. Typical British engineering, I growled.

Made in Glasgow by a hallowed yacht-equipment manufacturer, the windlass conformed perfectly to Robson's Law of British Appliances. Formulated in Oxford thirty years ago by Stuart Robson, a Rhodes Scholar from British Columbia who now teaches at Trent University, Robson's Law holds that the objective of a British appliance is to indicate a function, not to perform it. A British street light, for example, does not illuminate the street; it illuminates its own base, thus indicating a street light in that location. British central heating devices don't heat the room: they simply warm their own surfaces, showing that they *are* central heating devices. By the same token, the anchor windlass adds a fetching salty touch to the decor of the foredeck, but it doesn't actually crank up the anchor; it just looks as though it *should*.

Lulu came forward, and together we worked out a better way to lead the anchor cable. I cranked again, and the line started to come aboard. The more I cranked the windlass, the more cowed and obedient it became, until finally the anchor came in sight. We were sailing again. We worked our way slowly west of the ferry lanes.

An hour later we were becalmed again, drifting eastward.

Anchor and wrestle again with that damned windlass? The hell with it: we would just drift. Around four o'clock we felt the first stirrings of a northwesterly—exactly the breeze we did not want. But at least it would get us back into Wood Islands, which was now a mile or so to the west of us. The sea had gone flat. *Silversark* inched towards the shore.

An hour later we were approaching Wood Islands from the southeast—but making good progress westward.

"We're only doing two knots through the water," I said, "but the Loran says we're making nearly four over the bottom."

"The current must have changed," said Lulu. "Let's go on."

"We'll probably get into Charlottetown in the middle of the night," I said. "Or maybe even tomorrow."

"I don't care. We didn't intend to go to Wood Islands in the first place. I certainly don't want to go back there."

Fair enough. We tacked on in the light breeze, riding the current and working steadily westward. And then, at six forty-five, with a sudden sustained gust, the wind shifted to the south-west, giving us a fifteen-minute canter before it settled down. This was more like it. We eased the sheets a trifle, and *Silversark* slipped quickly past the seaside farms. The sea was still calm.

"Whale!" said Mark. "Over there!" A pilot whale was browsing, and a couple of dolphins broke the surface, then a seal.

The sun dropped into the sea, an intense red disk above the flat water, painting smooth bands of yellow, gold and blue in the clear western sky. At nine-fifteen, with darkness coming on, the wind increased sharply. I lowered the genny and set the working jib. The wind slowly veered into the west. Still carried by the current, *Silversark* bucked into a short, heavy chop. We put on sweaters, oilskins and watch caps.

At ten-thirty we passed Point Prim, but the breeze had veered so far into the west that we could not fetch its light buoy without a tack. I scrutinized the chart. A direct course for Fitzroy Rock would take us through relatively shallow water over the Point Prim reef, but nothing that would endanger us. We altered course. I turned on the phone and called the Charlottetown Yacht Club. They had no berths available, and they closed at eleven o'clock—but we could tie up at the fuel dock overnight.

On a close reach, *Silversark* flew into Hillsborough Bay. Suddenly we were in steep, breaking seas; just as suddenly we were through them. So we had crossed the reef. The wind was still rising, and I doused the jib. At Fitzroy Rock we picked up the outer range lights. From below, Mark alternately listened to Pink Floyd and called off water depths, speed and distance to the Spithead Rock buoy. Far off to port, the Blockhouse Point lighthouse pulsed every four seconds from the entrance to Charlottetown Harbour.

We turned at Spithead Rock to follow the second range. The wind was blowing hard. *Silversark* charged into the narrow entrance and abruptly lost the wind in the lee of the point.

The waterfront was in shadow, its feeble lights lost in the glow from the city beyond. But I could see the square outline of the Prince Edward Hotel, and the yacht club had to be somewhere in front of it. As we sailed out from under the bluffs, the wind came howling back. *Silversark* raced into the darkness. Ten or 20 yachts would be moored in there. I dropped and furled the main as Mark brought the spotlight on deck. Under the jumbo alone, *Silversark* was still moving very fast.

Where *was* the yacht club? Where was the fuel dock?

The spotlight picked up the pale grey shapes of moored boats. We were close. Conferring in quick shouts, we chose an aisle between the boats and headed directly towards the shore. There were feeble lights on the gas pumps of the fuel dock, off to starboard. The route was clear, and the shore was very close—

"Hard a-starboard!" I called, and dropped the last sail. "Head for those dim lights!" Lulu swung the tiller and glanced over the side. Waves were breaking on wet rocks just a few feet to port. *Silversark* sailed right on, carried by her own momentum and the pressure of the wind on her broad transom.

With a mooring line in my hand, I climbed outside the lifelines. Our berth was a low floating dock just a few inches above the water, with a couple of four-by-four samson posts sticking up from it. *Silversark* rushed down on the wharf. We had held the jumbo too long; we were moving too fast. With a cluster of boats around us, and a Coast Guard ship looming up beyond the yacht club, we would have only one chance . . .

"Starboard! Not too much—port, port! Hold her there!"

I jumped down onto the fuel dock, surged the mooring line around a samson post and snubbed hard. *Silversark* slowed abruptly. Coming on deck at that moment, Mark thought I had stopped the boat with my bare hands. Lulu tossed a stern line. I wrapped it around the post, and *Silversark* swung around the end of the dock, presenting her port side to the whistling wind.

"Welcome to Charlottetown," I panted.

WILLY HARRIS

AND THE

ELECTRIC

ACADIAN

Charlottetown has blossomed during the past 20 years. The Island's only incorporated city, it is the market town for the Island's farmers and fishermen, and both groups have been doing reasonably well. It is the Island's seat of government, and it harbours a number of federal organisms, notably a CBC station and the headquarters of the Department of Veterans Affairs. Its educational institutions include the University of Prince Edward Island, a veterinary school and the headquarters of Holland College, a wide-awake community college. It is, in short, The Compleat Vest-Pocket Capital City.

That first morning, while Mark slept in, Lulu and I headed for the Prince Edward Hotel, stretching our legs and looking for coffee. The morning was cool but sunny and the water was dappled. The red-and-white bulk of the Coast Guard ship *Sir*

Charles Tupper lay up against the wharf next to the yacht club. We heard the faint tinkling of wind chimes. Through the waterfront's nineteenth-century brick buildings and modern low-rise condos and offices runs a waterfront boardwalk with a blue stripe painted down the middle of it. Following the blue stripe gives you a full tour of the waterfront.

"Silver Donald!"

We looked up. A man was standing among flowering plants on the balcony of a condo overlooking the yacht club's finger piers. The wind chimes were swinging behind him. It was Brian Cudmore.

"I was down to your boat, but you weren't awake yet," he called. "Welcome back to Charlottetown!"

Brian is a prominent haberdasher, an ardent sailor and a devoted Islander. He came down to the boat later that first morning for a coffee and a reunion. His boat was moored in the Brudenell River for a week. Would we like to use his slip in the marina? Indeed we would.

Small, says Brian, is certainly beautiful. And interesting.

"We get almost every federal department," he said. "Anything that wants to be national tends to come here, so we get exposed to everything that has to make a coast-to-coast tour, and that's invaluable. People here are much more involved in national issues than a suburban person in Ontario. There's a daily non-stop to Ottawa—75 or 100 people every day going back and forth."

Not your typical town of 20,000. But this *is* a capital city, and this is where The Deal was made. Later that summer, Canada's leaders would meet at the Prince Edward Hotel to forge the abortive Charlottetown Accord. The Accord was designed to renew the agreement concluded here in 1864, which led directly to the creation of Canada three years later. Confederation is almost an industry in Charlottetown. The Confederation Centre of the Arts, the Confederation Court shopping mall, Confederation Inn, Confederation Dining Room: nation building is to Charlottetown what steel is to Hamilton. Confederation is the thing Canadians know about Charlottetown.

We stayed in Charlottetown a week, moored in the heart of the city. Coffee at the Prince Edward became almost a daily ritual. The Prince Edward is the Island's one large, flossy modern hotel. It has been through several financial storms, but it anchors the whole waterfront renewal scheme. In its ground-floor shopping arcade is a quiet open area with tables and chairs among the pillars and potted plants. An adjoining food boutique serves a variety of coffees. We would walk over, often in drizzle or mist, sit at our table feeling raffish and piratical as we watched the tourists go by and then get on with our errands or pleasures.

Coming to the Charlottetown Yacht Club was like coming home; I had stayed there for a month in 1974 in *Hirondelle*. Stinky Sam was sulking when I got there, and I discussed my frustration with Plum MacDonald, a genial, cherubic-looking boy in late middle age and a major source of energy for the Charlottetown Yacht Club. Plum had something to do with lounges, taverns and entertainment, but his friends, who were numerous, left the details vague. Prince Edward Island had puritanical liquor laws in those days—there was only one liquor store in the province east of Charlottetown—but everyone seemed to be able to find a drink. Was Plum involved with convivial public services performed just north of the law? I have no idea. But he knew everyone, and he was a warehouse of practical information.

"You need a little diesel in that boat," he pronounced. "Call Sonny Soper in Dartmouth. I'll get you the number. He's got a nice little Volvo diesel, all rebuilt, and I think he'd let it go pretty reasonable." He did: that's how I found Sweet Sue. Before I left, I gave Sam to the yacht club as a door prize for one of their summer functions.

To install the new diesel, Plum referred me to George Waller. George was a brilliantly inventive machinist, probably the most respected marine machinist in the Maritimes. He worked in a dark little shop at the end of a lane off University Avenue. His special forté was converting engines for marine use. Datsuns, Mercedes diesels, tractor engines: if the engine ran and it could be shoehorned into the boat, George would build new manifolds and exhaust systems, alter the generator bracket, rebuild whatever was needed to make things fit. His own little day cruiser was powered by the only Toyota marine engine I ever saw.

George and I worked together for several weeks. He had a gruff manner, which I suspect was rooted in a shy nature. He also had an acute sense of social class. "I don't like working at the yacht club," he told me once. "I don't like working for people who wouldn't like to see me at the front door of their house." I was surprised, because the Charlottetown Yacht Club seemed to me about as inclusive as any urban yacht club I ever saw; my friends there included not only businessmen and professionals, but also tradesmen, railway workers and the secretary of the local YMCA.

For all his skill, George Waller was squeezed into retirement by the metric system. Like other self-employed tradesmen, George had assembled his tools and equipment over a lifetime, keeping his eyes open and pouncing on bargains. Over the years, he had acquired his tools at a cost far below their replacement value. Then the government decreed that all measurements would henceforth be metric and imposed fines for non-compliance. George added up the cost of reequipping his shop. It would be financial lunacy; his business would never repay it. So he closed his doors.

I had seen George only occasionally over the intervening years. I wanted to have him aboard, but I was too late. He was in hospital, dying of cancer, past the point of receiving visitors. And Plum MacDonald had died just a few days before we arrived. The yacht club veranda was not the same sunny place without Plum sitting in a wooden chair, a cloth cap over his Churchillian pate, telling stories and giving advice.

Many Charlottetown sailors have moved a few hundred yards farther up the harbour to Peake's Quay, a full-service commercial marina with gift shops, restaurants and a big bustling bar overlooking the moored boats—a good place for a pub lunch. The yacht club, by contrast, is still in its funky little semi-finished building with its leaky roof. It has a small, cosy bar, an exposed anchorage, a small marina and a devoted but ageing membership. The club has drawn up plans for redevelopment, but the harbour bottom consists of 60 to 70 feet of soft mud, and the cost of building a breakwater and finger piers on that mushy foundation would be exorbitant. The club would need 200 boats to make the plans viable. Could it find them? Probably not. So the members enjoy what they have and put buckets around the dance floor when the rains are heavy.

The past seems very close in Charlottetown, and in some respects it seems better than the present. Most of the city's downtown buildings were built in the 19th century, some in the 18th century. They were owned by shipbuilders, marine surveyors, brewers, tanners, stone cutters, musicians, officers of the locally owned Union Bank and the Bank of Prince Edward Island. There were smiths, carriage makers, cooperages, saddlers and harness makers, watch makers and millers. People worked in meat-packing houses, a candy factory, a furniture factory, bakeries, import-export houses, brickyards and a soap factory. Later in the century, a local company named Bruce Stewart even produced make-and-break marine engines. A few of those trades have survived, but not many.

I stood in front of the Peake house, around the corner from the yacht club, and tried to imagine myself a boy of 14—Mark's age—in, say, 1856. The house would have been 20 years old then; it was built by James Peake in 1835 and 1836, just before his marriage. If Peake came by, no doubt I would doff my cap, for Peake was a big man in Charlottetown, a shipbuilder and merchant, a director of the Bank of Prince Edward Island, a Member of the Legislative Assembly. Peake had been launching 13 ships a year, selling some in Europe and using others in his import-export business between Charlottetown and Plymouth, England. One of them, named for his daughter Fanny, had carried the '49ers to the California gold rush.

To the west, at Pownal Street, I would have seen the home of James Purdie, another prominent merchant. The house had earlier been a school, a store and a hotel. Purdie had purchased it from Samuel Cunard of Halifax—soon to be Sir Samuel Cunard, Bart.—who had moved to England to start a transatlantic steamer service from Liverpool to Halifax and Boston.

But as a 14-year-old boy I think I would probably have walked the other way, half a block down muddy Water Street past the inns and warehouses and workshops toward James Peake's new brick office building at the corner of Queen Street, handy to his wharves and shipyards. I would squint up at the traceries of masts and rigging along the waterfront, smell the smoke from the steam-boxes and the sharp tang of turpentine and Stockholm tar, hear the ring of the caulker's hammers driving oakum into a ship's seams. A horse and dray might pass, carrying barrels of molasses and leaving road apples in its wake.

At Queen Street I might see Peake's barque, the *Castalia*—known as "Peake's Ark"—which had gone aground in 1838 and been hauled ashore to be used as a warehouse and sail loft. Looking two blocks up Queen Street, I could see the recently completed Duncan Mason Building, owned by another leading shipwright and merchant, James Duncan, whose ships were loading cargoes in Liverpool and Rio de Janeiro.

Everywhere I looked, I would see the world's work going on, with all its colour and variety. It would be clear to me that if I kept my eyes open, learned my trade and seized opportunities when I saw them, why—why, I might become a man like Peake or Duncan, with ships and buildings and business interests half-way around the world, with a gracious home in the centre of Charlottetown. And what more could any man ask?

Every one of the buildings in that imaginary walk is still in use—not because of sound planning, but because Charlottetown essentially stagnated for many decades. When I first visited it during the winter of 1967, the "cradle of Confederation" was a run-down, dispirited place reached by an uncertain ferry and a long rough road. I declined an attractive job there: the place just seemed too isolated, and too depressing.

Years later, I talked about the city's unparallelled stock of 19th-century buildings with Eddie Rice, then an alderman and executive director of the PEI Council of the Arts, an ardent conservationist who had gone into politics "because they tore down the Bank of Commerce building."

"This is a city you can get your mind around," he said. "But it's fragile." A city like Halifax can lose a block of heritage buildings without losing its character, but in Charlottetown, "the scale of the town is crucial. One or two buildings could destroy it." But Charlottetown had been spared the mindless development of the 1960s and 1970s, and by the 1980s it had become "more sensible to recycle than to build."

In short, said Rice succinctly, "Poverty preserves."

Eddie Rice lives in a yellow-and-white waterfront mansion at

2 West Street, which he bought in 1981 for $70,500. (He has restored it lovingly, and recently refused $295,000.) Nearby is the 21-room West End House at 18 West Street, which was not good enough for James Peake, Jr., the son and successor to the Water Street merchant. Young Peake sold it, and the buyer moved it here. There is a glorious 25-room house at the corner of West and Kent. This house, known as Beaconsfield, was built in 1877 on the lot where West End House once stood. This is the house that young Peake built.

Beaconsfield is a fairyland of cupolas and gingerbread, stained-glass windows and plaster mouldings, marble base-boards and fancy fretwork. Fit for a queen, one might think, or at least for Queen Victoria's daughter, Princess Louise, who was a guest here in 1879. She brought her husband, the Marquis of Lorne: he was Governor-General of Canada. Alas, Peake lost his fortune and the house passed to the mortgagee, Henry Cundall, in 1885. It served as a nurses' residence and a YWCA before the Heritage Foundation of Prince Edward Island acquired it during the Island's centennial year—1973, not 1967.

The house is not normally open to the public, but I went inside one time to visit Ian Scott. At that time Scott was director of the Heritage Foundation, which publishes the engaging semi-annual *The Island Magazine* as well as Irene Rogers's *Charlotte-town: The Life in its Buildings*, to which I am much indebted.

Ian Scott traced the Island attitude to buildings and land back to July 23, 1767, when the Colonial Office in London granted the entire island by lottery to 64 British merchants, military officers and minor nobles. They were required to settle at least one "foreign Protestant" per 100 acres within ten years, and to pay a small annual "quit rent" to the Crown. Few of these instant landlords met even these modest requirements, and only a hand-ful ever saw the Island, but their ownership of the land made Islanders into tenants on land they had cleared and developed with their own hands. As Islanders bitterly noted, it took just a day to give the Island away; it took a century to buy it back.

The Land Question became the overwhelming issue in Island life and politics, breeding widespread civil disobedience and occasional violence. Tenants occupying huge areas of the island simply refused to acknowledge the rights of the landlords. They withheld their rents and became self-governing enclaves. When the police and the sheriffs dared to venture there, tenant farmers would spread the alarm for miles by blowing an eerie wail on conch shells, and the men of the district would gather to face down the authorities.

The Land Question was the burning issue behind the drive for responsible government on the Island, and it even figured in the Confederation debates, a full century after the infamous lottery. One of the Island's terms for joining Canada was a loan of $800,000 from the federal government to buy out the remaining landholders, a project not completed until 1895.

As a result, Scott said, "the ownership of land is a theme to which Islanders are particularly sensitive. Perhaps it's part of the reason for the pride in home ownership, for the fact that homes and even barns here are kept up so well—repaired and painted and so forth. People have a great pride in their homes, and we have a greater percentage of people who own their homes outright, no mortgage, than anywhere else in the country."

Sensitive indeed. In the 1970s, when much of PEI seemed to be in danger of being bought up by off-Island speculators and summer residents, the province passed legislation forbidding non-residents to own more than ten acres without the express permission of the provincial Cabinet. (Islanders grumble, admittedly, that the Cabinet never refuses permission.)

And during our visit to Charlottetown, Premier Joe Ghiz had just returned from the last constitutional negotiations before the Charlottetown meetings which produced the fateful Accord. Each province had its cherished, non-negotiable requirements, and Ghiz's had to do with the preservation of his government's control over land ownership. If the general rights of Canadian citizenship were going to override the rights of Prince Edward Islanders to control the ownership of land, Ghiz argued, the constitutional deal was not going to fly in Prince Edward Island. He won the point, and the Island's land laws were grandfathered into the Charlottetown Accord.

The architect of Beaconsfield was William Critchlow Harris (1854–1913), the Island's most celebrated architect. The British cherish their Wrens and Nashes, but before the advent of Arthur

Erickson, Raymond Moriyama and Ron Thom, Canadians hardly seem to have noticed their architects.

The Island is an exception. Its architectural tradition began with an Englishman, John Plaw, who arrived in Charlottetown in 1807. None of Plaw's work is known to have survived, but his notebooks and his lectures to carpenters and builders inspired a generation of early builders. Isaac Smith, a Yorkshireman, came a little later. Smith designed Province House, the legislative building; Government House, the residence of the Lieutenant-Governor; and the Point Prim lighthouse, the first on the Island, which we had passed in the night.

But it was Willy Harris, more than any other, who set his mark on the Island's buildings. The stone house on the same intersection as Beaconsfield is another Harris design, and there are plenty of others in this part of Charlottetown. On one block of Brighton Road, between Ambrose Street and Greenfield Avenue, every single house was either designed or renovated by Harris.

Harris also designed 20 Island churches, of which 16 still stand. One of them is just off the Trans-Canada Highway at Crapaud, and it is a highlight of the drive from the capital to the Borden ferry. The most notable of Harris's churches is All Souls Chapel at St. Peter's Anglican Cathedral on Rochford Square, just a block away from Beaconsfield. The cathedral was erected when Harris was just a boy, but All Souls Chapel, built onto its west side, is all Harris.

The chapel is built of Island sandstone, a material of which Harris was particularly fond, and it shows his usual Gothic Revival tastes. The exterior was built in 1888 to 1889, but the interior details were added slowly over the years, always to Harris's designs. The stained glass windows were ordered from Kempe of London. The walnut altar, like the rest of the elaborate woodwork, was carved by Island craftsmen working with H. & S. Lowe, a firm of builders long associated with Harris.

The interior also houses 18 fine paintings, the first of which—an ascending Christ—was executed in 1890 and hangs behind the altar. The last two were hung more than a quarter of a century later, in 1917.

The painter was the architect's brother, Robert Harris (1849–1919), the first Island artist to make a living from painting and the first Island Fellow of the Royal Society of Arts. Harris is known particularly for his portraits, and for *Meeting of the School Trustees* and *Harmonium*, a tender portrayal of his wife at the harmonium, both of which hang in the National Gallery of Canada.

Robert Harris's most famous painting is familiar to almost all Canadians: the group portrait of the Fathers of Confederation. The original hung in the Parliament Buildings, but it burned with the building in the fire of 1916. All we now have are an oil sketch in Charlottetown's Confederation Centre and a 12-foot preliminary drawing, which the Centre was showing while we were prowling the city. It had not been seen by the public since 1883.

The Confederation Centre actually replaced the Robert Harris Memorial Gallery, built by his widow in Queen Square, just four blocks from All Souls Chapel. Queen Square is the heart of the city, and its centrepiece is Province House, the legislative building where the Fathers of Confederation met in 1864. The room has been restored to its 19th-century condition, with many of the original furnishings. I went up and had a look at it. I expected to feel something. I didn't. But this is where The Deal was made.

We went across the street to Apothecaries' Hall for ice cream. This whole block retains its traditional storefronts—but behind them rises a square glass office block. Most stores have an entrance on the street and another into Confederation Court Mall. Hidden behind the small-town facade, the mall is, in Brian Cudmore's opinion, "the best-kept secret in Charlottetown."

Apothecaries' Hall, a 19th-century drugstore, is now the home of Cows, a chain of ice-cream stores, which also sell a range of whimsical cow-theme gift items, like T-shirts showing cows in various social dilemmas—preparing for a steamy date, chewing over the constitutional debate or attending the University of Cowvendish. Cows sells by mail order and advertises in papers such as *The Globe and Mail* and *Financial Post*. The ice cream is excellent. The proprietary waffle-style cones are even better.

Cows has three stores in Prince Edward Island and one in the Channel Islands. With 250,000 copies of the second catalogue out, mail-order sales are strong, and Japanese investors are interested in Asian franchises. The concept is udderly wacky—Ralph Lauren in an Island pasture—but in a wacky world it seems to work.

Behind it all we find—who else?—the Electric Acadian.

"I am Cows," says Marc Gallant. "It's my package. I have a corporate partner, Scott Linkletter, who deals with the money end of it, but I came up with the concept and I have complete control on the creative side."

It figures. When I first met Gallant, he was a kid from Rustico working as a writer and photographer on Réshard Gool's 1970s alternative newspaper, *The Square Deal*. He was among the first to see the potential in Charlottetown's heritage buildings; he wheedled enough financing to purchase and renovate an old warehouse into offices, and then found himself desperate for tenants. As he told me at the time, he solved the problem by lying in wait for Premier Alex Campbell, seizing him by the arm as he emerged from Province House and steering the Premier through his building. Fortunately, the Premier was impressed. The government rented offices, and the project survived.

Gliding back and forth between business and the arts, Gallant carved out a *fin de siècle* life-style, interspersing Island summers with European winters, flitting between Rustico and the Greek islands, the Pacific, the Channel Islands. Modishly dressed, dark and blocky, with brooding eyes above a bushy drooping moustache, he became an exotic bird of passage, hatching improbable projects. Moving between continents like a faxed message, the Electric Acadian emerged as a citizen of the global village, picking up impulses in the ether, surfing on trends, merchandising products wherever he saw a niche in popular taste.

Was Lucy Maud Montgomery's *Anne of Green Gables* wildly popular in Japan? Very well: Gallant developed an *Anne* colouring book and sold it to a Japanese publisher. It made big money. Were the baby boomers reaching the age of nostalgia? *More Fun with Dick and Jane* was the adult sequel to the boomers' school primer. The bland artwork and the repetitive language are familiar, but Dick and Sally are suburban yuppies; Baby is divorced and drives a K-car. The book sold more than 300,000 copies. If trolls could become a craze, why not cows? Wouldn't frenzied, anxious yuppies buy into that soothing and nostalgic image?

Knopf published the book in New York. Its sales have been satisfying. More important, it launched the concept he and Linkletter are now exploiting.

Marc Gallant kept on travelling—to Asia, New Mexico, Florence. "I've wintered in a different place every winter for 20 years," he muses. When we saw him, he was building a dream house on a secluded Rustico peninsula, and ordering a houseboat.

"It's going to be 51 feet long, and somewhere between 26 and 30 feet wide," he said. "It'll be about 2,000 square feet—the ultimate party boat. It should be ready next summer. You'll have to come over for the launching party." In the meantime, he was heading for the University of Perugia for two months to study Italian, and then driving his van south for the winter.

ANNE,

WITH AN

"E"

The Japanese fascination with *Anne of Green Gables* took many Maritimers completely by surprise. It was easy enough to understand the Japanese interest in the West Coast, in New York, even in the Rockies. But *Anne of Green Gables*? A sentimental children's novel set in late Victorian Prince Edward Island?

Nevertheless, there they were, growing in numbers throughout the 1980s: planeloads of Japanese setting down in Charlottetown like flocks of migrant birds, picking through the Anne country like sandpipers in shallow water and spraying yen like water droplets on grateful tourist operators. But the Japanese were not alone: the Anne industry just keeps growing. True, more than seven million copies of 16 Montgomery titles are circulating in Japan, and a passage from *Anne* is in the Japanese secondary school curriculum. But Anne does not captivate only the Japanese: *Anne of Green Gables* and its successors have been published in more than 15 languages and in many millions of copies. The book has been twice made into a ballet and twice into films; it has been presented on stage in London, New York, Osaka, Nairobi and Java, among other places; and the recent Kevin Sullivan TV series has presented the story to a vast new audience.

Anne is everywhere on the Island: in bookstores and gift shops, on the stage, in the National Park. The province recently embossed the freckle-faced redhead on its license plates. Montgomery's manuscript is on display at the Confederation Centre, and the musical-comedy version of the story has been playing in the Centre's theatre for more than 20 years. It is the longest-running show in Canadian history.

Anthropologically interesting, at the very least. In a detached, investigative frame of mind, we went to the show.

The "freckled witch of a girl"—Montgomery's phrase—promptly nailed me, too.

The musical is fresh, funny and affecting. Anne's story seems to speak directly to the child in all of us, with our memories of hurt and misunderstanding, of being blamed for errors while trying desperately to please, of feeling lonely, powerless and unwanted. She also speaks to the adult in us—unduly realistic and almost numbed by experience, bearing the weight of the world on our shoulders, longing for the fresh perception and the capacity for wonder which children bring into our lives. In the musical, as in the book, those two outlooks collide—and in their collision lies a deep humour with a savour of melancholy.

As Anne ages, the shadows lengthen. But Anne's impulsiveness and imagination have become her servants, not her masters, and Marilla is dependent on her. The world transforms itself, and the baton of responsibility is passed to the next generation.

Anne is really an archetypal fable about ancient values and the eternal conflicts between continuity and innovation, self-fulfilment and duty, imagination and realism, power and justice. Anne Shirley triumphs through the quality of her character, her ability to dance between these opposites. She is Cinderella in puffed sleeves and Island homespun: the unwanted orphan who ultimately becomes the benign ruler of the realm. Like other fairy-tales, her story is endlessly charming because it speaks to deep fears and cherished dreams.

The three of us sat in the theatre alternately gasping with laughter and moved by the show's poignancy. Lulu looked at Mark and at me, amused by Anne's ability to touch parent and child at once, effortlessly bridging a gap of 40 years.

But she bridges much larger gaps of culture, sex and language, too. Like all great fables, she melts human divisions, bringing us together to celebrate our brief lives in defiance of our certain mortality.

At intermission, I suddenly thought: Tom and Bev Grove must be here. Tom is a bassoonist, Bev a violinist; in winter they work in Halifax, but they spend their summers with the Confederation Centre orchestra. Lulu had the same thought. We looked up. Tom Grove was walking towards us. After the show, we met them backstage and went to *Silversark* for a nightcap.

We talked about boats, about planes and about *Anne*. The Groves own half a dozen rental cottages at rocky little Duncan Cove, near Halifax, and Tom has tinkered with innumerable boats, ranging from a fibreglass day sailer to an ex-Navy torpedo boat. He understands the Water Rat philosophy—but Duncan Cove, though a spectacular setting, is not a good harbour.

It does have a tolerable airport, which Tom built for his own Piper Cub. He used to bring the plane over to their rented Island farm each summer—but not this year.

"I gave it to my son," he said. "I think I'm going to get a glider. I spent a lot of last summer gliding—up there in the Piper Cub, chasing thermals with the engine off. It was wonderful—quiet, peaceful, and if you got into a good thermal you could just go up and up and up."

After nearly two decades of playing the *Anne of Green Gables* score, they still find the show fresh and alive.

"It's a wonderful show," said Bev. "It isn't great music, but it works. I still enjoy the show, even after all these years."

"That's right," said Tom. "The music works for the show. The strength is in the story and the characters, particularly Anne—and those we owe to Lucy Maud Montgomery."

"Every line in the show comes straight from Montgomery, did

you know that?" said Bev. I didn't. The music is by Norman
Campbell and the lyrics by Don Harron. The two wrote the
script together.

"You should come to the crew party with us," said Bev. "Are
you free tomorrow? It's over in Rocky Point, across the harbour."

"Come see the farm, too," said Tom. "Come stay overnight.
We've got four big bedrooms, and there's nobody there."

Lulu and I looked at each other, and at Mark.

"We'll come to the party," Lulu said. "But I think we'd rather
sleep on the boat."

Lulu knows I am a domestic animal: I like to sleep in my own
bed. But as we curled up in the delta berth a little later, we
remarked on the fact that people often invite us to sleep ashore,
and we rarely accept. It's a positive pleasure to sleep aboard: our
berth is comfortable, and we like the lapping of the waves against
the hull, the gentle motion of the boat, the sound of the breeze in
the rigging. We designed that interior to suit ourselves, and it
works remarkably well.

"Must be a pretty fair boat," I said.

"Mmph," said Lulu.

Next day we visited Green Gables House, in Prince Edward
Island National Park, a narrow 25-mile strip of sand dunes and
beaches on the Island's northern coast. We wanted to try some
North Shore harbours, but the *Sailing Directions* were daunting:

> The harbours are small and shallow, with narrow
> entrances through sand bars, which become impass-
> able in a heavy sea. All harbour entrances break in a
> moderate sea and in some areas it becomes impossible
> to locate the best channel . . . The channels through
> the bars are likely to be blocked or shifted by storms.
> Leading lights may be shifted without advance
> notice, and buoys moved, or lifted . . . With few
> exceptions, the anchorage is poor along this coast.

Yes, indeed. In 1883, when Lucy Maud Montgomery was
eight years old, the people of Cavendish were transfixed to see a
great ship, with all sails set, driving headlong towards the beach

at the height of a roaring storm. The ship grounded about 300 yards out, and the crew instantly cut away her rigging; her three towering masts fell with a crash that could be heard ashore.

She was the *Marco Polo*, built in Saint John, New Brunswick, in 1851—one of the greatest of Canadian ships. In her early days, under the notorious Bluenose captain "Bully" Forbes, she sailed from Liverpool to Australia in 68 days and was back in Liverpool less than six months from her departure. An almost demonic character, Forbes drove the ship so hard that he terrified the crew, bestriding the poop deck with pistols in his hand, threatening to shoot any man who tried to shorten sail.

But by 1883 *Marco Polo* was a tramp, sailing from Quebec with a load of lumber. In a gale in the Gulf, she sprang a leak too strong for her pumps to clear, and her captain deliberately drove her ashore. Little Maud Montgomery stood on the shore and watched the ship die. The wreck was the subject of an essay which placed third in a competition when she was 15.

Would we visit that tricky coast? The opinion at the yacht club was unanimously opposed—especially for a boat without an engine. Well, we would drive up, look at a couple of harbours for ourselves, and we would look at Green Gables, too. En route we would drop Mark at the race-track.

For Mark, sailing remained distinctly less interesting than RC—radio-controlled model cars. He had already dragged me to East Coast Models to pick up parts for the ungainly vehicle which shared his berth. A steel building in Southport, across the river from Charlottetown, the whole store was stuffed with costly toys for grown-up boys. Huge models hung from the ceiling— Spitfires and Dakotas, sloops and speedboats, racing cars. Some were electric-powered, like Mark's; others had tiny gas engines running on nitro-methane. They were controlled by hand-held radio transmitters which looked like Darth Vader weapons.

While Mark discussed the merits of different tires with one clerk, I asked another about the business. It was only three or four years old, and it had begun in the owner's basement. But RC was booming—a new trend, which the Electric Acadian had unaccountably missed—and now East Coast Models employed four people full-time and did a substantial mail-order business across Canada and down into the United States, in direct competition with the major American suppliers.

"You should come to the races on Sunday," said the clerk. "At the Petro Canada in North River. Starts about noon."

RC is a costly hobby; Mark's car was nothing very special, but over the years he had sunk close to $500 in it. The engine he *really* wanted was a microscopic V-8, which sells for more than $3000. (No, I told him firmly, there is no point in dropping hints about *that*.) At the North River race meeting I saw how serious a hobby it could be. Young men drove up in pick-up trucks and vans and produced complete pit facilities: portable work-benches with specialized tools, parts cabinets, spare bodies and engines, different tires for different road surfaces, canisters of compressed air to blow their cars clean, special grips to hold their cars while they altered and exchanged servos and engines.

The track was defined by painted two-by-fours on the parking lot. Snarling like big bees, the cars whirled around the track, streaking down the straightaways, caroming off the rails and spinning out on the turns. Crouching low to the ground, I took some video footage of them. When you see the action on a monitor, it looks like Grand Prix competition.

Mark was in catnip. We left him to his ecstasy and drove to Cavendish, the heart of the *Anne* country.

In Cavendish, we did not stop at the Green Gables Post Office or play the Green Gables golf course. We passed up Matthew's Market and we did not eat at Marilla's Pizza. We did not spend $1.00 Adults/50¢ Children to gaze on the foundation—all that remains—of Lucy Maud Montgomery's Cavendish home. In the Anne world, you can buy videos, figurines, posters, hats, book-marks, buttons, scarves, CDs, sweatshirts and purses. You can taste Marilla's plum jam and stay at Shining Waters Country Inn, the home of Rachel Lynde. (You can also stay at the Bosom Buddies Cottages, the Kindred Spirits Country Inn, Anne's Windy Poplars, the Anne Shirley Motel or the Avonlea Cottages.) You can subscribe to an Anne of Green Gables newsletter or join the Kindred Spirits of PEI association.

The Anne kitsch is bad enough, but the spin-offs are truly bizarre. Cavendish boasts, if that is the word, a Ripley's Believe It Or Not Museum, wax figures at the Royal Atlantic Wax Museum, radio-controlled boats at Cranberry Village, a 37-acre fun park called Rainbow Valley, a Ferris wheel and bumper boats at Sandspit Amusements, a Country Bear musical show at the Enchanted Castle—not to mention King Tut's Tomb and Treasures.

Tourism has been part of Charlottetown's economy at least since 1829, when Thomas Hyde opened the Queen's Head Hotel at 27 Water Street—the house Cunard once owned—and noted it was "peculiarly adapted to the accommodation of private families who may visit Charlotte Town during the summer months." And tourism is a major theme in the Urgent Conversation.

Travel is the world's fastest-growing industry, and arguably one of its most attractive. Travellers do not foul the air or the water, except marginally; they are relatively modest consumers of energy and they do not swill down irreplaceable resources. True, tourism tends to generate low-paying seasonal jobs, and it contributes to the general erosion of local cultures. But the Maritimes offer a safe, unique experience to travellers, and if one is looking for an industry one could do much worse.

Still, when a community surrenders entirely to tourism, it undergoes subtle changes. It lives not by its own idea of itself, but by the ideas of it held by others. It is sprayed with a coat of Quaint Paint—quick drying, sets like iron, looks just like the original. It becomes a museum of itself, as the poet Bill Howell would put it. The illusion created for transient visitors becomes the reality in which people live and work. People become clichés: horny-handed fishermen or laconic farmers who set off the decor of wharf or barn. Who can calculate the cost of such a transformation?

We should be asking the question, whether or not we know the answer. Meanwhile, we were tourists ourselves. Our objective was Green Gables House, the Victorian farmhouse in which Montgomery set Anne's tale. Despite a certain bureaucratic stuffiness, Parks Canada is good at maintaining shrines. Near the house are the Haunted Wood, Lover's Lane, the Birch Path and the Dryad's Bubble, all impeccably labelled. The grounds are spotlessly maintained. The house itself contains Anne's dress with the puffed sleeves, Marilla's amethyst brooch, Montgomery's typewriter and scores of people from the cars and buses parked in ranks in the parking lot.

We shuffled shoulder-to-shoulder up the steep staircase and

through the narrow hallways, peeping into roped-off rooms full of period furniture. Voices gabbled, bodies pressed, guides explained, the slow stream of flesh moved relentlessly through the shrine. We were happy when it disgorged us at the back door, handy to the Green Gables Tearoom and Gift Shop.

The gift shop was doing a roaring business, but the tea-room was blessedly quiet. We ordered chowder, tea biscuits and tea. Our waitress was named Mikiko Motoishi. She came from Kyushu, in southern Japan. She had been in Prince Edward Island for a couple of months, and she liked it, although she was finding the summer chilly. A recent letter from her mother told her that the temperature in Kyushu was thirty-five degrees Celsius, day after day.

"What brought you here?" asked Lulu.

Mikiko giggled. "Anne of Green Gables."

"What will you do when you're finished here?"

"I would like to live in a house by the water," said Mikiko. "*Here.* But first I must find my husband here."

We decided not to visit the Anne of Green Gables Museum at Silver Bush (in Park Corner) and Anne's House of Dreams and the Avonlea schoolhouse (at French River) and the Lucy Maud Montgomery Birthplace (in New London) or Grave (in Cavendish.) Instead we turned west and went to look at Rustico Harbour.

We drove to the harbour entrance and then walked to the breakwater. The brisk westerly breeze had an unbroken fetch clear from the Gaspé peninsula, and the resulting wave trains made the harbour look downright scary. Seas were breaking on the bar a quarter of a mile out, and the channel approached the breakwater through the surf at an oblique angle and ran close under the breakwater to the shore. It turned sharply left, parallel to the beach, before abruptly turning right into the harbour proper. You could pitch a stone across it all the way in, and the current was pouring through the gut, bearing buoys over sideways. Gulls and ducks were standing on sandbars on the other side.

"We could possibly sail in, but we might be here for a month waiting for a wind to go out again," I said. "And there's no room to make a mistake. You wouldn't dare try it in the dark."

"Are the other harbours better or worse?" Lulu asked.

"They tell me this is one of the better ones."

"No, thanks," said Lulu. "Let's skip it."

We zipped back to Charlottetown, avoiding the main routes. Most of the Island's back roads are paved—a necessity in country where cars sink to their floor pans in the red ooze of early spring. Aside from red sandstone, the Island has no rock at all; gravel for concrete comes in by barge from Nova Scotia. The back roads wind through shallow valleys, green and billowing with their crops of oats, hay, potatoes, tobacco. Tiny hamlets like Wheatley River and Ebenezer are perhaps the true Anne country, with their almost palpable aura of settled patterns of living and accepted scales of value.

We scooped up a protesting Mark from the race-track and drove out to pick up the Groves at their Rice Point farmhouse— right on Northumberland Strait, on the opposite side of the island from Cavendish and Rustico.

"Tough life," I said, looking around the lovely old house on the shore, set off from its neighbours by fields of barley and private woodland and with its own secluded beach. "The grim penury of the struggling musician."

"Oh, we suffer," said Tom. "No question about it, we suffer."

We drove on to Rocky Point, overlooking the entrance to Charlottetown Harbour, near the site of Port Lajoie. This was ancestral ground: one of Lulu's Terrio ancestors was baptized here in 1750, during the last years of the French regime in what was then called Isle St-Jean. We found the Anne of Green Gables party at the summer home of three brothers named Flynn— three unpretentious cottages among the spruce trees at the top of a bluff. In a clearing at one side, people were pitching horseshoes and playing volleyball. Packs of kids chased across the lawns and into the bushes. Earlier in the afternoon there had been a three-legged race and an egg-and-spoon race.

Under a tent along the back of a cottage, an assembly line was producing food—steaks, potato salad, green salads, rolls. Members of the *Anne* crew worked their way through the crowd, pouring drinks from pitchers of wine and a lethal fruit punch based on Quebec alcool. Between two of the cottages, a quintet of musicians from the Charlottetown Festival orchestra was playing Dixieland and old standards.

Fellers she can't get
Are fellers she ain't met;
Georgia named her, Georgia claimed her,
Sweet Georgia Brown!

The faces were oddly familiar: Marilla, Mrs. Blewett, Anne
herself. In jeans and batik skirts, in shorts and Nikes.

Below the bluffs a little sloop was slowly beating into the
harbour. I recognized the boat from the yacht club: it was Tom
Walker's. Tom and his wife like to sail her out behind St. Peter's
Island, in water too shallow for anyone else. Their little twin-
keeler sits upright when the tide goes out, and the Walkers wade
ashore and have a picnic. When the tide comes in, the boat floats
and they sail home.

I found myself eating a second piece of strawberry shortcake,
reflecting on the taste of the berries, like the sweetness of the
brief Maritime summer itself. Other Maritime seasons are glorious, too—October especially—but we have only two short
months when people can get together to talk and play beside the
sea, to drink wine and make music, to eat lobsters and strawberries and watch the children flying across the grass.

"Dear old world," says Anne, "you are very lovely, and I am
glad to be alive in you." True, I thought. Life doesn't get much
better than this.

"Silver Donald!"

"Rich Wilson!"

Rich Wilson is an *homme du théâtre* whose path crosses mine
every year or two. In moments, the conversation had expanded to
include Hank Stinson, who played the mailman and the station-
master in the show, and his wife Rowena.

After two decades, the show has its own history and mythology. In this first season under Jacques Lemay as artistic director,
it was distinctly sunnier than Walter Learning's version a year
earlier. This was also the first season in which Glenda Landry
appeared not as Diana Barry but as Mrs. Spencer and Mrs.
Sloane. How could someone play a schoolgirl for 20 years?
Everyone laughed; Gracie Finley had continued to play Anne
when she was north of 30 and pregnant with her third child.

I asked why the show appealed so much to the Japanese.

"General MacArthur," said Rich Wilson. "That's what I've

been told. During the occupation he was looking for a book which would give a flavour of North America and would also show how a person could be independent and strong-willed even within a very rigid system. His wife was a great *Anne of Green Gables* fan, and he got the book onto the curriculum for all the schools."

Lulu and I had speculated that this compact little island, with its trim farms and tidy flower gardens, would itself feel comfortable and familiar to the tidy, island-dwelling Japanese.

"Maybe so," said Hank. "You know, Rowena and I toured Japan with the show, and we were treated like royalty. It's the first foreign country I've ever visited where you didn't have to establish that you were *not* American—the Japanese simply didn't care. But to be from *Prince Edward Island! That* was something special."

"I had another idea," said Rowena. "The two main religions of Japan are Shintoism, which is basically nature worship, and Buddhism, which is a later import. Now you look at Anne—at first she's Shinto, naming the trees and ponds and worshipping nature, but later she's Buddhist, sacrificing herself to preserve the social order of Green Gables."

"Green Gables itself is really a character in the piece, too," said Hank. "Somehow that has something to do with it."

"The story's so *funny*," said Lulu. "Maybe we share our sense of humour with the Japanese, too."

I wanted to hear more from Japanese people themselves about *Anne*'s appeal to them, and the next morning, in the lobby of the Prince Edward, I met a Japanese guide named Shinobu who now lives on the Island full-time. So I asked her.

"It's very difficult to say," she said. "It appeals to different things in different people."

Well, did the example of individuality and rebellion in a heavily structured society have anything to do with it?

"Yes, that's part of it," she said. "And . . . do *you* like *Anne of Green Gables*?"

"Very much."

"Why?"

Well, I said, hmm. I like her strength of character, her ability to create a home for herself despite the obstacles—and I find it not only touching, but very funny.

"Yes," she said. "For us, too. But for me, now, it's not so much *Anne of Green Gables*. It's this island. I love *this island.*"

Mikiko. Shinobu. How many others? This, too, is one of the changes that tourism brings, and it will greatly enrich life on the Island.

The next generation will include some patriotic Islanders who are half Japanese. And if their hair is red, their mothers will feel especially blessed by Heaven.

THE

MIGHTY

SPUD

A cruise has a certain rhythm, hard to define but easy to feel. One could easily stay in Charlottetown for a month, or a year—but after a week, it was time to go.

I had been gleaning advice from yacht club veterans like John Simmonds, whose graceful wooden 28-foot Cheoy Lee was new when I first met him, nearly 20 years earlier. Among the club's most active cruisers were John and Mike Day, a father and son who had built their 38-foot Bruce Roberts sloop out of steel. *Daydreams* weighs 13 tons; she was supposed to weigh ten tons, John concedes, but they over-built her. She sails fine, but she lies lower in the water and takes more spray aboard than she should. Her 30-horsepower diesel engine has enough fuel to reach Boston under power. She has all the usual electronics, plus an electric anchor windlass, a microwave oven, an electric stove. The hollow keel is filled with massive batteries.

"I'm an electrical contractor." John Day shrugged. "My motto is *Live better electrically.*"

With their dog as bosun, John and Mike voyage at every opportunity. They were in Summerside when we arrived, and they went to Shediac the next weekend. They were heading to the Magdalens in August, to Cape Breton in September. John wanted to take her south for the winter, but he couldn't afford to.

Dave Mosher sails *Blitz*, a 7000-pound 35-foot Kevlar rocket. She is not much heavier than *Silversark*, but her tapering, whip-like carbon-fibre mast is half as tall again as ours. She does more than seven knots to windward. Dave had recently sailed the 40-odd miles from Charlottetown to Summerside in four hours. With a racing crew of 13, he was flying a spinnaker and surfing downwind at 11 knots.

"Ride the currents," he said. "The currents change 15 minutes after the tides. They change first along the shore and later in mid-channel. Stay inshore to catch the tide early, far out if it's going to change against you. The tides run in and out around both ends of the Island, and they meet at Borden. The rising tide runs west on this side of Borden, and east from there on.

"You're going to Summerside? Leave on the last two hours of the falling tide. That'll carry you out of Hillsborough Bay, and then you'll pick up the rising tide going westward. By the time it changes you'll be at Borden, and you can ride the *falling* tide westward, too. Work the currents and you'll easily cut an hour off the trip, maybe more."

We looked at the tide tables. The tide would be low the next morning at nine-fifteen: we should sail, then, at seven-fifteen. Good: that gave me time to go see Harry Fraser and talk about potatoes.

"I tried Centennial Russets," Harry Fraser once said, "but I found they looked sickly, and they had a tendency to hollow heart." It sounded like a wailing country-and-western song:

> Centennial Russet, now we got to part,
> You're sickly lookin', got a hollow heart . . .

Harry Fraser thinks potatoes, eats potatoes, broadcasts about potatoes, lectures on potatoes, does research on potatoes, writes about potatoes, strives to *understand* potatoes. He phones around the world for potato news: what's the state of the potato market in Algeria, Argentina, Antigua? When Shakespeare wrote, "Let every eye negotiate for itself, and trust no agent," Harry Fraser thinks the Bard had potato contracts in mind.

Harry lives in Hazelbrook, just east of Charlottetown, surrounded by potatoes. As editor and publisher and proprietor of *Fraser's Potato Newsletter*—"The Publication for Potato People"—Harry Fraser has the duty and pleasure of finding out anything pertinent to the welfare of potato growers and brokers in Canada and the United States.

Harry's newsletter, now 25 years old, was actually at the forefront of a trend. General magazines have been dying, specialist magazines are thriving. Goodbye, *McCall's* and *Star Weekly*; hello there, *New Mother* and *PC Week*. Newsletters extend the trend. Subscriber-supported, slim, pin-point focused and desktop-published, they constitute the fastest-growing branch of the periodical publishing industry.

At least 100,000 newsletters are being published, and they cover topics you would never think about and might never want to know about. (My particular favourite is *Last Month's Newsletter*, published—late—by the Procrastinator's Club of America.) Since they accept no ads, newsletters aren't cheap—but investors, consumers and corporations will pay well for information which may generate profits, save money or deflect lawsuits. *Food Chemical News* costs US $390 a year, but food companies consider it indispensable; *The G Note*, a Toronto investment letter on small-capitalization companies, costs $480 for seven issues. By those standards, *Fraser's Potato Newsletter* is a bargain: US $75 puts it in your mailbox every Monday morning—two pages of foolscap paper full of facts, printed on both sides and mailed to nearly 2000 potato people

Harry Fraser's world is dominated by 10,000 growers, a mass of information and a hell of a pile of spuds. Did you know that potato production was down last summer in Texas, Washington and California? And that Idaho's 1992 production could be as much as six hundred million pounds less than in 1991? No? Then you couldn't have foreseen the rising prices later in the year—and if you had a barn full of Netted Gems, you might have sold them too cheap.

But the newsletter is not only about prices and markets. Weather conditions, tariffs, diseases, government policies, biological experiments, lawsuits, profiles of potato people and the odd contest also crowd Fraser's pages. Who said, in 1944, that "We can't can 'em, but we sure as hell can freeze 'em"? The answer: O.P. Pearson, a food-packing engineer in Corinna, Maine. How right he was: as of July 1, 1992, the United States held 1,127,199,000 pounds of frozen potato products. Four of Fraser's readers correctly identified Pearson, too.

Fraser's Potato Newsletter thrives on statistics; Harry has been known to address conventions on such inspirational themes as "A Practical Look at Potato Statistics." More than once, he has come up with accurate estimates of potato production long before government statisticians.

"We have good sources." Harry grins. "The credit for that belongs to our readers, subscribers and contacts, who keep us informed."

That network of contacts is the newsletter's strength. Harry is constantly on the phone, and he travels frequently to potato-growing areas throughout North America. Still boyish at 52 despite his half-height reading glasses, he works in what would be the basement of a 25-year-old bungalow if it were not built into a south-facing hillside, with a glass wall overlooking the potato fields and the Trans-Canada Highway. He has been here since 1960, when his potato-farming father, Jock Fraser, dispatched him from Woodstock, New Brunswick, to put in a potato crop on the neglected acreage which Jock had just purchased. Harry was not thrilled. He had a degree in business administration from the University of New Brunswick, a management trainee's job with Canada Life and no particular interest in deserted potato farms.

"My father needed help on this farm, and I came over," he recalls. "Well, after I'd been here a while you couldn't get me to move." He married Janet, then a young schoolteacher, in 1962, and settled down to raise three children and a million potatoes.

By 1967 he had noted that most farmers grew only a few acres of potatoes, didn't have enough information to bargain effectively with buyers and couldn't afford to ferret out the information for themselves. The buyers were specialists, and they used information to govern the market and bamboozle the growers. Harry Fraser had written for his high-school paper, and for a small country weekly. In March, 1967, *Fraser's Potato Newsletter* made its way to 43 subscribers, mostly in Prince Edward Island.

It was "pretty primitive at first," Fraser remembers, "and it was restricted to the Maritimes. But then Ontario and Quebec got interested, and it grew from there. Once you have new areas you have to go there and meet the people, see what their concerns are." Huge irrigation projects in Washington and Idaho, for instance, have opened up tremendous acreages and helped Moses Lake, Washington, grow from 2,000 people to 20,000 in 25 years. Harry Fraser toured there each of the past three summers.

"It's fantastic what they can do out there," he declares. "They get 550 hundredweight to the acre in what used to be sagebrush. Those are the highest yields of any place, double what we get here. But they don't get that much more money from it because the processors pay less for Western potatoes; they're just too far from the markets in the East.

"The story we're going to be watching out there is water. There's very little water in the Pacific Northwest right now. They had to ration it in June in the Klamath basin, and some growers had to write off their wheat in order to save their potatoes. If they don't get a lot of rain or snow this winter it's going to be a huge problem for them."

To an outsider, Fraser's potato-centred world seems faintly comic, but it matters a lot to Canada. Though Holland is by far the world's leading exporter of potatoes, Canada is second, and 60% to 70% of our exports come from the floating potato patch which is our smallest province.

The potato we know, *Solanum tuberosum*, is native to the Andes, where it was cultivated by the Indians 8,000 years ago. Spanish conquistadors encountered it about 1570, but Europeans were suspicious of it, as they were of the tomato; both belong to the same family as the mandrake and deadly nightshade. In the early 1800s, Lord Byron deplored the "sad results of passions and potatoes," which were thought to be powerful aphrodisiacs.

One authority argues that the vast work-force required by the Industrial Revolution could not have been fed without a cheap, adaptable staple. In France, potatoes were popularized in the 1760s by Antoine-Auguste Parmentier, whose name is remembered in many potato dishes *à la Parmentier*. Today the potato—eight species, with about 5,000 varieties—is grown in 130 countries. In the Philippines, potatoes in a housewife's shopping cart are a sign of high status, and in the Dominican Republic, a wealthy person is "in the potatoes."

Prince Edward Island's potato industry had already begun by 1771, when colonial governor Walter Patterson was boasting that the harvest had been a "phenomenal success." By 1800, the island was shipping potatoes to Nova Scotia and New Brunswick, and by the 1830s potatoes were among the Island's chief exports.

By the end of the last century, Islanders had 44,000 acres in potatoes, but low prices and high costs drove that down to 32,000 acres in 1920. During the Roaring '20s, however, rising prices and new varieties—notably Irish Cobbler and Green Mountain—revived the industry. In 1930, at the peak of that revival, 54,000 acres produced nearly 12 million bushels.

Cavendish Farms, the agribusiness arm of the Irving industrial empire, has operated a processing plant on the Island for a decade. McCain's, the New Brunswick potato giant, recently opened a processing plant near Borden. Since their arrival—which guarantees a solid local demand—potato acreage has risen from 72,000 in the early 1980s to about 85,000 today. The limit, says Harry Fraser, is about 90,000 acres—roughly one-fifteenth of the Island's total area. The plants may be a mixed blessing: wary Islanders suspect that the new processing plants are securing their supplies by quietly picking up land under other names, circumventing the Island's land-ownership laws.

Despite the new processing capacity, much of the unprocessed product still goes abroad. It is an odd experience to sit, as I once did, in a dusty office in a Queen Street house and listen to potato dealer Morley Smith trying to call the Hotel Carib in Puerto Cabello. Venezuelan phones are whimsical, and Smith failed to get through. It didn't bother him: he had spent half his life calling to out-of-the-way places like the West Indies, South America, Europe and Toronto, and being awakened in the middle of the night by potato importers returning his calls without allowing for the time differences.

Smith's company, H.B. Willis & Co., are not only potato dealers, but also shipping agents, exporters, stevedores and ship charterers. Their business is moving potatoes—some to Upper Canada, but far more to Brazil, Jamaica, Algeria, Italy and elsewhere. In a good year they may charter between 30 and 40 ships to carry them.

Seed potatoes are the Island's chief export, and the heart of the Island's seed-potato production is the Elite Seed Farm near Alberton, owned by the PEI Potato Marketing Board. The farm occupies every inch of Fox Island, 350 fertile acres connected to PEI only by a causeway. You enter by walking (or driving) through a pool of disinfectant. Isolated by water, upwind from the rest of the province, blessed with rich sandy loam and winter temperatures which annihilate soil microbes and leftover buried spuds, Fox Island is an ideal spot for antiseptic horticulture.

Potatoes come in seven levels of purity, beginning with pre-Elite I and II and descending through Elite I, II and III to Foundation, Certified and Table grades. The first three grades are produced only at the Elite Seed Farm; Elite II and III are grown by carefully selected farmers elsewhere, under close government inspection. Each grade descends from the grade above it; seven years from now, the descendants of this year's pre-Elite I will be in the supermarkets.

I asked Don Northcot, my guide, why the offspring of a Russet Burbank was still a Russet Burbank.

"Cloning," said Northcot.

Cloning? Captain's Log, Stardate 24543 . . .

"No, no," said Northcot. "Cloning is nothing new." Farmers always seeded their fields by cutting up potatoes, leaving at least one eye in each piece and planting the chunks. The new plants develop from the actual flesh of the previous generation. That's genuine cloning, as traditional as an Irish jig.

Until the early 1980s, the Elite Seed Farm bred its seed stock by an exacting version of that traditional method. Eyes were cut from thousands of selected spuds, grown during the winter in the greenhouse and put through a nasty round of testing. If they passed such horrors as the polyacrylamide gel electrophoresis test, the latex agglutination test and the enzyme-linked immunosorbent assay—known to close friends as ELISA—the parent spud got chopped up and planted in the spring. But if ELISA looked into an eye and saw any impurities, the parent spud was ruthlessly expelled from the Elite.

More recently, however, the Elite Seed Farm has moved into tissue culture—which really *is* like science fiction.

Northcot took me to a small basement room, scarcely larger than a closet. It was lit by fluorescent lights and held at a constant temperature and humidity. It contained 10,000 tiny potato plants—and scores of them were descended not just from the same spud, but from the same eye. In a lab, Northcot cut the eye out of a Kennebec—research is a cruel business—and with a fine scalpel peeled away its outer layers before putting it under a microscope. While I watched, he cut to its core, finally excising a tiny white heart-shaped bud.

"This is called the meristem," he explained. "It's the growth point of the eye." Away from the microscope, the meristem was almost invisible. It looked like a very small flake of dandruff, but it was just as magical as the beans from which Jack grew the beanstalk. A meristem can be planted in a nutrient gel—and when it grows, a technician can section it and produce half a dozen more. He can do this again and again, and the number of plants increases geometrically—6; 36; 216; 1,296; 7,776; 46,656; 279,936, and so on. And all of them exactly alike, all clones of that one meristem.

Just to demonstrate the point, Northcot and his colleagues once took a single meristem and produced a ton of potatoes a year later. It could have been a hundred tons "if we'd had enough people to do the work."

Oddly enough, the tuber itself—the part we eat—is actually a stress reaction. Take a tiny potato plant, give it a couple of cold nights, and it instantly forms micro-spuds. Just for fun, Northcot once raised an Alpha potato plant under stress-free conditions, with ideal nutrients in an ideal environment. It produced no tubers. Instead it grew ten feet tall.

Such a plant could propagate only by using the potato's *other* reproductive system. Like a pea or a sunflower, a potato produces blossoms and seeds. Why can't a grower use those seeds instead of cloning the parent plant? Northcot smiled. Those seeds offer all the wild diversity of nature. The offspring of a Red Pontiac might look like a long black snake, a bright red cherry, a miniature pineapple or a Yukon Gold—all random dippings from the great genetic pool of wild potatoes. Potato farming is dicey enough without the risks posed by such flights of genetic fantasy.

The potato's biological foes sound like the nicknames of the criminals in a Batman movie: purple top wilt, blackleg, ring rot, hollow heart, spindle tuber, common scab, silver scurf. The insect predators sound equally vile: wireworms, cutworms, seed-corn maggots, flea beatles and eelworms, also known as nematodes.

With such an array of enemies, it's a wonder that the poor old tuber survives—and that fact, oddly, gives Prince Edward Island an important edge in world markets. It is easy to grow table potatoes in the tropics, but not *seed* potatoes; the climate is too hospitable to parasites, viruses and predators. Aphids lurk in the jungle all year round, and soil microbes live forever. On Fox Island, however, the frigid winters clean the environment. So, while the Island's table potatoes flow largely to consumers in New England and central Canada—Bud the Spud from the bright red mud, rollin' down the highway smilin'—Island seed potatoes compete vigorously in the tropics and around the world.

Since half the crop goes offshore, into world markets, *Fraser's Potato Newsletter* keeps a sharp eye on production in Holland and France, our major competitors in such Mediterranean countries as Algeria and Greece. It monitors government regulations in other countries and reports on the shipments arranged by Morley Smith and others like him. *Fraser's Potato Newsletter* has subscribers in a couple of dozen foreign countries—overseas buyers and brokers, chiefly—and in every province of Canada and every state of the Union.

Every one? Alaska? Hawaii?

"There's a Frito Lay processing plant in Hawaii." Fraser grins. "And Alaska has 500 acres in potatoes. We're in a world market, and we're moving a lot of potatoes. Look, every two weeks, except in midsummer, the Maritimes ship 20,000 hundredweight to the West Indies." The slack period occurs when the old crop is gone and the new one isn't harvested yet. To solve that problem, Dr. Don Young developed a new variety of potato, the Shepody, at the Fredericton research station of Agriculture Canada.

The king spud of North America is the Russet Burbank, known in Canada as the Netted Gem. The Shepody is a short-season Russet which matures early, filling the late summer gap between old crops and new. Its potential is enormous—and that, Fraser hints, may be why the United States banned PEI seed potatoes in 1989, though the ostensible reason was a virus known as PVYn.

"PVYn is found in every country where potatoes are grown, and has been for three decades," declares Fraser. "It doesn't show up in the tops of potatoes, and it doesn't affect the tubers at all. It's thought to be destructive to tobacco, though we're not even sure of that, and it wasn't very widespread. More than six million leaves were tested for it last year, and 96 growers were told to disc up their fields and destroy their potatoes—and it turned out that only ten were actually infected."

Three cases were later discovered in California and one in Florida. But when PVYn was found in Island potatoes—probably brought by smuggled European potatoes—the US federal government promptly banned the import of Island seed.

"That snuffed out one of the most promising new markets of a lifetime," Fraser says. The Columbia River valley and western Idaho were clamouring for Shepody seed, and only the Island had it in quantity. Those growers were eventually supplied from Alberta, Idaho, North Dakota and Minnesota. Prince Edward Island could and did sell offshore, and the ban was expected to be lifted in late 1992—but by then the Island's competitors had captured that huge market.

A dastardly plot against the Island? Harry Fraser shrugs—but the newsletter is not reluctant to chastise the federal government for its obsequiousness to the Americans, nor to nail the American government for tilting the level playing field when it fears the other side might win.

The Shepody is only one of dozens of commercial varieties—and Harry Fraser carefully monitors the steady stream of new ones coming from the research labs. Ranger Russet may be a good new variety for French fries. Norchip and Atlantic were bred for potato chips, and Superior "has obliterated Irish Cobbler in the east." He knows just how many acres are planted to Snowden, Yukon Gold, LaRouge. Each has its strengths and weaknesses. Superior boils well. Russet Burbank bakes well.

Red Pontiac likes mucky soils. Hi-Lite may be good for both fresh and French-fry markets.

"New varieties are always coming out," Fraser says. "The Russet Norkotah has gained popularity in many areas. It won't grow rough like the Russet Burbank often does, but it doesn't have the same cooking qualities, either. Now these are all white-fleshed potatoes, but we're going to have to get into yellow-fleshed potatoes. Look at Brazil, for example: that's a market of 40 million people who like yellow-fleshed potatoes. And in England they like a yellow-fleshed potato called the King Edward."

Bring up the orchestra, now. Let's hear the strings swell in a great crescendo:

> Spuds of hope and glory,
> Tubers of the free . . .

PASSION PLAYS

AND

FERRY TALES

"How are we going to get out of here?" asked Lulu. It was seven-fifteen on a pearly golden morning.

"We'll figure it out," I said, trying to figure it out.

Imagine yourself in a shopping mall parking lot. One end of your aisle is blocked. You have to back out, turning as you go and avoiding the cars parked directly behind you. Then you drive down the length of the narrow aisle, swerving right to avoid a long truck, and then left at the end, to avoid a school bus which half-blocks the exit.

Easy? Sure. But now do it without an engine, in a puffy wind.

"I'll cast off and hold onto the stern line," I said. "The wind will back her out and turn her into the channel. As soon as she's clear of *Blitz*, haul the sails in tight. I'll jump aboard and hoist the jib."

"We're going to sail out."

"Yep," I said, with a confidence I was far from feeling. The other "cars" in the parking lot were a million dollars' worth of yachts; the long truck was a rusty steel dock, and the school bus was a floating breakwater.

"Are we going to clear the *Tupper?*" asked Lulu, looking at the towering red bulk of the Coast Guard ship tied up just outside the marina.

"Probably. If not, we'll have to tack—fast. And then tack again."

"Hmm," said Lulu. "Let's go."

It worked perfectly—but once we cleared the breakwater, we found ourselves crabbing slowly towards the *Tupper.*

"We'll have to tack," I called from the foredeck.

"No," said Lulu. "You and Mark fend off, and we'll just slide along her side."

"All right."

Mark and I hurried to the rail and pushed against the tall steel topsides of the ship as *Silversark* eased her way past. If she had touched, it would have been no more than a caress.

We were passing an open porthole in the ship's side when a Coast Guard seaman stuck his head out for a morning glance at the hills and the harbour. Instead, he found himself nose-to-nose with Mark.

"Good morning," said Mark, with impeccable politeness.

"Er, good morning," replied the sailor, blinking.

Clearing the ship, we sailed out into the harbour. The wind was southwesterly, and we beat down the harbour, making long legs and short ones. The falling tide was carrying us, tugging at the anchored yachts and making the buoys lean downstream. In forty minutes we were under the bluffs at Rocky Point, trying to spot the Flynn cottages among the trees, remembering the party:

> Georgia named her, Georgia claimed her,
> Sweet Georgia Brown!

Heeling sharply, we beat on into Hillsborough Bay, butting into short blunt seas rolling in from the Strait. The bay spread out around us, that lovely Island topography of red bluffs capped by dark green spruce trees and light green fields, with the low bulk of Governor's Island squatting alone on the water.

In the middle of the bay, the wind began to fade. I dropped the jib and raised the genny, and *Silversark* picked up her skirts again. Mark yawned, went below and fell asleep. Looking back at the harbour entrance, I saw the white sails of a sloop beating out in our tracks. John Simmonds, I guessed, in his Cheoy Lee, who had planned on sailing this morning to River John, Nova Scotia. He would probably catch us somewhere near the mouth of the bay, and I would call him on the VHF and say goodbye.

We sailed on, nosing into a steadily falling wind, holding to the west side of the bay, close to St. Peter's Island. A long bar runs south from the Island, so we held our course as we passed it, heading well out to sea. And the white sail was keeping to the east side of the bay on a steadily diverging course.

"John Simmonds, John Simmonds, this is *Silversark*, over."

A crackling voice, barely within range.

"*Silversark*, this is John Simmonds, over."

"John, I just wanted to say goodbye, and thank you. It's been a treat being back at the yacht club, over."

"Been a pleasure to have you. Come again soon, over."

"We will. Thanks again. Over and out."

"Have a good sail. John Simmonds out."

But it was not going to be a good sail: we were steadily losing the wind. With the genny flapping and filling, *Silversark* ambled towards the sea buoy off St. Peter's Island.

"Look," said Lulu. "What's that? It looks like a liner."

I jumped for the binoculars. The thing sat on the horizon like a great white apartment block. Through the binoculars it reshaped itself into a cruise liner, a rarity in these waters. As we watched, it grew larger and larger, approaching us at 15 or 20 knots, bound into Charlottetown. It passed us a mile away, moving steadily up the bay and leaving us bobbing helplessly in the Strait.

We were becalmed. Again.

But it was summer at last. As the wind had fallen, the sun had strengthened—and now, in early August, for the first time this summer, the weather was actually hot—*hot*, by God! It was a strange, ill-remembered sensation.

Well. We took off our shoes and socks, changed into shorts and settled into the familiar routine of waiting, reading and watching for wind. We peered at the shore through binoculars, trying to identify the Groves's farmhouse. I got out the phone and tried to call them, as promised: a pretty thought, calling from the sea to the shore, but there was no answer.

Becalmed. Nothing to do but wait.

I lay on deck thinking about Charlottetown. I was glad to be back at sea and sorry to leave the city—and yet I knew we had seen only its smiling face.

It has other faces. I came to Charlottetown once to report on a chilling, inscrutable murder. On July 20, 1981, three young men crept into the glebe house at Kelly's Cross, a cluster of a dozen houses and a general store on a back road midway between Charlottetown and Summerside. When they fled, Father Clarence Roche lay dying, bludgeoned by a four-foot length of pipe.

By all accounts Father Roche was an exceptional priest— tough, self-sufficient, uncompromising and yet deeply accepting and forgiving, with an "awesome" devotion to his calling. He had spent 13 years at Charlottetown's Basilica before being posted to Kelly's Cross. He was involved in sports, in youth and marriage counselling. He was much in demand as a counsellor— people trusted him and listened to him—and he had touched the lives of thousands of Islanders. They loved him, but they also saw something extraordinary in him: a fierce personal austerity, an unswerving imitation of Christ. "More than anyone else I know, he was trying to lead the life of a saint," a close friend told me. "While he was dying, he would have forgiven whoever killed him."

The Island's instinctive reaction was that no Islander could have committed such a murder; outsiders must have done it. But Islanders *had* done it. Stephen and Brian Laviolette and Jackie Lund were small-time criminals, denizens of a world of race-tracks and drugs, beer and break-ins, car thefts and siphoned gas. I talked about that world with the late Carl Sentner, whose book of short stories, *Everywhere I've Been*, vividly evokes a netherworld of bootleggers, pool halls, wasted days and squalid nights. Like other seaports, he said, Charlottetown does have a twilight stratum of punks, tavern brawlers and petty thieves.

"The Island milieu is in Charlottetown and Summerside,"

Sentner said, "and I've talked to cops who say Charlottetown is known in police circles as a really bad-ass little town. The deviant behaviour that goes on at four or five in the morning in Charlottetown is something else—but you have to be there to see it." When I reported those comments, they provoked the mayor and the chief of police to denounce both Sentner and me for gross calumny. A well-placed Mountie, on the other hand, distinguished between the Islanders' "fairly low tolerance for crimes against persons" and their much more lenient attitude towards "some kinds of low-level activities," which breeds "a reluctance to co-operate with the police on minor crime." Yes, exactly: Maritimers do distinguish sharply between misbehaviour and genuine crime.

Eventually, a jury found that Lund and the Laviolettes had gone to Kelly's Cross to rob the glebe house, that Clarence Roche had interrupted them and that they had killed him in the ensuing scuffle. All three were given life sentences; Stephen Laviolette, who was then 25, would serve a minimum of 15 years before parole; his younger brother, then 18, and Jackie Lund, then 20, would do a minimum of ten years.

A tidy explanation, but inadequate. For here was Stephen Laviolette standing in a Charlottetown courtroom and saying he had approached the priest *ten days earlier* with robbery and violence in his heart, and Clarence Roche had overwhelmed him with sheer spiritual force.

Roche was "fearless," said Laviolette, "the type of person who would stare at you with not a bit of fear" because "he was so close to God." On that earlier occasion, Stephen Laviolette had cut the telephone wires and he had a knife in his hand, which he was prepared to use, but neither of the Laviolettes had "the guts" to deal with such a man. "I didn't have it in me to do it and Brian didn't have it in him to do it." Instead they turned and left.

What tragic magnetism brought Stephen Laviolette back ten days later, *intending*—as he admitted—to kill Roche? What karmic tie bound the two of them together? For Roche was not killed in a scuffle. When he opened his bedroom door, Stephen was already crouching in the hall. He immediately hit Roche in the right temple, and Roche moved towards his murderer, saying, "Don't do it." All three of them heard him say it, and for his friends, the meaning of that extraordinary plea is clear: *Don't commit this sin, don't stain your soul with my blood.* His last words, they feel certain, were addressed not to his own plight but to his murderer's. But Laviolette hit him again—six times in all, according to the police pathologist—and he fell.

Clarence Roche emerges as an extraordinary man, engaged in a profound spiritual venture, with his vision fixed on vast and final things. And Laviolette seems an almost Shakespearean character, doomed to destroy what he could not dominate, moving—as he told the court—"in a sort of trance," like a man under a spell.

That moment in the hallway in Kelly's Cross continues to haunt me, and not just for its horror. Like a flower springing from a battlefield, Clarence Roche's last moments have an electrifying and exemplary quality about them; the strange and provocative beauty of this Island passion play cries out for a Sophocles or a Dostoevsky.

I put some of these thoughts into a CBC radio commentary soon after the trial, and several months later I received a letter from a listener who had been moved by the talk. He wanted to thank me for it. His return address was Dorchester Penitentiary. His letter was signed Stephen Laviolette.

From our present position we could almost see Kelly's Cross just behind the shoreline, five miles inland from the tiny port of Victoria. We drifted on in the warm sunlight, keeping well offshore to avoid Tryon Shoals—"a hundred and five sandbars," as John Day said, "all of them shifting, and the buoy is three miles out to sea." I had a healthy regard for the sands along this shore, for somewhere nearby were the remains of the schooner *Theresa*, once owned by my mentor, Leonard Pertus. He lost her in the 1920s, running her onto a sandbank on his way into Victoria. She was rotten, and when they pulled her free the next day, her keel floated right up beside her.

I thought again about Carl Sentner, about the yawning gulf between *Anne of Green Gables* and *Everywhere I've Been*. Not the least of the Island's fascinations are its layers and depths, the interplay of vastly different realities. When the British took it over, they divided it into three counties: Kings County in the east, with Georgetown for its shiretown; Queens County in the

centre, with Charlottetown (named for King George's consort) as
its shiretown; Prince in the west, with its shiretown in Princetown. (The locals always preferred "Malpeque" to "Princetown," but the post office duly kept delivering mail to
"Princetown" as late as 1945.) The grid of downtown streets in
all the 18th-century Maritime towns reflects the same genteel
obeisance to royalty: there is always a George Street, a Queen
Street, a Charlotte Street, a Brunswick Street (Charlotte came
from Brunswick), a King Street or King Square, and so on.

Yet under that gentility lay the cynical reality of the absentee
landlords. Islanders learned early that gentility was a veneer and
that they would survive by their wits and their cunning. The
genteel rules were not a code that deserved their assent, but
simply a fact of life to be dealt with. That duality, it seemed to
me, had become ingrained in the Island's culture.

The wind arose in the east, gentle and reliable as a grandmother.
The water was absolutely flat, and the rising tide was giving us a
good lift. *Silversark* moved softly but steadily, like a trotting cat.
We came to the Tryon Shoals buoy at six-fifteen. Far ahead, we
could see the ferries shuttling back and forth from Borden to
Cape Tormentine, New Brunswick, their superstructures white
in the sunlight against a low bank of charcoal clouds far away to
the west. Behind us, just visible on the horizon, a gun-metal line
marked the coast of Nova Scotia.

"This is a unique spot," I said, looking around just before I
went below for a nap.

"Why?" said Mark.

"I think it's the only place in Canada where you can see three
provinces at once."

The nine-mile narrows between Borden and Tormentine, the
shortest distance between the Island and the mainland, is the site
of the "fixed link," a recurrent fantasy of politicians, planners
and engineers. The idea of a bridge or tunnel boils up every
generation or so; from 1965 to 1969, the governments actually
built approach roads before reality took hold again. We are going
through another such fever now, and I will offer some odds.

Will construction be commenced? Three to two in favour.

Will it be completed? Five to one against.

If completed, will it cause fewer delays than today's ferries? Seven to one against.

Will it be constructed on time and on budget? Two hundred to one against.

Oh, yes: and will the cost to the Canadian taxpayer be no more than the current ferry subsidies, as its promoters promise? A sucker bet: the project will suck up funds like a vacuum cleaner.

But it's easy to understand the enthusiasm. Communication with the mainland has been as vexatious a theme in Island life as land tenure—and its history is almost as long. In winter the Strait is virtually impassable for as long as five months.

The shallow waters along the shore freeze in December, forming "bord" ice. Sea ice forms offshore, both in the Gulf of St. Lawrence and in the Strait. Wind and waves break the ice up, drive it together, push ice fragments and water onto existing sheets of ice. Ice fields collide, says one witness, "with a grinding roar that can be heard for miles. Blocks weighing tons are upended and thrown back on themselves; in effect, the edges of the fields are rolled back and overlapped until ridges of ice sometimes thirty feet in height are formed."

The first ferries to traverse this shifting, treacherous jumble of ice and gelid brine were little convoys of iceboats—narrow lapstrake rowing boats about 18 feet long. They had two runners on the bottom, scalloped to provide hand-holds, and steel-shod to withstand dragging over rough, abrasive ice. Each was crewed by six men. Each carried a compass, emergency firewood, food, small triangular sails and steel-tipped oars. Both sides of the vessels were fitted with short chains and leather harnesses, and the crew and male passengers alike would don the harnesses for the trip.

The boats scooted across the bord ice, rowed across the slushy open water and then ran their bows up on the edges of the ice fields. The harnessed men jumped out and dragged the boats across the ice, between the crags and over the hummocks. Occasionally an ice cake would capsize, tipping a man into the freezing water; then the harness kept him from drowning.

In good weather, the iceboats could make the crossing in a couple of hours. In poor weather the crossing could mean exhaustion, frostbite, madness and death. The main function of the iceboat service was to carry the mails. It continued well into the twentieth century: the last iceboat crossing took place in April, 1917, and for many years thereafter even the steam ferries carried iceboats on deck—just in case.

Prince Edward Island stayed out of Confederation in 1867, and when Canadian ministers came to offer "better terms," Premier R.P. Haythorne demanded year-round steam navigation across the Strait. The Canadians agreed. Noting "the isolated and exceptional condition of Prince Edward Island," the 1873 terms of union promised "efficient steam service for the conveyance of mail and passengers, to be established and maintained between the Island and the mainland of the Dominion, Winter and Summer." Winter service across the Strait had become a constitutional *right*.

That didn't mean the Island was actually going to get it. The following century resounded with complaints of bad intentions, bad management, bad vessels and bad faith. The ferry issue brought endless federal-provincial consultations, tunnel proposals, joint addresses from the Island legislature to the House of Commons, secessionist movements and appeals to the imperial government in London.

The Island had something to complain about. The roster of failed ferries is astonishing: the old wooden steamer *Albert*, the early icebreaker *Northern Light*, the iron-sheathed Newfoundland sealing steamer *Neptune*, the all-steel icebreakers *Stanley* and *Minto*.

The vessels could be ice-bound for weeks. On January 12, 1903, the *Stanley* left Summerside for Cape Tormentine. The ice carried her 100 miles to Arisaig, Nova Scotia. A month later, the *Minto* found her 21 miles east of Pictou, still frozen in—and now the *Minto* herself was caught. In late February, the *Minto* escaped to Georgetown, picked up coal for the *Stanley* and was trapped again. The sealing steamer *Newfoundland* came to the rescue; she was caught, too, and the three ships drifted in slow, lazy circles, like dolls on a rotating music box. When the *Stanley* eventually broke free and towed the *Minto* into Pictou, the *Stanley* had been trapped in the ice for 66 days.

The most notable of all the early ferries was the *Earl Grey*, launched in 1909—a magnificent and powerful ship, with a sharp clipper bow designed to split the ice. She had mahogany panelling, plush velvet upholstery, electric lights, steam heat—and, in her stern, a private suite for Governor-General Earl Grey himself, who used her in summer as a vice-regal yacht. She was sold to Canada's Russian allies in 1914; under the names *Kanada, III International* and *Fedor Litke* she served Russia magnificently, becoming the first vessel to sail from Vladivostok via the Northern Sea Route to Murmansk, and on another occasion carrying scientists within 400 miles of the North Pole. At least two of her captains wrote love letters to her as they left her, and when she was finally broken up in 1959 her bridge was taken to the Maritime Museum in Moscow.

The first rail-car ferry, the well-loved *Prince Edward Island*, came into service in 1915, and served for 54 years. Her bow and stern were cast of heavy steel, and she wore a girdle of one-inch steel at her waterline. A bow propeller allowed her to weaken the ice ahead of her by creating turbulence underneath it, or to push herself astern when hard-pressed by the ice. She was joined by the *Charlottetown* in 1931—the first ferry with an automobile deck—and in 1940 the two ferries shuttled back and forth across the Strait 2,772 times.

But the *Charlottetown* was wrecked early in the war, and with German submarines prowling the coasts of the Maritimes, the Island's winter service depended entirely on the venerable *Prince Edward Island*. From 1941 to 1947 she essentially *was* the Northumberland Strait service—and the demands were heavier than ever. The annual number of crossings doubled between 1938 and 1945. The ship carried fuels and manufactures to the Island, carried fish, livestock, turnips and potatoes to the mainland and even rescued the frost-bitten crew of an RCAF plane, which had run out of fuel and ditched on the ice.

But when the war was over it was no longer unpatriotic for Islanders to gripe a little. More than 70 years ago, the Canadian nation for which many of them had so recently fought and died had promised "continuous communication" and "efficient steam service." And where was it?

Ottawa's reply was MV *Abegweit*, the beloved Abby—7000 gross tons of nimble, muscular, ice-battling ship. She could carry a complete passenger train, 60 automobiles and 950 passengers. Her interior boasted brass, mahogany, walnut, oak, plush upholstery and frosted glass, and her dining room was staffed by white-jacketed waiters. Her plates at the waterline were as thick as those of the *Queen Elizabeth*, and she had special water-filled ballast tanks, which she could alternately fill and empty to rock herself free from the grip of the ice. She had eight diesel engines driving two propellers in her bow and two in her stern; the bow propellers chopped and chewed their way through, or allowed the ship to back away from the ice.

In 1950, the railway unions went on strike and took the CN ferry workers with them. The airlines and the privately owned Wood Islands ferries became hopelessly overloaded. The Island's supplies of flour, groceries, drugs and even liquor began to run out, while tons of potatoes and other perishable farm produce lay trapped in Island warehouses. Citing the constitutional promise of "continuous communication" and "efficient steam service," the Island Cabinet threatened to secede.

Between the Wood Islands route and the Capes route, four ferries now served the Island in summer. But they were clearly not enough—and in 1962 Islanders welcomed *Confederation*, a 60-car ferry with loading doors at both bow and stern.

By then the ferries were carrying more than a million passengers and almost half a million vehicles annually. In 1968, the $14 million icebreaker *John Hamilton Gray* arrived. She could carry 475 passengers and 165 cars, and she was soon joined by the $4.2 million *Lucy Maud Montgomery*. The noble old *Prince Edward Island* was finally retired for good.

The Island's tourist trade took off between 1969 and 1972, increasing traffic by half in just three years. Two new summer ferries joined the fleet in 1971: the high-speed, high-capacity *Holiday Island* and *Vacationland* carried 155 cars each, and loaded and unloaded vehicles two lanes at a time. And in 1983, a new *Abegweit* arrived—the same length as the *Gray*, but much more powerful. Her passenger facilities included a shop, vending machines, a games room and four different lounges; ferry buffs were particularly pleased by the nostalgic Abegweit Lounge, fitted with frosted-glass mahogany doors and brass lamps from the earlier Abby. The old ship, meanwhile, was sold to Chicago's Columbia Yacht Club for use as a clubhouse. When she sailed from PEI for the last time, in early April, 1983, she had been in service for 35 years. She had made 123,207 crossings, and sailed 1,145,585 miles on Northumberland Strait.

With the new *Abegweit*, accompanied in winter by the *John*

Hamilton Gray and serving as back-up in summer to the *Holiday Island* and *Vacationland*, the PEI service had evolved into the ferry service Maritimers know today, carrying nearly two million passengers and more than 100,000 tractor-trailers a year. But the future of the ferries was cloudy: fixed-link fever had broken out again.

The project had been investigated in the 1890s and the 1920s, but the cost was prohibitive. In 1965 the federal government went so far as to call for tenders to build a $148 million bridge, tunnel and causeway, but after an election, federal enthusiasm declined. It flared up in August, 1966, when another rail strike tied up the ferries, but in 1969 it was formally abandoned.

In 1985, two Nova Scotia businessmen proposed to build a bridge and operate it themselves, charging a toll and collecting a subsidy equivalent to that of the ferries. After 35 years, the crossing's cost would be retired, and the bridge would be given to the government, ending the subsidies forever. When the federal government agreed to consider the concept, proposals emerged from major contractors and engineering companies around the world.

A lively debate arose on the Island. Anti-link groups like Friends of the Island were concerned about ecological damage—to the $100 million lobster fishery in particular, but also to other fish, to birds and to the potato crop. They also worried about the Island's relaxed, trusting life-style.

"Our whole tourism industry is based on image, on a certain ethos," said professor David Weale of the University of Prince Edward Island. "If you greatly increase road traffic and cottage development, what does that do to your tourism in the long run? How long is it before that intangible quality of being a clean, pastoral place is eroded?"

Islanders for a Better Tomorrow, however, rejoined that the trucking industry could save as much as $5 to $6 million a year, chiefly in lost time, while 125,000 more tourists would visit the Island, spending between $5 million and $10 million annually. The project would create about 2000 jobs during the construction phase, and about 75 long-term jobs at the toll gates and in snow removal and emergency services.

But the 600 jobs associated with the ferry service would be lost—and those jobs contribute $15 million a year to the Island economy. Nearly 90% are held by Islanders. And the ferries lose money only because the fares are absurdly low. The service costs about $34 million annually; only $14 million comes from fares. If the car-and-driver fare were $25—much less than comparable Baltic ferries charge—the ferries would make money. Islanders would howl of course. The ferries are part of the Trans-Canada Highway system, and there are no tolls elsewhere on the Trans-Canada: why should there be *any* tolls on the ferries?

The Island has a constitutional right to "continuous communication" and "efficient steam service." Would a fixed link be as reliable as the modern ferry fleet? Aside from holiday weekends, one never waits for a ferry today, and the service rarely shuts down unless the weather is bad enough to close the roads as well. Cape Breton's Canso Causeway is only half a mile long and protected by high hills, but storms close it several times each winter. The PEI link would be nearly 20 times as long, and its bridges would be far higher, far more exposed.

As one Islander said, the question "has obliged us to think about what we want to be as a province." In a plebiscite held in February, 1988, Islanders demonstated their mixed feelings about the project. They approved it, 60% to 40%.

We found Islanders remarkably quiet about the link.

"The fixed link has become like religion and politics," one Islander said. "You don't talk about it because it's too divisive. You've got family members not speaking to one another because of it. If you talk about it, everybody's going to get angry, and nobody's going to change their minds. What's the point?"

In March, 1993, the Federal Court agreed with Friends of the Island that the governments must obtain a full environmental assessment on this specific design, which will delay the project and may even kill it. Otherwise it will probably die for the traditional reason: it is simply a dumb investment. The developers claim the costs will look something like this:

- $840 million to build the link itself, assuming that the designated builder, a transnational consortium called Strait Crossing Inc., stays within its budget.
- $20 million in assistance for Borden and Cape Tormentine.
- Settlements for 600 displaced ferry workers. If these averaged $50,000 each, the total would be $30 million.

- $40.8 million for new highways associated with the bridge.
- More millions, perhaps, for damage to the fishery; Strait Crossing Inc.'s obligations are capped at $10 million.

And there's more. Strait Crossing will have a completion bond of only $200 million; that's the most the government can recover if Strait Crossing fails to complete the job. And the federal government is giving Strait Crossing unlimited guarantees to cover overruns, and to prevent any default on the bonds Strait Crossing will issue.

The proponents' own figures yield a total cost—which will ultimately be paid by taxpayers and consumers—of close to $900 million. If we took that money and invested it at 7.5%, the interest would be $67.5 million a year. That's almost enough to subsidize *three* fleets of ferries, forever.

One final bet. Sometime between the years 2010 and 2040, a bureaucrat or an engineer will take the ferry from Tormentine to Borden, and she'll think: wouldn't it be marvellous if we could just have a bridge or a tunnel across here? Why not? *Why not?*

And fixed-link fever will strike again.

THE AEOLUS

OF

SEACOW HEAD

I woke up, yawning, and went on deck. *Silversark* was creeping over a placid sea just east of Borden. There were tall clouds far off the port bow, over New Brunswick, but the sky above us was clear. At seven-thirty in the evening the colours were luminous: gold, grey, blue, silver. A ferry pushing a white bow wave like a moustache was converging with us, heading for Borden.

"I wonder if we should go into Borden," I said. "It's still a long way to Summerside. We'll be entering at night again."

"Boredom," said Mark. "I don't want to go into Boredom. I want an interesting city."

"Summerside's got plenty of buoys, doesn't it?" said Lulu.

"Oh, yeah."

"Then let's go on."

The view from the bow was of flat calm seas. "We've been sailing three days," said Lulu, "and we're only a half-hour's drive from home."

"Fog?" I said. "Fog? There's no fog in Northumberland Strait in July."

"This year there is," said Dave Bateman (right). And once again the wind had died. Dave looked over the side and snorted. "Even the jellyfish are passing us."

The Water Rat (Tony Eastman) embodies the spirit of the early cruisers—idiosyncratic, self-sufficient, craggily independent. He and his wife Bertha (left) are spending their retirement cruising the Gulf and Cape Breton coasts.

Doug MacNeil (left) had been building his boat for thirteen years. I knew he wasn't doing it to get it done. Like a true artist, he was working for the sense of accomplishment, the joy of the thing itself.

Silver Donald Cameron

Mark was delighted with *Marksark*. With its varnished mahogany and shining black paint, the new dinghy was stable, light and stylish—as pleasant to row as it had been to build.

The second major event at the 1992 Africville picnic was a sod-turning ceremony for the replica of Seaview African United Baptist Church. The church (below, left) was established in 1849, and it was Africville's only real institution—village council, police force and social centre all in one.

Bob Brooks, Picture Collection, Public Archives of Nova Scotia

The earliest regular boat service from PEI to the mainland began in December of 1827. Iceboats—small boats with runners and steel bottoms— were rowed or hauled across the Strait in winter. Each boat carried a compass, emergency firewood, food, small sails and steel-tipped oars.

Ferries eventually replaced the iceboats. The powerful ice-breaker *MV Abegweit*, the beloved "Abby" (below) was one of the most famous. In 35 years, she made 123,207 crossings and sailed 1,145,585 miles on Northumberland Strait.

When Ray and Juan Miller offered to take him on as temporary pit crew for the Grand-Prix hydroplane races, Mark was in ecstasy.

He happily sent us on the next leg of our trip and then tried out the driver's seat in *Deuces Wild*.

Silver Donald Cameron

In Bouctouche, the Acadian *fête nationale* included a *tintamarre*—"a parade where people walk along together and make a lot of noise, any way they can. Hell of a racket. Old Acadian custom."

"Can visitors join in?"

"Sure, if you feel like it." So we did—along with the mayor, André Goguen (below, right) and alderman Aldéo Saulnier (left).

Silver Donald Cameron

Bill and Pauline Boucher
(above) towed us out of
Bouctouche. And after we ran
aground in the channel, they
took us clear out of the bay.

Our run to the Magdalens took
54 hours and 82 lonely sea
miles. This lighthouse at Cap
du Sud was our landfall.

While we were in Georgetown we visited marine biologist Greg Keith and he showed us his mussel farm—an operation that needs the skills of both a farmer and a scientist.

The passage home was glorious. Strong winds on a bright day reminded Lulu of John Wayling's earlier comment, "Life doesn't get much better than this!"

Good enough. Borden has scanty facilities for small boats; it would be a tedious place for a stay longer than a day or so.

"That ferry's probably wondering about us," said Lulu. "Better give them a call."

"Hello, fairies, this is a leprechaun calling," I said.

"Smart ass."

I picked up the VHF, identified *Silversark* and called the ferry. It was the *Holiday Island*.

"We're bound for Summerside," I said. "By the looks of things we'll pass well astern of you."

"I was wondering what you were doing," said the ferry skipper. "I thought you were stopped."

Nice talk.

"No, no," I said. "We're just making very slow progress in very light winds."

As we passed the Borden range lights at eight-fifteen, the wind veered to the southeast and blew sedately but more purposefully. The wake began to gurgle again. I went forward and braced the genny out with the boat-hook to catch every puff.

Back in the cockpit I took the tiller while Lulu and Mark went below to eat. In a Charlottetown health-food store we had discovered a useful line of dried soups; you add hot water, let it sit and in minutes you have something almost as thick as a bowl of stew.

The sun was low, and I could see the double flashes from the lighthouse at Seacow Head, six miles ahead. We would hold our course past the lighthouse till we reached the fairway buoy, with its Morse A light. Then we would sail north-northeast up Bedeque Bay to Indian Point and northeast into Summerside Harbour. The wind was picking up, and *Silversark* was bowling along nicely, the genoa straining forward. Just to be safe, I thought, I should take that genny in before dark.

A scatter of raindrops fell on the deck—huge round ones, making little puddles the size of nickels and instantly penetrating my sweatshirt. The ferry terminal astern was still in sunlight, but we were sailing fast under a canopy of grey.

Lulu and Mark pulled on their oilskins and came on deck. I went below and gobbled my soup. It was raining seriously now, pattering on the deck.

The wind picked up sharply, and *Silversark* surged ahead.

"Look at her go!" cried Lulu, grinning in the rain. I could just make out her face.

I pulled on my oilskin pants and my safety harness and put my right foot in its boot.

BANG! Flap flap flap—

"Don! The pole's gone!"

I scrambled on deck, leaving my jacket and my left boot behind. The boat-hook had broken under the strain from the genny. One broken end hung from the clew of the sail. Clipping on my lifeline, I reached overboard and grabbed it. The other end hung awkwardly from the mast, like a broken arm. A third piece lay on deck. I picked them up and passed them to Lulu, then jumped to the mast and cast off the genoa halyard. The big white sail sagged and scalloped on the forestay, flapping like thunder. "Sheet!" I shouted, scrambling forward, stumbling on my lifeline. I clawed the sail down and stuffed it into its bag, snatching glimpses around me as I worked. My glasses were streaming with water, and a fold of the sail knocked them askew.

The wind had backed to the east; it was blowing like hell. The night was black as a bandit's heart. The lighthouse at Seacow Head was just forward of the beam.

But there were two red flashing lights up ahead to port. We were going to pass inside them. All wrong: the rule is Red to Right, Returning from seaward, and we were certainly Returning. They weren't on the chart; there weren't any red flashers outside Bedeque Bay. So what were they? Had I made some hideous error in navigation? I dragged the sailbag aft and dropped it below.

The wind intensified, hitting us at gale force, shrieking and screaming in the rigging. The boat heeled sharply: I clutched the mast. Damn, damn, *damn!*

"I'm going to drop the main!" I yelled.

"Yes! And put up the jumbo!" Lulu shouted.

Clinging to the mast and swearing, I cast off the main halyard. The sail collapsed, flapping furiously. Staggering on the deck, I got a couple of sail ties on it, then struggled forward to the jumbo. *Silversark* was pitching and rolling heavily. How does the wind get the sea up so fast? I clawed at the lines. The dinghy had shifted position, fouling the jumbo sheet. I pushed it back and hoisted the sail. *Silversark* moved forward again, lurching through short, rough seas. I stared into the dark, trying to force my eyesight through the blackness. Seacow Head light was still winking at me.

And so were the two red bastards.

I called through the companionway to Mark, stationed at the sounder and the Loran.

"How far to the fairway buoy?" I shouted.

"Two point three miles!"

"Bearing?"

"What did you say?"

"Bearing!"

"Three-three-five!"

"Speed?"

"Four point six knots!"

"Depth?"

"Thirty-eight feet!"

"See the Morse A, Lulu?"

"Not yet!"

"What are you steering?"

"Three-three-five."

Mark's facts computed properly. Lulu was on course. But we'd been worried about the accuracy of the compass earlier in the day. We had to trust it, but . . . Navigation is all about information: gathering data, evaluating it, fitting it together. I remembered Luke Batdorf: bringing quality information together at the right time to make good decisions. Well, the current decision was to hold our course. Maybe—

The rain stopped.

The wind died.

Silversark was wallowing aimlessly, all but becalmed. Lulu and I looked at each other.

"What the hell is going on?" I said, my voice loud in the suddenly quiet night.

"Huh!" said Lulu.

Damn glasses: everything blurred and fuzzy. But where was the white dit-dah of the Morse A? *And what were those red lights?*

We waited, wary of the wind's intentions.

"We might as well get the main on her again," Lulu said. "We're not going anywhere like this."

"Easy for *you* to say," I said. "I have to hoist it."

"Well, do you want to wait some more?"

I sighed.

"No," I said. "We can always drop it again. Or reef it." I clambered back on the main deck and raised the main again. *Silversark* began to move once more.

Hand in hand with a rain shower, the wind pounced on us again—a little more northerly, but lighter than the earlier squall. We sheeted in and waited. This wind was heavy and puffy, but tolerable: a rebellious servant, but not a master. We left the main and jumbo set, and sailed on.

"Have you figured out what those red lights are?" asked Lulu.

"Not a clue."

"Why don't you call the yacht club?"

"Good idea."

I dropped below and scanned the charts. The old Chart 4406 showed no buoys, but no dangers either. Chart 4459 was brand new, updated just a month earlier, and it didn't show them, either, but it ended just beyond Seacow Head.

I called the yacht club in Summerside. Through the static, I heard the barman call Jerry Prowse. I lost him and called again, lost him again and called once more. We switched to the VHF, with no better results.

"Are you in distress?" he asked.

"No, I just can't figure out—" But Jerry was gone again in a blizzard of static.

"Don," called Lulu, "those buoys are *amber*."

Amber? I vaulted on deck. Sure enough, as the air cleared and we sailed closer to them, the colour of the buoys had resolved itself into a deep yellow.

"Cautionary buoys of some kind," said Lulu.

"Scientific buoys, maybe. But they're not a problem, anyway." In fact they marked the location of the electric power cables from the mainland; they were a warning not to anchor.

"I think I have the Morse A," Lulu said, pointing just off the port bow. "Isn't that it?" Faint and weak in the darkness, a white light was flashing. Dit-dah. Dit-dah. Dit-dah. Just as it should be, just where it should be.

We sailed right to the fairway buoy, and Mark saved it on the Loran. We tacked up into Bedeque Bay, ticking off buoys, Mark calling out the speed and distance as we went. It was a wet, plunging ride in the sloppy night, the bow pointing into the ghostly loom of light over Summerside. At the first range lights we altered course, steadily closing with the leisurely flashes from the tall lighthouse on the long low spit of Indian Point.

We rounded the spit and picked up the inner range lights. The forward light is mounted on a shed on the Public Wharf. The yacht club lies behind the wharf, but we were in no mood to jig around looking for the perfect mooring. There were no ships at the Public Wharf: we would go there and review the situation later.

The little cutter beat on up the harbour, the wind almost dead against us, Mark calling out the depths. Twelve feet, ten, nine, ten, eight, *tack*. The wharf came closer and closer—a huge concrete structure covered with warehouses, fendered for ocean-going ships loading up with potatoes, much too massive and brutal for a little yacht. No matter. I stood on the pulpit with the mooring lines. Mark came on deck as Lulu veered parallel to the wharf, just inches away.

I jumped ashore. Mark dropped the sails. I surged the mooring lines around the bollards while Lulu and Mark fended off.

Summerside. At last. It was midnight.

While Lulu tidied ship, Mark and I went looking for a better berth. Near the shore, the wharf took a little inward jog.

"Right in there," said Mark. "That'd be a good place for us."

"I wonder if there's enough water," I said.

"We could ask someone," Mark said. "What about those guys?" He pointed at two cars with their hoods open and their owners attaching jumper cables.

We walked over to the cars. The man nearest us was bent over a fender. I coughed to draw attention to myself and tapped him on the shoulder. At that instant, the other car's engine roared into life. The man jumped like an ambushed alleycat.

"Jesus, are you a ghost?"

I apologized, laughed, explained.

"I'm pretty sure there's plenty of water there, but I've only got a speedboat. Maybe you should ask someone at the yacht club."

We went back to the boat and called the yacht club. A young man named Spencer Sheen answered the phone. He was the only one there, and he didn't know, either. We went on deck to discuss it.

A car drove up to the boat. My victim got out.

"I just checked," he said. "There's 30 feet of water there at low tide, minimum. You're in a great spot here. Everything's right handy—laundromat, restaurants, whatever you need. There's a 24-hour Tim Horton's right up the street."

"Great. Thanks very much."

"No problem." He paused, then laughed. "My God, did you ever give me a shock there. Can't remember when I've been so scared." He got into his car. "Well, enjoy your stay in Summerside."

He drove away. Two minutes later, another car drove up. It was Spencer: he, too, had determined there was 30 feet at the new berth, and he would tow us into the club tomorrow.

He drove away. Lulu and I looked at one another.

"I think I like Summerside."

"Me, too."

"What about coffee?" said Mark.

Why not? And so three weary but chipper people walked down Water Street at one in the morning, wearing seaboots and oilskin jackets. We swaggered into Tim Horton's, feeling very salty, and ordered hot chocolate and doughnuts.

"Nice," said Mark. "This place is very civilized."

SILVER

FOXES

"The PEI Triangle!" cried Spencer Sheen. "Summerside-Borden-Shediac! There's always squalls off Seacow Head."

We were sitting in the cockpit in the sunlight, sheltered from the brisk southerly wind by the jog in the wharf. It was blowing too hard to tow us, Spencer said, but the wind was supposed to go southwest. There would likely be a lull as it shifted, and he would tow us then. In the meantime, if we wanted showers at the club or laundry or anything . . .

We walked over to the club past a clapboarded mini mall on pilings and the national exhibition centre. The long, low Silver Fox Curling and Yacht Club stood facing a perfectly protected marina behind a stone breakwater, just on the other side of the Public Wharf. At the doorway, Mark caught sight of a poster.

GRAND PRIX HYDROPLANE RACES—

"Hydroplane races? Here? This weekend?"

Well, um. We'd seen the posters elsewhere, and we'd hoped to avoid what sounded like a noisy and tiresome event.

"Grand Prix?"

Well, yes.

"You knew about this?"

Well, um . . .

"And you didn't tell me?"

Well, look, hydroplane races are just funny-looking boats with noisy engines chasing around in circles. And this is Wednesday, the races are Saturday and Sunday, we should really be gone by then—

Forget it. Hopeless. Persuade a 14-year-old to sail away just as the hydroplane races were starting? Impossible.

Sigh.

We showered and came out to the sun-deck by the bar. It was almost lunch-time, and the place was filling up with people who obviously weren't on vacation. I asked the bartender to point out Jerry Prowse, last night's contact—a quiet, silver-haired man, retired from the military. I thanked him. He had wondered whether he should go looking for us, but his trimaran only had an outboard engine, and anyway we weren't in distress.

"How's J.J. Vincent these days?"

I turned. J.J. Vincent, our neighbour, is a bushy-bearded ex-naval man who single-handed his tiny yellow bilge-keeler as far as the Gaspé coast in 1984, leaving a trail of friends behind him. The man who had asked was short and cheerful, with a grizzled beard and a quick grin. He was wearing a striped navy-blue and white dress shirt and a red tie. He looked prosperous and con-fident: a doctor, perhaps, or a small businessman.

"J.J.'s fine," I said. "He didn't launch this summer. He was waiting for the weather to settle down, and it never did."

"Tell him Dick Wedge was asking for him," he said. "I see your boat tied up at the public wharf."

I nodded. Had I met this man before?

"You don't want her in the marina?"

"Well, I do, but we need a tow, and Spencer was waiting for a lull in the wind to bring her around."

"He's not going to get it," said Dick, shading his eyes. "Your boat's hopping around a lot. In fact you'd better move her now, before that chop starts smashing her on the wharf."

I followed his gaze. We could see *Silversark*'s mast above the wharf, jerking angrily forward and back. The wind had veered, building up a chop and pinning the boat against the wharf.

"I'll get the club launch and tow you in," said Dick.

But nobody at the club had the keys. Dick drove off to get them from someone else while we ran back along the waterfront. The wharf was built for ships, not small boats. *Silversark* would be rolling against open pilings and concrete. When we got there, the wind was strong and the chop was steep and aggressive. Our two-by-six fender board had been broken against a piling, and only our light fenders were keeping the boat from smashing her topsides and rails.

We fended off with our hands and feet for a long 20 minutes until Dick and two others came charging around the end of the wharf in *Te Amo*, the club's beefy fiberglass tender. *Te Amo* had a powerful engine, a big set of steel towing bitts and a heavy towline on a reel. Sweeping in close beside us, they tossed us the towline and slowly pulled *Silversark* clear of the pilings. In the hard silvery sunlight, the tossing water looked like pea soup with pewter highlights. Dick kept glancing over his shoulder, his necktie flying like a scarlet pennant in the wind.

Secured in the marina, we broke out the Scotch and drank some in the cockpit. Dick turned out to be the owner of Enman Drugs, the only local non-chain drugstore. A couple of years earlier, he had hired a younger pharmacist, a woman, to run the drugstore with him, allowing him to half retire. It was a wonderful decision, and he was delighted with his young colleague, but while he was disengaging from the drugstore he had started not one but *two* new businesses upstairs above the drugstore, a secretarial service and a computer business.

"I computerized the drugstore in 1984 and 1985," he said. "A pharmacy's a natural for computerization because there are so many repetitive operations. But I couldn't find a property management program I liked, so I decided to have one written. That's how I got into the software business. Now we do sales and service, training, all kinds of things. I'm supposed to be semi-retired and I'm working seven days a week. I haven't had my boat in the water for four years." The cellular phone on his belt warbled. "Tell him to hold on," he told the phone. "Tell him I'll be there in half an hour."

Dick belongs to the Coast Guard auxiliary, a network of fishermen and boaters around the coast trained to aid small boats in distress. While his own *Whitecap* remains ashore, he sails *Trinity*, a sloop which belongs to a friend who lives in Halifax. She is hardly a rescue tug, but one blustery night she was the only boat available when a cabin cruiser called in with engine trouble. When Dick found the cruiser, her skipper looked down loftily at the little sloop.

"You're going to tow us with *that*?"

"Listen," said Dick. "Halitosis is better than no breath at all. Do you want a tow or not?" The man accepted.

The Coast Guard work gives him a network of nautical friends all over the Maritimes. He had heard about *Silversark* while we were still building her and had recognized her at the wharf. He examined her with approval, but he thought we should have a canvas dodger to shelter the cockpit. We agreed. He sketched out the dodger he had designed for *Whitecap*—a better arrangement than any we had seen.

We wound up at the Wedges' for dinner. Mary Wedge has a deceptive, grandmotherly demeanor; the Wedges *are* grandparents, several times over: the ideal grandparents, in Mark's opinion. They live on 18 acres of waterfront a mile above the yacht club, in a much-enlarged summer home—the only one-storey house in Prince Edward Island with an elevator. A section of the carport floor is supported by four long threaded rods; an electric motor turns a long bicycle chain, which turns four nuts welded to the rods and to bicycle sprockets. As the motor runs, the floor slowly descends, carrying firewood, tools, building materials, engines and boat equipment into the basement.

Whitecap stands on a trailer beside the house, looking forlorn. She is a Morgan 34. Over hors-d'oeuvres on the patio, Dick told how they bought her hull and deck from Charley Morgan in Florida, loaded her on a trailer and towed her home with the family car. At the New Hampshire border they found themselves stalled. It was a Friday night.

"You can't drive through New Hampshire and Vermont at night or on a Saturday with a ten-foot-wide load," Dick recalled. "You can't drive *anywhere* on a Sunday. And we were broke.

"We got into a shopping centre and I saw a bank of phones—a whole wall of them. Well, somewhere I'd learned that if you deposited a dime, called the operator and *immediately* hung up, the phone would refund the money from the last long distance call. So I went along the wall with my dime, and collected $18 or so—enough to buy a meal, anyway.

"Then, while we were eating, two guys approached us and wanted to know about the boat. They turned out to be a couple of off-duty New Hampshire policemen, and they led us through the back roads all the way to the Maine border.

"But there was a Maine cop right at the border, and he wasn't letting us go *nowhere* in Maine in the dark; he made us stop right there till daylight. He was serious about it, too, he cruised by us every now and again until dawn.

"So this was Saturday, and we got through Maine and across the border into New Brunswick—but then it was getting dark again, and we'd been warned about the Moncton cops. So I called a couple of boaters and they got *20 cars* and met us on the highway. We put ten in front of us and ten behind, and we went through Moncton in the dark in this long stream of cars, and no cop could get close enough to give us a ticket.

"At the ferry, the purser didn't know what to charge—you know, here's this 34-foot boat, ten feet wide, taking up half the car deck—so he called the skipper.

"What's the problem? said the skipper. *Well, it's a guy with a boat on a trailer.* Boat on a trailer, the charge is seven dollars, said the skipper. So that's what they charged us, the same fare they'd charge for an outboard skiff. We got home at midnight, and all our friends were waiting at the yacht club to celebrate."

To help them finish the boat they hired Johnny Williams, the legendary boat builder from Murray Harbour, the man who measured the deck of my schooner and built a dinghy to fit. He charged me $75. It was a great little dinghy, and I hated to let it go.

"Yeah, yeah, Johnny was great, but Johnny *changed things*," said Dick. "He never built the boat the way it was on the plans. You never knew what the hell he was going to do—and it wasn't always an improvement." Johnny booked into a boarding house in town and worked on *Whitecap* for weeks. Then it came time to fiberglass the house to the decks, "and the day we started that,

Johnny packed up his tools and went home. He didn't want anything to do with fiberglass."

Clearly, we had found the perfect guide to Summerside. One afternoon I dropped into Dick's shop to send a fax. He was just going home, and on the way he took me on a tour in his little pick-up. For decades, the main industry in Summerside had been the air base—the second-largest employer on the whole Island, with 1,200 employees and a $40 million payroll. Military towns have a tidy, well-managed, middle-class look about them, and much of Summerside retains that scrubbed, military look, especially in the belt of look-alike bungalows and small apartment buildings near the air base.

We drove out to Highway 2, which bisects the Island from tip to tip, Tignish to Souris. To the south we could see the sun-washed surface of Bedeque Bay, on Northumberland Strait, while to the north were the dark blue waters of Malpeque Bay, on the open Gulf—the source of the Island's most famous oysters and the site of the largest Mi'kmaq Indian settlement in the province.

Not far from the highway a huge steel framework, like a vast hangar, was rising from the red Island earth.

"The new GST processing centre," Dick said. "That's what the federal government gave Summerside to replace the air base."

There's The Deal again: the government spends vast amounts on the military infrastructure in Atlantic Canada—not really for defence, but for high-level welfare. And what the feds take, the feds must also give: that's The Deal.

"Will the GST jobs take up the slack?" I asked.

"It'll be *better* than the base," Dick said. "They say it's going to have 500 or 600 employees, but I say it'll have 1,000 within a couple of years. And they'll be permanent. That air base was really the worst thing that ever happened to Summerside. It kept people coming and going. You could see it at the yacht club—a fellow'd move in, join the club, crew with members for a couple of years, then he'd buy a boat. And just when he was getting to be useful, he'd be transferred. The GST people will come here and stay here. You'll be able to count on them to take a long-term role in the community."

Meanwhile, the former air base has been turned into an industrial park which intends to specialize in aerospace. An appealing idea, on the face of it, but Slemon Park, as it is now known, has a familiar reek of politics. Its privatization was managed—for a $500,000 annual fee—by a consulting company, Rambri Management. Rambri's president, Donald MacDougall, is a former president of Labatt's. He is also a defeated Tory candidate, and his sister, Pat Mella, leads the PEI Tories.

Slemon Park is an enormous piece of real estate, almost a small town in its own right. It includes 253 houses, an airport, a hospital, three hangars, a dental clinic, hockey and curling rinks, an indoor pool, bowling alleys, tennis courts, rifle ranges and more than 100 other buildings. It is assessed at $45 million, but estimates of its true market value range from $200 million to $800 million.

On Rambri's recommendation, all this was turned over to a private, for-profit company, Slemon Park Inc. for an unknown amount. A Rambri employee then became president of Slemon Park, and Donald MacDougall became its chairman. Slemon Park is supposed to induce other companies to move in and create jobs, but only two have done so—and they have received $8 million in grants, plus a 20-year tax holiday. The jobs they have "created" include several union jobs transferred from Montreal. The Summerside jobs are not unionized, and the pay, say the workers, is significantly lower. Meanwhile, Ottawa and the provincial government had ponied up $21 million plus tax write-offs to support Slemon Park's operating costs and improvements. The governments have also announced a $30 million jointly funded program to foster an aerospace industry on the Island.

So what will it finally cost to "privatize" this air base? Something north of $300 million, possibly as much as $1 billion. It will be largely wasted, and the waste will be blamed on Summerside—as though Summerside had anything much to do with the whole fiasco.

And, while Slemon Park sits virtually empty, the government spends thirty million dollars—*thirty million!*—on a new building right across the road where it will process the paperwork for the Goods and Services Tax. And it lectures the rest of us about belt tightening and fiscal probity.

Oboy.

Dick and I drove back into the leafy residential grid of old Summerside, beside the harbour, among spacious Victorian and Edwardian houses—Harris houses, some of them. Dick pointed at an elegant old mansion.

"That's the Stone House. It's the only one in Summerside. I think there's only three on the Island. It's a fox house."

A fox house. The story behind that phrase is the great boom-and-bust story of the Island—a vulpine version of the Klondike.

In 1883, a 33-year-old farmer named Charles Dalton bought two wild foxes from John Martin. They were unusual foxes: black, with silvery highlights in their fur. Dalton lived in Tignish, at the extreme western tip of the Island. He later became a druggist, and he was always an outdoorsman. He had a keen instinct for business opportunities. He had conceived the notion that foxes—black foxes in particular—could possibly be bred in captivity. He had tried it before, with limited success. He wanted to try again.

Black fox fur had always been enormously valuable; in mediaeval Europe, royal decrees barred most people from wearing it. A fox tail, or "brush," was the personal badge of Henry IV and Henry V, who flew it from the tip of a lance in battle. The Abenaki Indians considered one black fox pelt to be worth forty beaver, and in 15th-century Russia, two black fox pelts could buy fifty acres of cultivated land, five horses, ten milk cows, several dozen hens and a new house—with enough left over to throw a good party.

Dalton's foxes produced two litters and then ceased breeding. He consulted with a hunting and fishing companion, Robert Oulton. They concluded that the foxes should be bred in conditions as much like the wild as possible, so they built large pens on an island Oulton owned in Cascumpec Bay. Here the foxes reproduced enthusiastically, and by careful selection, said Dalton, he and Oulton "succeeded in producing absolutely perfect, blue-black pelts, heavily furred, that were readily competed for, at very high prices." By 1888, they were sending pelts to the London fur market. One pelt is said to have gone for $1,878, and been resold for over $2,800. At the time, you could hire a full-time farmhand in PEI for $26.60 a month.

About 1900, Dalton and Oulton sold a pair of breeders to another friend, Robert Tuplin, who formed a partnership with Captain James Gordon. Meanwhile—as often happens—others were trying to breed what became known as silver foxes, too, and another Island family succeeded, a father and son by the name of Rayner. These pioneer breeders are still known as the Big Six.

For some years the Big Six kept their secrets to themselves, quietly enjoying their handsome profits. But in 1910 the lid blew off. Dalton and Oulton sent 25 pelts to London. They got a cheque for an astronomical $34,649.50, and suddenly *everyone* wanted to be in the fox business—not just in PEI, but everywhere.

There was only one source of breeding stock: western Prince Edward Island. In 1910, Frank Tuplin, Robert's nephew, sold a pair of breeding foxes to a "large firm" for $10,000. The firm was probably Holman and Company; just a year earlier, it had refused Tuplin $30 worth of credit for groceries. Fox farms proliferated all over the Island and beyond. In 1912, proven breeders were going for $18,000 to $35,000 a pair. Not many people could amass that kind of money, so companies were formed expressly to buy and rear foxes. Dalton sold his own holdings—not Oulton's—to such a company for $500,000. Tuplin sold 22 pairs for $250,000. The demand seemed endless: whole carloads of live foxes, each rail car with its own caretaker, were being pulled out of Summerside, destined for Minnesota, Oregon, Norway, Russia.

In the early years the fox companies paid dividends of 500% and more, and they were numerous enough to support a Fox Exchange—like a stock exchange—in Charlottetown. In early 1912, a pair of breeders were sold for $20,000; a few weeks later their five pups sold for $20,000. These were normally cash transactions, and Tuplin had men with hobnail boots crushing piles of money in order to close a suitcase full.

Many of the fox breeders spent their new-found wealth on the ostentatious Summerside homes which are still known as "fox houses." Cars were forbidden on the Island, but towns made their own rules, and Summerside allowed them. The speed limit was seven miles per hour. Frank Tuplin bought a huge Pierce Arrow with license number eight: the first seven cars were in Charlottetown. He swapped two foxes for one of the largest and finest homes in Summerside, a house which is now the International Hall of Fame of the Fox. He wintered in Florida—and sold foxes while he was there. To improve his rudimentary education, he hired a tutor from England at $10,000 a year. When he had completed one big deal at his farm five miles out in the country, his lawyer had missed the last train. Tuplin hired a special train to get him back to town.

Meanwhile foxes were stolen and smuggled; red furs were dyed black; unborn pups fetched thousands of dollars. Fox-farming magazines appeared; companies were formed to produce and market fox feed; governments established fox research stations; courses in fur farming appeared in universities. For one glorious moment, Prince Edward Island was said to have the highest per-capita income in the British Empire.

Fox farming was a speculative mania like the 17th-century tulip frenzy in Holland, the South Sea Bubble in England, the stock market in the Roaring '20s. In fact it went on *into* the Roaring '20s; even when the music stopped on Wall Street in 1929, it kept playing on the fox farms of Tignish and Alberton and Summerside. True, sales of breeding stock fell off, and the price of pelts dropped—but in the mid-1930s breeders were still fetching $400 to $850 a pair, and though pelts averaged $62, some very fine ones went for $500 and up.

Prices continued to fall, even though several new strains came on the market—white-faced foxes, blue foxes, platinum foxes. But fox was no longer exclusive. As early as 1934, fox tails had become a youth fad, flying from car aerials and bicycle handlebars. By the time the Second World War broke out, the market was saturated, and the fashion-conscious had turned to another fur-bearer, the short-haired mink. Other furs were reaching the market: chinchilla, sable, even rabbit. What Dalton and the others had created, in fact, was not just the fox-farming industry, but the *fur*-farming industry—and the silver fox had become, in a sense, a victim of its own success.

F. J. Lockerby entered the fox business in 1913, two years before the birth of his grandson Lloyd. Lockcroft Farms—in Hamilton, on Malpeque Bay, half a dozen miles from Summerside—is the oldest continuous fox-farming operation on the Island, and probably the oldest in Canada. Lloyd Lockerby is 77 now, but he still raises foxes in partnership with his son Ian, the fourth generation of fox-breeding Lockerbys.

Lloyd is a big quiet man, with a farmer's ruddy face and a hand that simply envelops mine. He is known as "a wizard with foxes." Even after all these generations, the foxes are still wild animals, and most breeders handle foxes with three-foot tongs which close around the fox's neck like a collar. Not Lloyd.

"I handle them with my bare hands," he said. "You have to be careful—they'll bite, and they're very quick. But I believe that handling them with tongs develops an antagonism."

Not only did Lloyd grow up with foxes, but he also took a degree in agriculture from Macdonald College in 1938, when a dollar was worth a dollar and a bachelor's degree was an achievement. He worked for the PEI Department of Agriculture and the Canadian National Silver Fox Breeders' Association—which is still headquartered in Summerside—as fur grader, secretary manager and president.

The Lockerbys have attended every Charlottetown fur show but one since the shows began in 1929; in the 1992 show they cleaned up once again, being named Premier Breeders as well as collecting numerous lesser prizes. The corner of the living room, in fact, was heaped with trophies, ribbons and medals. I mentioned that, and Lloyd smiled and said the attic was full of them, too. He was wondering what to do with them. He thought maybe he should give them to some organization which could use them.

The Lockerbys kept a few foxes through the long decline from the 1940s to the middle 1960s, when almost all the Canadian ranchers had "pelted out," killing their fox herds and leaving the business. In Scandinavia, however, the governments were supporting the breeders, doing research and expanding their holdings. Canadians, said Lockerby, believe that Canada still has the best quality—the best character, the best colouring, density, blending and silkiness. Perhaps they do: a Norwegian came out from the Norwegian Fur Breeders' Association in the early 1960s to buy top-quality breeding stock to introduce some new genes into the Norwegian gene pool. When he found what he wanted, the Norwegians sent out a veterinarian who accompanied the foxes back to Norway.

In the meantime mink was the rage, and the Lockerbys got

into that, too, though Lloyd never liked mink and was happy to eliminate mink from his operations when the time came.

"To me, a fox has individuality," he said. "They're all different. Mink have no individuality. They're just like a bunch of rats." A fox can make a good pet; the Lockerbys had one called Tidy for years. She lived in the house like a dog, but she produced a litter every year as well.

During the lean years, the Lockerbys were down to five female foxes, and they were feeding them as cheaply as they could. It was impossible to make money with them; the price of a pelt was less than the cost of producing it.

"Then in the late 1960s I got the impression that the trend was changing, and that long-haired fur was coming back," Lloyd remembered. "The Scandinavians had a head start, of course. There were only about six farms left producing foxes on the Island at that time.

"Anyway, we expanded the fox herd and eliminated the mink—and by the mid-1970s, there was a market for all the breeding stock you could produce. One year in the early 70s every female pup went for breeding—none of them were pelted. That year foxes were selling from $1,000 to $1,500 each, and the prices were rising every year. Pelts went as high as $360, and they were regularly $250 to $300."

And then the market collapsed again. By 1991, a pelt that cost $50 to produce would fetch only $42 on the market.

What had happened?

Climate, life-styles, the stock market. Mean temperatures are gradually rising; the winters really are not as cold as they once were. Today we don't walk to work or stand waiting for street-cars; we enter our heated garages and drive to heated underground parkades. The stock market crash of 1987 hammered the wealthy, leading them to forgo expensive luxuries.

"And the animal-rights people have put a fear into the fur-buying consuming public world-wide," said Lloyd. "They were going around spray bombing people in furs, letting animals out on ranches, that kind of thing, and they had media support. But I think that's changing. The animal industry has finally recognized that the animal-rights objective is to eliminate the *whole* animal industry. If they had their way there'd be no cattle, no hogs, nothing. We'd all be vegetarians. So the industry's doing a lot of education, especially of the media, and I think they now see that there are two sides to it, at least."

Will the silver fox come back yet again? Nobody knows. During the past few years, more ranchers have been pelting out. There were five fox ranches in Hamilton a decade ago; now, once again, there is only the Lockerby farm.

Silver foxes make an interesting passage in the Urgent Conversation, and what they show—like radio-controlled cars and newsletters and software—is the impossibility of predicting what's going to work. Some Island farmers are now growing ginseng; Saskatchewan forest companies are producing chopsticks. The mesh of the world is always moving, opening new niches and closing down old ones. If you have a million people thinking of possibilities, nosing out opportunities, they will find surprising things to do. You need a culture which encourages them, and you need plenty of resources for fledgling ventures—advice, research, financing, training and the like. You have to let people try. You have to let them fail. But some will succeed.

I saw Lockerby foxes later, on another farm. They were gorgeous animals: sleek, sinuous, fine-featured and alert, the silver highlights in their fur glinting against the glossy black. No wonder men like Lloyd Lockerby speak of their foxes not only with admiration, but also with affection.

It is a peculiar kind of love these men bear for animals they raise only to kill and skin, but something deep and emotional motivates the handful of ranchers who still keep silver foxes. On the Island, the silver fox symbolizes art, science, wealth and beauty. When Lloyd Lockerby goes out to work with his 25 remaining foxes, he engages his heritage. He will not easily consent to its eradication, nor to the elimination of the animals which his family has brought to such a pitch of perfection.

Besides, the market is fickle. Who knows? It may yet, once again, turn in his favour.

DEUCES

WILD

The hydroplanes started to come into town a couple of days before the weekend races. We saw them here and there, sleek and polished, propped up sideways on their trailers. With two sponsons thrusting forward and a thick body aft, they looked like lobsters designed in a wind tunnel. They were painted scarlet and canary yellow and metallic burgundy, plastered with the decals of their sponsors. Chrome exhaust stacks and superchargers poked through their engine nacelles, sending Mark into flights of joy.

Inspired by their example, Mark resolved to try outboard power on *Marksark*.

The dinghy had worked out beyond my expectations. Varnished mahogany inside and glistening black outside, it was stable, light and stylish. It fit on the foredeck so unobtrusively that it seemed it had always been there. It was as pleasant to row as it had been to build.

Mark clamped the little Evinrude on the stern, fastened the safety line and pulled the starter cord. *Marksark* took off at a canter, buzzed halfway across the marina and died. Mark pulled the cord again. Once more *Marksark* sprinted forward, only to subside halfway back. Mark tried again. Same thing.

The dock-side experts made their suggestions. The fuel mixture was wrong. Mark tried it at various settings: it made no difference. The cooling system was blocked. Maybe so, but in a 25-yard dash it couldn't possibly be overheating and seizing up. The spark plug was defunct. Mark and I went into town looking for a new spark plug, and found one. We installed it. No change.

It was clearly an excellent motor, provided your voyage was not longer than 75 feet.

Passers-by on the dock began making witty remarks.

"It's a marine engine," I explained. "Don't you understand? That's What They're Like."

Tiring of these motorized spasms, Mark gave up on the engine. He stood on the finger pier, shading his eyes and looking towards the Public Wharf. The earliest of the hydroplanes were tuning up on their trailers. Supercharged and tuned for wide-open performance, they idled with a violent pulsing rasp. *rrRRAAAKK-raak-raak! rrRRAAAKK-raak-raak! rrRRAAAKK-raak-raak!*

"I wish I could get over there," he said longingly. "I'd do *anything* to get in there with those hydroplanes."

"Anything?" I said. "Do dishes for a year, mow the lawn—?"

"You know what I mean."

"Yeah, I do."

I wonder, I thought. Elmer Cormier's in charge . . .

I had been repairing the damage we had suffered during the squall at Seacow Head and at the Public Wharf—working in Dick Wedge's shop to make a new boat-hook out of electrical conduit pipe, buying a green, springy two-by-six to make a new fender board. When I was boring holes in the new fender board, Jerry Prowse came by, found out what I was doing and took the board to his own shop to round off its edges with his router.

Earlier, when I was bringing the board back from the lumber yard—walking through the parking lot of the waterfront shopping centre with an eight-foot plank, feeling very conspicuous— a man pulled up beside me in a car and started to talk. His name was Graham MacKay. He was descended from three generations of Nova Scotia lighthouse keepers, but he himself worked in the brown wood-faced building next to the marina, which housed the Land Registration and Information Service.

LRIS is a project of the Council of Maritime Premiers, the structure through which regional cooperation usually takes place—if it takes place. LRIS was a splendid venture, but it has been neglected and cut back in recent years; the federal funds which covered 75% of its costs have dried up, and rumour has it that the organization will soon be privatized.

In the early 1970s, when I first encountered it, LRIS was at the forefront of geographical science. Its objective was to computerize almost everything that was known about land in the Maritimes—topography, vegetation, buildings, soil composition, drainage, history of title, ownership, everything. Every package of land would be precisely described and labelled. The information could be merged, overlaid, separated or combined, and it could be provided to users as maps or data or both.

If you wanted to know the percentage of New Brunswick covered with pavement, LRIS would tell you. If you wanted to find good grape-growing soil beside a lake, with a southern exposure, the computer would give you a list of such spots. If you dreamed of water frontage where you could see the sun setting into the sea, with a sandy beach before your building site and a stand of pine trees behind it, LRIS would take your money and give you a list of places where that combination of features might be found. It could tell you who owned them, and which ones might be coming up in future tax sales. It knew where major gypsum deposits could be found near deep water and where the geological structures were favourable for finding oil, tin, amethyst.

You would be able to tell the computer that all the railway tracks in PEI had been ripped up, and it could instantly generate a new map with the railway tracks removed. It could calculate the area of federally owned land in Albert County, New Brunswick, and identify houses in Bathurst with back-yard hedges. If your eccentric interests required a map showing all the lighthouses, shopping malls and garbage dumps with an elevation greater than ten meters above sea level—or one showing the track of your voyage—you could have it. You can see a sample at the front of this book.

The system would have revolutionized title searches: instead of articled clerks poring over folio volumes in rural courthouses, a quick inquiry to the computer would establish, immediately, who held title, whether the title was sound and what changes had occurred in the boundaries. The lawyers were less than ardent in their enthusiasm.

Graham MacKay took Lulu, Mark and me through the building one morning. In a big ground-floor room, people were peering into large precision machines. The people were called photogrammetrists, and they were practising a highly technical, very specialized craft. The machines were stereoscopic viewers, which worked like a child's ViewMaster. Each eye was looking at a slightly different aerial photograph. They invited us to look through their eyepieces. We saw overlapping photographs with a common point of reference. With finely calibrated knobs, you moved the two photos until the two points of reference merged, and suddenly trees and hills leaped up at you, valleys and lakes fell away.

The photogrammetrists went carefully over each three-dimensional image, interpreting the information for the computer. They would stop on a spot and tell the computer that the spot was three and a half metres higher than the reference point and that it had spruce trees on it, or that it was part of a paved highway, or that it was a summer cottage four feet above sea level. It was time-consuming, exacting work. Meanwhile, in other LRIS sites around the region—for LRIS jobs are distributed among the provinces—others were entering information about soil composition, geological structures, land tenure and so on.

Graham took us upstairs to the computer room, where banks of mini computers were storing and digesting all this information. On request, they would feed the information to a plotter in an adjoining room. Each plotter had four styluses, with jewelled points of varying widths, which carved lines and symbols directly into broad sheets of negative film. These were the masters from which new maps would be printed.

When LRIS began, nothing like it had ever been done before. The project would have provided invaluable information for Maritime business, industry, government, researchers and private individuals. But it was also new technology, and it could have been exported to every jurisdiction on earth. Maritimers would have been installing the system in Dakar, training operators in Shanghai, delivering seminars in Auckland. We could have sold software updates and built academic institutes around it. The Maritimes could have become *the* place to study geography, cartography and certain kinds of computer imaging.

Perhaps it was too new, too difficult to understand. For whatever reason, LRIS fell from favour. Others seized the opportunity, and our competitive edge was lost. LRIS will still benefit the region, but it will never achieve its original potential.

It is easy to excoriate the three governments for failing to see the opportunity, but I did not really understand it myself, either. Did anyone not immediately involved have any conception of what computers were all about and how the information economy would reshape all our lives—and how fast that would happen?

But if it was not obvious then it is obvious now—and we still have not learned. Our most precious capital is the intelligence of our people, and we will not invest in that. We will pour a billion dollars into a ribbon of concrete stretching across Northumberland Strait, and we may well sink another billion into Summerside's abandoned air base while squandering four billion more on attack helicopters. Those are choices. We are choosing *not* to spend that money on our crumbling universities, on industrial research, on film and software and music—the places where the information economy is growing. The new giants of the world economy are not General Motors and Inco, not even IBM and Xerox: the new giants have names like Microsoft, Intel, Sony, Bertelsmann, Disney.

Canada suffers less from financial poverty than from intellectual poverty. In the middle of a second industrial revolution, we stand paralyzed like rabbits in the headlights of an onrushing car. It is not the collision that kills the rabbit. It is the rabbit's own terminal stupidity.

By Saturday morning the marina was jammed with cruisers, speedboats and yachts from Charlottetown, Shediac, Pictou, Cocagne. The Public Wharf was covered with hydroplanes, and the air was thick with the *rrRRAAAKK-raak-raak! rrRRAAAKK-raak-raak!* of their engines. I went for a shower in the yacht club and found everyone in the shower rooms speaking French. A naked man came out of a shower stall and asked me a question. I answered in French, and then realized he had spoken English.

"Sorry," I said, "I just assumed everyone was French here."

"That's okay," he said, towelling his head vigorously. "*On est bilingue.*"

"Yeah, but I wish I spoke better French," I said.

"Well, this is a good place to learn. *Au revoir.*"

I found Elmer Cormier, the Summerside Hyundai dealer who was in charge of the race arrangements. He arranged a press pass, and I walked over to the Public Wharf. If I had to watch hydroplane races, I wanted to understand as much as I could about them—and maybe I could find a way to get Mark closer to the action.

Behind the chain link fence were acres of hydroplanes. People in coveralls swarmed over them, tuning, adjusting, polishing, tinkering. The sound of the engines was like a wall of sound: violent, harsh, deafening. Tall cranes stood on the wharf like giant arms with yo-yos hanging from them, swinging boats off the wharf and setting them into the water as their races came up, then lifting them out immediately afterward.

In the smallest hydroplane class, 2.5 litres, the boat weighs at least 850 pounds including the driver, and is powered by a Ford Cobra or Pinto engine. The top speed is about 105 mph. The 5-litre boats weigh 1,200 pounds and can do 125 mph. The big daddies, the Grand National Hydroplane Class, otherwise known as the Grand Prix boats, use a big GM engine, weigh 1,800 pounds and can top 150 mph. Grand Prix engines have superchargers, known as "blowers"—air pumps which blow far more air into the combustion chamber than the engine could draw in on its own. Each class runs three qualifying heats on the Saturday, with a final run-off among the eight top boats on Sunday. As with Grand Prix auto racing, the boats compete in a circuit of races, towed behind their owner's campers and motor homes. The circuit includes three Quebec towns—Chambly, Aylmer and Valleyfield—as well as Picton, Ontario; Cocagne, New Brunswick; Detroit, Michigan; and Summerside.

Looking at the crowds and the glitz, I heard someone say, "That's a wonderful hat." The speaker was a lithe, middle-aged woman walking between the hydroplanes on the wharf. She stopped in front of me. "Do you mind telling me where you got it?"

"Not at all," I said. "It's made by an entertaining maniac in Toronto named Alex Tilley. He wanted a good sailing hat and couldn't find one he liked, so he decided to build the best sailing hat in the world."

"I'd love to get one," she said.

"Easy," I answered, sweeping off my hat and reaching into the crown. Because these encounters happen fairly often, Tilley provides the owners of his hats with "brag tags." I handed one to the woman.

"Most Tilley Hat Wearers, *and the person beside you is a prime example,* are interesting people of sterling character," she read. "And it gives you the 800 number to order it." She looked up with a merry ripple of laughter. "What a marketing concept! I'm Juan Miller, by the way, my husband and I own *Deuces Wild.*"

Deuces Wild—also known as GP 22—was right beside us, a red and yellow Grand Prix boat with a glittering 1,250-horsepower engine. On the back bumper of its trailer were the words *Blown alcohol hydroplane,* an immediate answer for a puzzled motorist wondering what on earth was ahead. Juan's husband, Ray, turned out to be a retired executive with Ford Financial Services—and, at 60, the oldest rookie driver in any major motor sport. He was a handsome man, tanned and fit, standing on the wharf in his red racing suit with his crash helmet in his hand. I spoke to him briefly, but his mind was somewhere else.

Juan noticed that I had a video camera.

"We've never been able to get good video of a race," she said. "We're always down on the dock with the boat at the start. Do you think you could shoot some video for us?" Of course, I said. While we waited for their race, Ray and Juan idled around the wharf together, talking softly.

The smaller boats came and went, swinging over our heads in slings, settling in the water, then roaring off into the harbour.

They have tiny fins on the tips of their bow sponsons so that the driver can make out the end of his boat in the flying spray of the race course. The bow sponsons just kiss the water occasionally, and only the propeller is fully immersed; the boat actually flies above the water on a cushion of air.

That explained the small fins, no more than the area of a dinner plate, thrusting downward near the stern on the port side. They prevented the boat from flying off sideways on the turns— and they were only needed on one side because the race course was always counter-clockwise, so the port side was always the inside of a turn.

That fin took me back 40 years. I had installed one myself when I was 14, the same age as Mark. The very first boat I built had been almost a hydroplane; it was a sea sled, a square box with a blunt, rolled-over nose and a foredeck, powered by a four-cylinder, 5.5 horsepower Evinrude Zephyr engine. I have the plans yet: I could build another tomorrow. With the engine flat out and my weight up forward, the sled would plane, lifting herself onto the surface and screaming over the water. I leaned out over the foredeck, steering her in long slow curves by shifting my weight from side to side, my hair streaming back, tears pouring from my eyes. I have no idea how fast she was going— possibly 15 mph—but I never had such a sensation of speed before or since.

When I turned the sled more sharply, though, the sharp corner of her hull dug into the water and the sea poured over the side. To stop that, I rigged a couple of angled blades along the corner. That stopped her from digging in, but it also allowed her to skitter sideways like a rock skipping on a pond. To stop *that*, I made a little sheet-metal fin and screwed it to the bottom.

Just like the one on *Deuces Wild*.

If anyone should understand Mark's passion for these boats, their uncompromising quest for raw speed and power, it should be his father. For was not that small boy alive in me yet? To be honest, didn't something in me lift with joy as those engines snarled and bellowed, and the boats lit out for the race course, trailing plumes of spray?

Ray Miller's heat was called at last. *Deuces Wild* rose overhead, descended to the water and was gathered in with boathooks by her pit crew, George and Faye Henley. Ray and Juan went down the ladder to the float. Ray put on his helmet and slid into the cockpit, buckling himself in. George squatted on the deck beside him, touching things on the engine, talking to Ray. Ray nodded, staring straight ahead.

The five-minute gun sounded. Ray started his engine: an explosion of sound, dropping to a low wet growl. I framed *Deuces Wild* in the viewfinder. Ray cracked the throttle, and the boat inched forward. Then he opened her up. *Deuces Wild* gave a deep, hard-edged snarl, and I got the best shot of my life. As I swung with my camera, the boat moved forward, lifted out of the water and took off as though shot from a gun, solid water pouring over her deck and sponsons before she disappeared in a tower of spray.

I tried to imagine what it was like out there, flying over the water, trying to see through torrents of water while the world flashed by. "Things happen very fast at 150 miles an hour," Ray had said. The lead boat has a huge advantage in clear vision and solid water; all the following boats are roaring through spray, their propellers revving wildly in a frothy mix of air and water churned up by the boats ahead. Pit crews tune the propellers for this, changing pitch and diameter for the expected conditions. All the same, the trailing boats may be turning up more RPMs than the leaders and yet still be falling further behind. If the propeller comes out of the water in turbulent conditions, the engine can quickly rev up from 8,000 to 12,000 RPM and tear itself apart. Racers who can afford it carry two or more engines, and their crews can switch engines between heats.

Half a mile out in the harbour, the boats buzzed and snarled, pulling tall rooster tails behind them. As the leaders pulled ahead, the boats spread out almost evenly around the course, making it difficult to tell who was leading. Ray was soon back, skimming towards the wharf and then abruptly cutting the power. GP 22 slumped down into the water and coasted to the dock. He had placed third, a good enough finish to put him in the finals the next day.

The Millers and Henleys came over to *Silversark* for a drink before dinner. The moment they were in the cockpit, Mark pounced. Why did they use methanol for fuel? Would nitro-methane give more power? How did a supercharger work? What did they think of his design for a rotary engine? It should be more efficient than a Wankel, but it had too many moving parts . . .

With the race behind him, Ray was relaxed, amused and interested. Mark struck him as "intellectually hyper." Methanol, he explained, is a cool fuel with a low flashpoint, far less dangerous than gasoline but just as powerful. The real power comes from the supercharger, which rams amazing quantities of fuel and air into the engine; when it starts, you can see raw fuel pouring out of the exhaust pipes. The blower boosted the engine's power from 500 horsepower to 1,250.

"Your boy is really interested," said Juan quietly. "He knows a lot about it."

"That's putting it mildly," said Lulu. "He's absolutely obsessed with engines and explosives."

"If you're going to be here tomorrow I can get him a pit pass," she whispered. "He could be part of our crew for the day."

Lulu and I looked at each other, delighted and appalled. We had intended to sail for Shediac in the morning; we had a favourable forecast and a long way to go. But if Mark ever even found out about that offer, he would never forgive us.

"Let's see if we can arrange it," Lulu whispered.

"Come over to our motor home later," said Juan. "We can look at the videotape and work out the details."

They went to a banquet, Mark stayed on the boat, and we went to the Wedges'. The marina was packed with boats from Shediac—big cruisers, open runabouts, sports cruisers, sailboats. Walking down the finger piers that morning I had seen young men sprawled in sleeping bags on decks and curled up on cockpit seats. I didn't know them, but Dick would. If we sailed in the morning, could Dick and Mary send Mark on a Shediac boat that evening?

"No problem," said Dick. "I'm sure I can. And if I can't, we'll bring him over ourselves. We have to pick up our granddaughter in Sackville in the next day or two anyway. Drink?"

Well, sure. We talked about the voyage ahead, about the Acadians. After Summerside, almost all our ports would be Acadian communities. The Gulf of St. Lawrence is really an Acadian sea: the Acadians encircle its waters as the rim of the glass encircles the rum. Acadian villages speckle the west coasts of Cape Breton and Newfoundland, the north shore of Nova Scotia, both coasts and both tips of Prince Edward Island. The Gulf coast of New Brunswick is solid Acadian, and so are the Magdalen Islands. Even the North Shore of Quebec was settled by Acadians from the Magdalens.

"We're everywhere," said Dick. "You didn't know I'm Acadian?"

"Wedge? Acadian? What about the coat of arms on the door—"

"That's all bullshit. Some company wrote offering the coat of arms of the Wedges, family motto, fake genealogy, all that stuff. It was so stupid I bought it just for fun. No, really, my family comes from Mont-Carmel, just west of here, but when we moved into Summerside they took me to be baptized, and the priest said, *We're not having any French names in this parish.* So he changed my name. Our name was Aucoin, 'at the corner,' so he called me Wedge, and the whole family changed their name, too."

"Do you speak French?" asked Lulu.

"I get along all right. I studied a couple of years in Quebec. Anyway, look, no problem with Mark. Just give the Millers our number. We'll take care of it."

We picked up Mark and went to the Millers' motor home. We watched the video and told Mark what we had arranged. Ray and Juan were smiling.

"Yes!" cried Mark. *"Yes!! Awesome!"*

LOVE

BOAT

I rowed out of the marina at nine-thirty the next morning, while Lulu steered. We tied up at the Public Wharf, just where GP 22 had been the day before. We said goodbye to Mark and raised the three working sails. Delighted with my video of the race, Juan returned the compliment by taping our departure. I cast off, pushed the boat away from the wharf and jumped aboard. Lulu sheeted in as I got the fenders on deck. Once clear of the wharf we tacked and headed down the harbour, with a last wave at Juan and Mark. Juan got it all on tape.

We beat down the harbour, enjoying the sunny morning, cutting close under the lighthouse at Indian Point, heading for the Miscouche Bank buoy which marks the limit of a broad belt of sandbanks running out from the west side of Bedeque Bay.

The wind slackened. We had been promised a moderate
southwesterly, going southerly in the evening. We looked at one
another and changed the jib for the genny, anticipating another
idle day in the Strait, another late-night entrance in hard winds
and rain. But the wind held, light though it was, and at the buoy
it turned southerly. Instead of a close reach or a beat, we were
going to have a nice gentle downwind ride to Shediac. I checked
the steering compass against the hand-bearing compass: it
seemed to be reading a couple of degrees north, so we steered a
little towards the south. With these winds it would be easy
enough to gain more northing later if we needed it.

We slipped quickly along the shore past the Acadian village of
Mont-Carmel, with its massive church overlooking the Strait.
With a fair wind, the day was warm. We changed to shorts and
T-shirts. By noon it was downright hot. We slipped off our
T-shirts. Then we slipped off our shorts.

I looked at Lulu, standing at the tiller, wearing her Tilley hat. I
gave a tug on my own Tilley. I knew I was leering.

"Hmm . . . " said Lulu, grinning.

"Quite," I said.

"We've never made love on deck."

"And the Evil Magician is otherwise employed."

"Hmm . . . "

I moved towards her and touched her shoulder.

"Lobster buoys," said Lulu, looking ahead.

"Lobster buoys?"

"Thousands of them."

I stood up. Lobster buoys floated all around us as far as the eye
could see. The lobster season in the western part of the Strait had
just opened, and the sea looked like a mine field. An American
sloop passing through Summerside had warned us about the
buoys, but I had forgotten. They had run down a buoy at three in
the morning. The line had passed between their stern-post and
their rudder. They had spent an hour poking and tugging, and
the skipper had been ready to go over the side in scuba gear when
it finally came free. It had stopped them as efficiently as an
anchor, too, and they had a big boat.

Damn.

"You'd better go forward and keep a look-out," Lulu said.

"Aw . . . "

"Donald," said Lulu. "The welfare of the ship comes before . . . anything else."

My dejected Tilley went forward, taking me with it. Lobster buoys are vividly painted and patterned. Here, because the currents are so strong, they are set out in pairs. I had never seen so many, but I had no enthusiasm for the artistry and imagination they showed. Singly and in clumps, they stretched out to the horizon. The Evil Magician had placed them cunningly.

"Port," I said. "Just a bit. Five off to port, well ahead—"

The little ship swept onward, borne by the tide and hurried by the breeze, doing a slalom through the buoys. Far behind us, a big ketch came out of Summerside, sailing much too close to Miscouche Bank but clearing it without incident. I turned the binoculars on her: she was *Ronara J*, a Fisher motorsailer from St. Peter Port, Guernsey, in the Channel Islands. She seemed to know these waters much better than we did.

"Why don't you take the helm and I'll make lunch?" Lulu said.

"Lunch," I said, "is not what I had in mind."

"Lunch," said Lulu, "is what is offered."

She went below to make sandwiches. I stood on the cockpit seats, peering over the bow, weaving among the buoys. The coast of the Island was falling away from us, retreating into the deep recess of Egmont Bay. Somewhere over there, at Cap-Egmont, were two little houses and a chapel all built of glass bottles set in mortar, the work of a retired Acadian fisherman and carpenter named Edouard Arseneault—a funny, quirky effusion of the creative spirit. The Island is full of surprises.

I found myself thinking about the things we had not done in Charlottetown and Summerside, the people we had not seen. We hadn't seen Hilda Woolnough—and we would never see Réshard Gool again.

"You know, Réshard missing is a good piece of the Island missing," said Lulu.

"I was just thinking about Hilda," I said. "She came down to the boat, and we were gone with the Wedges or something."

"That's terrible," said Lulu.

It was. Lulu's introduction to the Island, almost, had been a party thrown for us by Réshard and Hilda at their farmhouse in

Rose Valley—a great party, the tables covered with Hilda's gourmet food and Réshard's homemade wine, all of it bathed in good music and good talk. We had just been married. "Your Island wedding party," Hilda had said, smiling and sipping wine.

Hilda is a highly respected artist whose works hang in places like the National Gallery of Canada; Réshard was a political scientist by profession, a writer by vocation, a publisher by circumstance and a talker by temperament. His origins were faintly mysterious, but his ancesters were from various spots around the rim of the Indian Ocean: Malaya, Persia, South Africa. He was quite beautiful, with his olive skin and his dark liquid eyes animated by his bottomless *joie de vivre*.

Réshard was born in London, grew up partly in South Africa and partly in a boys' boarding-school in Scotland, studied in Toronto and Hamilton, taught in Regina, Jamaica, Charlottetown. There was a marriage somewhere that I knew nothing about, and a dark and lovely daughter I met briefly in a Charlottetown garden. There was his passionate pursuit of Hilda— "camouflage of woman round pert of bird," he called her in one of his poems. He invaded her Mexican studio once while still wearing his long johns from Regina. *I just thought I'd drop in,* he said. *You bastard,* she said later, *I could have been in bed with someone.*

But you weren't, he grinned. And who could resist such assiduous courtship? They married: and in 1967 they moved with Hilda's children to Charlottetown, where Réshard taught political science at the University of Prince Edward Island. They never moved again—though they travelled widely during sabbaticals and vacations, living at various times in Mexico, the Canary Islands, Europe, India.

They were a generous, forceful, talented couple, and their impact on their beloved Island home was enduring. Hilda devoted years to the revival of the Island's craft traditions and to the establishment of innovative galleries. Réshard founded a news magazine, *The Square Deal,* and a literary press, and sponsored an endless series of visits and public readings for writers he admired. He published Carl Sentner, Frank Ledwell, Leon Berrouard. In 1973, he organized a national reading tour by seven Island poets to celebrate the centennial of Confederation on the Island. He taught politics through the study of literature, encouraged and published Maritime writers, criticized and appraised the region's artists, implored and hectored and cajoled government agencies for better arts support.

Réshard and Hilda lived in Charlottetown, in a dark old house on University Avenue, until they bought the farmhouse and renovated it. It was stuffed with their eclectic collection of books and works of art, with comfortable chairs and wood stoves, cascading plants and good things to eat.

"Never marry a man who can't cook," Hilda once told Lulu.

"No?"

"No. If he can't cook, he'll be no good in bed."

By then Réshard had largely withdrawn from university affairs and public controversies: he only wanted to write. He was a writer of baroque subtlety and sensitivity, and he loved language in all its forms—books, plays, poems, lectures, commentaries, polemics, letters, table talk, gossip, anecdote. He loved to talk, loved to tell stories, insisted that his conversations have substance: once, when Hilda upbraided him in the morning for dominating his guests the previous evening, he looked at her absolutely without apology, and explained, "But they had nothing to say!" His repertoire included a marvellous imitation of a heavily accented South African municipal politician bitching about the conduct of "shitty affairs at the Shitty Council."

He had written a couple of novels—*Price* and *The Nemesis Casket*—and he had finished another, *Capetown Coolie*, when he fell ill in the summer of 1988. He had had a stroke, and he had another just after Thanksgiving. It simply erased half his brain, leaving him speechless and paralyzed. In a Halifax hospital, he hovered for days between life and death. The doctors thought he would never go home again.

But by Christmas Hilda had him home for weekends, and a month later he was home to stay. She built a 65-foot plywood ramp from the house to the car, and for four months she devoted up to seven hours daily simply to *preparing* him for the day.

"Réshard couldn't speak, but that didn't mean he couldn't communicate," said Réshard's neighbour and protégé Leon Berrouard. He taught himself to sing without words, entertaining Hilda with jazz riffs and old pop songs. Hilda laughs when she recalls how they managed: Réshard, unable to remember the location or purpose of electric light switches, wheeling his chair

into a darkened room and pointing imperiously upward at the
light fixture, Hilda carefully teaching him how to achieve the
miracle of light.

"We had a two-and-a-half-hour row one time," she says. "Can
you imagine it? Réshard couldn't speak—but the way he
whipped that wheelchair around expressed *everything* he wanted
to say."

During his last four months, *Capetown Coolie* was accepted by
a major publisher, and the Prince Edward Island Council of the
Arts and the provincial government conferred a special award on
Réshard for his services to literature. At the reception, Hilda
reported, "he roared around the room in his wheelchair, wearing
his cap—naturally—and getting loads of attention. He loved it."

On April 29, 1989, Réshard and Hilda went into town with
Leon and Karen Berrouard to attend a screening of films by Rick
Hancox, a film maker Réshard had always admired and supported. He was clearly on the mend, and he could even speak a
few words. When they got home, Hilda poured a glass of wine for
each of the other three, and Réshard mimed that he wanted one,
too. No, said Hilda, you're not allowed to drink wine. But it was
good wine, not no-name plonk, and Réshard insisted.

"Oh, come *on!*" he said. Hilda relented.

The next day he suffered a third stroke, and they both knew he
was dying. They said their goodbyes. When Réshard began to
choke, Hilda took him to the hospital. He died in her arms.

"He looked beautiful, absolutely noble," she says. "He looked
like a prince." She kissed him. It was May Day. He was 57.

In August, Hilda and some friends organized a wake—another
glorious party at the Rose Valley farmhouse. The party flowed
out across the sun-decks and into the garden. Torches flared
against the spruce trees. There were computer artists and cura-
tors, poets and painters, impresarios and editors and plenty of
writers—Kent Stetson, J.J. Steinfeld, Joseph Sherman, Jim
Hornby, Marc Gallant. We ate barbecued trout, zucchini salad,
blueberry buckle, liver pâté, broiled chicken, fresh green beans,
strawberry mousse and cobs of sweet new corn done over an
open fire. We drank plenty of wine. An old friend said he could
sense Réshard's spirit among us.

"No," I said. "You wouldn't have to *sense* it. If it's not talking,
it's not Réshard."

He did seem to be there—partly, no doubt, because it was simply unthinkable that in that house, with that crowd, he could possibly be anywhere else.

We missed him later, whenever we came back to Prince Edward Island. There are places you always go, people you always see: touchstones of your experience of the place. *Réshard missing is a good piece of the Island missing.*

Yes, Lulu. Yes.

When I think of Réshard, I often think of poems—not his own poems, often, but the poems of the Island poets he loved and valued. Leon Berrouard, with his "Toothbrush Trilogy" and that other delicious poem—

> i told karen
> that i was gonna take her
> to a taxidermist.
>   then
> she told me
> she was gonna take me
> to a psychiatrist.
>   it began
> when our siamese cat
>   sat
> still and beautiful
> on our bookcase
> and i thought
>   he
> almost looks like
> a stuffed animal
>   &
> jokingly i said
> lets take him
> to a taxidermist
> so he'll always
> be like that, she said
>   O!
> how would you like it
> if i took you
> to a taxidermist

> &
> i thought
> she is beautiful too
>   &
> that's when
> i told her
> i was gonna take her
> to a taxidermist
>   &
> she told me
> she was gonna take me
> to a psychiatrist.

And Milton Acorn, the greatest of the Island poets, a shy and angry man who went through life like a piece of tumbling shrapnel, cherished for his gifts by friends like Réshard:

> Since I'm Island-born home's as precise
> as if a mumbly old carpenter,
> shoulder-straps crossed wrong,
> laid it out, refigured
> to the last three-eighths of shingle.

And John Smith, Réshard's colleague at the university, with that wonderful love poem I once sent Lulu by electronic mail for a Valentine's gift:

> Will there ever be time for me to cover you with kisses?
> Has anybody ever really done it to anybody else?
> What's your epidermal area?
> How much does a kiss cover anyway?
> Let's say no more than one square centimetre.
> They should overlap like shingles on a house.
> I'd like to take all day all night as long as need,
> do it the way an obsessive collector would lay down
>   postage stamps in a vellum file,
> stamps of the vanishing flowers and beasts and birds,
> games and faces, artifacts and butterflies . . .

Very appropriate, I thought, looking up at the genoa. Here we are, sailing along in the nude . . .

Suddenly I heard something odd. Oh, no: a lobster buoy

bumping along the side of the boat. Thinking about poems, I hadn't been paying attention.

Bump. Bump.

Maybe it'll float clear.

Maybe it won't catch in anything. There's no propeller—

Silversark slowed abruptly and stopped. The sails were still full and drawing. It looked as though we were sailing. But we were held firmly by the stern.

"%#&⋆@#$!!" I said, looking over the transom into the water.

"Where is it?" said Lulu.

"Jammed between the rudder and the skeg." I could see the yellow polypropylene deep in the water, streaming out astern.

I got the boat-hook and poked it down into the water. Missed. Again. Missed. And again.

"No luck," I said.

"What next?"

"Drop the sails and go overboard. Or maybe hook the rope up to the surface and cut it off."

"We can't do that."

"Well, if there's no other way—Good Lord, they must expect to lose some. They're right across the Strait. Look, we're a lot closer to New Brunswick than we are to the Island, and there's hardly been a gap in them yet."

"You'd think there'd be a channel for ships."

"I know, but there doesn't seem to be. I'm going to try again with the boat-hook, anyway."

I poked the boat-hook down and slid it along the rudder stock. I felt a momentary resistance—and then suddenly two buoys popped up to the surface and fell behind.

Silversark was moving again.

"How come you hit it?" Lulu asked.

"Not paying attention," I said. "Thinking of other things."

"Hmm."

"You know, there aren't quite so many buoys over here. The Evil Magician must have been distracted."

"Well," said Lulu, grinning.

"I'll have to keep steering," I said.

"But if I move—look, like this—" said Lulu.

"Yeah, and—that's it. We'll manage . . ."

When we regained consciousness, as Sergeant Renfrew would
say, the coast of New Brunswick was getting close.

"Look behind us," said Lulu, who had been looking behind us.

I looked. A cloud bank was rolling up from the south, high
and dark and cold-looking. It might well have some wind in it,
too. By the time we dressed, the sun was gone and a warm
southwesterly had sprung up: our three-knot amble was over,
and *Silversark* was skipping along at five knots in calm water,
close to the New Brunswick coast.

"What's Shediac Harbour like?" asked Lulu.

"Wide and shallow," I said. "They don't recommend anchor-
ing."

"So we're going to a marina?"

"Pointe du Chêne, I guess."

I called the marina on the VHF, explaining that we were
engineless and needed a spot we could sail into. Fine, said the
marina, there was a slip free inside the entrance, and they'd be
ready to take our lines. Soon we were sailing along a wide sandy
beach lined with big houses: Parlee Beach, a favourite summer
refuge of middle-class Monctonians. Once a fishing community
with some summer people, Shediac is now on a four-lane highway, which brings it within fifteen minutes of Moncton; more
and more, it is becoming a fashionable outer suburb.

We found the outer red buoy and made our turn for the
entrance. The water conceals shallow sandbanks, and the narrow
channel is marked by four buoys. It was evening, and the wind,
behaving like an authentic summer breeze, was slowly dying.

We eased our way up the channel, tacking back and forth,
Lulu at the helm, me watching the depths from the foredeck. On
this summer Sunday, Shediac's boaters had been out in force,
and a series of high-powered speedboats zipped by, rocking us in
their wake and rolling the wind out of our sails. Light winds are
trying enough, and heavy wakes make the situation worse. In
Europe, where Lulu learned to sail, such behaviour is viewed as
gross, boorish and uncivilized. In the Maritimes, where pleasure
sailing is more unusual, such niceties are not yet understood.

As two more powerboats roared up behind us, Lulu gestured
for them to slow down. They didn't get it: they thought we

wanted help, and they were happy to provide it. Circling around us like high-powered bees, they shouted instructions and asked questions. We were dead downwind from the marina entrance, but they had no concept of a sailboat's limitations: they kept pointing to the entrance and shouting that we were going the wrong way. In the tumultuous cross sea set up by their wakes, *Silversark* wallowed like a drunken rhino.

I have to confess it: I thought it was funny, this tumult of circular waves, sloppy motion, missed signals, incomprehensible shouts in French and English, everybody trying to help and making things worse. I tried not to laugh, but the harder I tried the harder it was. I hid behind the genoa, chortling helplessly.

"Lower the genoa!" Lulu ordered. I clawed down the big white sail. There went my cover. Lulu looked at me severely.

"Are you *laughing?*"

"No—no!" I choked. "Ab-absolutely n-not!"

She fixed me with a laser gaze, but said no more for the moment. Later in the evening she looked at me across the galley table with an expression like that of a judge about to sentence a particularly despicable criminal.

"You said you were laughing at the men in the boats," she declared. "But I suspect you were laughing at *me.*"

She impaled me on her most serious Anne-of-Green-Gables expression.

"This vexes me," she said.

But that came later. In the meantime, the power boats streaked off across the harbour, and a yellow-and-red outboard-powered Zodiac came alongside. Two sun-tanned young men were aboard. The Coast Guard.

"Hear you need a tow!" said the driver.

"No," said Lulu. "Who told you that?"

"Well, your engine's broken down, isn't it? That's what they told us at the marina."

"We don't have one," I said.

"No engine at all?"

"No."

"Do you want one?"

"Have you got one for sale?" Lulu asked.

The driver laughed.

"You're going to sail in."

"Yep."

"Well, the way you got that sail down, I don't think you're going to have any trouble. We'll stick around just in case."

We sailed along a narrow channel right beside the rubble breakwater, then made a switchback turn to starboard, with rocks on both sides. I pulled a few strokes with one oar, just to get us around. Inside was a broad basin with ranks of finger piers in the shore end. Off the port bow, by an empty berth, two men were waving us in. We tacked, paused, threw a line, and dropped the sails a little too late. *Silversark* charged into the slip as though determined to run right over the pier itself. Two more feet and she would clean off an electrical power stanchion. I stuck out a foot to fend off, but one of the men got a turn around a samson post on the dock and snubbed hard. *Silversark* stopped in her tracks, swinging heavily against the dock.

"Thanks," I said. "I thought we were going to knock that down."

The man laughed.

"Don't worry about that," he said. "Everybody knocks those down. This used to be my sister's berth, and she knocked it down. I pulled it out once myself—took off with my extension cord still tied to it." He put out a hand. "Welcome to Shediac."

"In daylight," said Lulu. "How peculiar."

COQUES FRITES

AND

CHIAC CHIC

Pointe du Chêne proved to be several miles from Shediac itself. The Wedges had not put Mark on a Shediac-bound boat; they arrived the next day with two grandsons in time for lunch. Mark was bursting: he had a baseball cap with GP 22 emblazoned on it. It had been Awesome. Ray Miller had placed second in the Sunday finals, and Mark had been at the awards dinner as part of the crew.

"Let's go to Gould's for lunch," Dick said. "They make the best fried clams around. Where are you heading next?"

"Ned Belliveau's place at Shediac Cape," I said. "But there doesn't seem to be much water in the harbour."

"Don't worry about it," said Dick. "Go wherever you feel like. They race Thunderbirds all over the harbour, and those

things draw as much water as you do. Anyway, if you do hit a
sandbank it's no big deal, you're not going to do any damage."

"Thunderbirds? The West Coast design?"

"Big fleet of Thunderbirds here," Dick said. "They build 'em
on a coop basis—build three or four every winter."

Shediac was a bright, busy town of 4,000, its main street
clogged with small-town services and chipper little boutiques.
The town is 85% Acadian, but almost everyone seems to shift
from one language to the other as easily as they shift a package
from one hand to the other. Gould's Fried Clams—Coques Frites
Gould—is just an enlarged take-out, but the clams really are
excellent; the Wedges used to sail over just for a feed of them.

Gould seemed like a strange name for Shediac, but a Halifax
friend, Dana Doiron, later explained it.

"They're Doirons," he said. "When Acadians anglicize their
names, they take an English name that means something similar
to the French name. LeBlancs become Whites, Levesques
become Bishops and so on. Well, the Doirons were translators.
They spoke both French and English, so you had to have them
around to do business, and they always seemed to get a little of
the gold as it went by. So they became known as 'd'or,' having to
do with gold, and when they anglicized they became Goulds.
There are thousands of Goulds in New England, you know, and
they're all Doirons from New Brunswick."

Dana's speech is impeccable in both languages, too—a major
asset in public relations. It's become genetic.

The Wedges dropped us back at Pointe du Chêne. We paid
the marina bill. The three of us sailed out much more easily
than two had sailed in. Mark stayed at the sounder as we
crossed the harbour: nothing less than eight feet anywhere, and
at low tide, too.

Ned Belliveau's home is shaded by trees, but we spotted his
brother Frank's summer cottage from across the harbour: an
apparent lighthouse, set on a low bluff right beside the water.
("It's only a summer home," Frank later explained, "so we only
needed something suitable for light housekeeping.")

We rounded up among some moored sailboats and dropped
the plow anchor. The bottom looked muddy, and the water was
shallow, so I launched *Marksark* and set the Danforth as well. We
rowed ashore and walked up the long, gently sloping lawn.

When I had been here before, working with Ned on a book about the ferries, I had looked out into the bay, wondering what lay to seaward and how one would sail in here.

The house had belonged to the family when Ned was a child, and had been sold. Decades later, he bought it back and made it into a retirement home—although "retirement" hardly seems the word for a man who can't seem to stop writing.

While Gertrude Belliveau talked with Lulu about life on a boat, and Mark made common cause with their granddaughter Jacqueline, Ned reminisced about journalism as he had known it in the heyday of *The Toronto Star* and *Star Weekly* when the newspaper had a circulation of one million and a handsome budget. He covered the Coffin case in Quebec, which radicalized a generation of Québecois, and is one of only two people still alive who were actually there—which led to a recent consultation with researchers from *The Scales of Justice.* He wrote stories from Rome, Sicily, Haiti, the Dominican Republic, Central America. Each time he filed a story he would send a proposal for another along with it. Each time the *Star* told him to go.

Ned left the *Star* to work with the Ontario Liberal leader John Wintermeyer—"far too honest a man to have been in politics"—and with a little Acadian down home in New Brunswick, Louis Robichaud.

"Robichaud's victory, coming after Lesage's in Quebec, told us the tide was running," he says. He joined Lester Pearson as a speech-writer, and then went into advertising. Presumably he prospered, and no doubt his relationship with the prime minister was an asset, just as his son Bill's advertising agency did well enough under Gerald Regan's Liberal regime in Nova Scotia to finance the late, lamented *Atlantic Insight* magazine.

The Belliveaus have five sons, all in public affairs or communications one way or another. Mike is executive director of the Maritime Fishermen's Union. Rick is Canada's consul-general in Shanghai. Tim had been running the information office at the University College of Cape Breton, but had just joined the Atlantic Canada Opportunities Agency and moved to Moncton. I didn't know Peter. They grew up in Toronto, but all except Rick were in or near Moncton.

Although Ned wrote in English, he was a *chiac* by birth. A corruption of "Shediac," the term is used in New Brunswick to describe any Acadian from the Moncton area. In a *Canadian Geographic* article on the Acadians and their language, Ned noted that the Acadians did not come primarily from Brittany and Normandy, but from Touraine and Berry, north and south of the Loire Valley. Their speech was influenced not only by the northern language which ultimately became standard French, but also by Provençal and Spanish—and by English, since the region had sometimes been ruled by English kings. And it had been a *literary* language—the language of Bossuet, of Pascal and Racine, the great writers of the 17th century in France. Above all, it was the language of Rabelais, a native of Poitou.

The Acadian forefathers arrived between 1605 and 1671, including Ned's ancestors and Lulu's, the Belliveaus and the Terrios—or Teriots, or Theriaults, or Terriaus: we have collected 17 different spellings of the name. They descend from Jean Terriot, a ploughman of Poitou whose son Claude was born in Port-Royal in 1637. Lulu belongs to the 12th generation of Terrios in Nova Scotia.

While England and France battled for their territory, the Acadians lived rather well, raising good crops from their dyked lands around the Bay of Fundy. Food was plentiful, birth rates were high—6.75 children per family—and mortality was low. By 1713, when the British took Nova Scotia for good, the Acadians numbered about 2,000. By 1755, when they were deported en masse, their numbers had risen to about 13,000. They were a distinct people, French by origin but rooted in the Maritimes; those who fetched up in France caused endless frustration to the royal bureaucracy, with their casual ways and their assumption that they were free people, entitled to come and go as they pleased.

Some escaped deportation, like René Terrio, Claude's great-grandson, who fled from his home on Northumberland Strait to Nipisiguit, now Bathurst, New Brunswick, where he was captured by the British and carried prisoner to Fort Cumberland, Nova Scotia, and then to Halifax. When the Seven Years' War ended in 1763, thousands of others returned. Their lands were occupied by British settlers, and they fanned out across the region, establishing scattered settlements along the shores of Nova Scotia and Prince Edward Island and along the Gulf coast of New Brunswick. By 1803, about 8,300 Acadians were once again living in the Maritimes; today there are more than 300,000, and thousands more in Maine and Québec. In all, more than a million North Americans can claim Acadian descent. Like the Basques, the Kurds, the Mi'kmaqs, they are a buried nation.

Through their long, often isolated history, their 17th-century language persisted, just as the English of the 17th century persisted in outport Newfoundland. The Acadians preserved their culture, as well. They could tell folk-tales dating back to the Crusades; some of their songs were written by mediaeval troubadours. They named their children not so much for saints, as in Québec, but for heroes and lovers of myth and romance: Ulysse, Hector, Narcisse, Roland. Or for ancient kings and emperors: Claude, Alexandre, Clovis. Or for admirable qualities: Placide, Patient, Fidel. Or for poets: Ovide, Omer. It must have been Acadians who named such features of my own home waters as Cape Argos and the rocks called Cerberus, Orpheus, Castor and Pollux.

But the deportation fragmented and marginalized them. Like the Highlanders after the Clearances, they were disorganized, dispersed and leaderless. Not until the end of the 19th century did Acadian leadership begin to reemerge. The dominant Acadian business institution was formed in 1903, the Assumption Mutual Life Insurance Company—but it was created in Waltham, Massachusetts, not in Canada. It moved to Moncton in 1913.

And only in our own day did the Acadians become a potent political force. In New Brunswick, Acadians constitute one-third of the population. In 1960, Louis Robichaud, a Liberal, became New Brunswick's first Acadian premier. His government reformed local taxation and education, declared the province officially bilingual, and in 1963 created the Université de Moncton. His quixotic Tory successor, Richard Hatfield—a unilingual Loyalist from the Saint John River Valley, a most unlikely supporter—developed an astonishing rapport with the Acadians, and entrenched those reforms. Hatfield's Tories were completely eliminated from the legislature in the 1987 election, but the reforms were permanent.

"In the long run, the most important thing may turn out to be the Université de Moncton," says Ned Belliveau. "In a single generation the Université de Moncton has created an educated Acadian community."

That generation of sharp, canny young Acadians is busily transforming Moncton itself. Once a tired old railway town, Moncton becomes more attractive every year, with brick sidewalks and cast-iron lamp posts, chic restaurants and a renovated vaudeville theatre. When Canadian National closed its repair shops and Eaton's shut down its catalogue-sales operation, Moncton lost several thousand jobs. But the city's motto is *Resurgo*: I rise again. It has replaced those lost jobs and added some new ones— and better jobs, too. In the middle of the recession, Moncton was humming: it had become the pace-setting Maritime city in terms of economic development. Shortly before we visited Shediac, the *Globe and Mail Report on Business Magazine* had singled out Moncton as one of Canada's five best business locations. Its strengths included first-class transportation and advanced communications, low-cost land and housing, a high quality of life, a pro-business attitude—and the largest and best-educated bilingual work force outside Quebec.

It also had one of the finest salesmen in Canada working for it: Premier Frank McKenna, backed by a sophisticated, wide-awake economic SWAT team.

"McKenna's incredible," a Nova Scotia development officer told me enviously. "When he hears about a company thinking of making a move, he gets an appointment with its top management. He goes in with a couple of aides. A whole team stands by the phones in Fredericton. When the company raises a problem, he says, *I think we can deal with that*. One of his aides makes a phone call and comes back in a few minutes with the answer. At the end of the meeting McKenna says, *Well, gentlemen, I think we've addressed all your concerns. May I take it we have a deal?* And he closes the deal on the spot."

The deal usually has to do with communications. Computers, fax machines, fibre optics and toll-free numbers make such "back-office" functions as telemarketing, billing and customer service as easy to operate from Moncton as anywhere else. Moncton's unanswerable competitive advantage is its Acadian work force, switching instantly from unaccented French to unaccented English, ferociously industrious, eager to please. For companies like Federal Express, CP Express and Camco Inc., they are the perfect people to answer the phone. Moncton's latest coup is Purolator Courier, whose new national service centre will create 400 jobs—no small number in a city of just 55,000. Best of all, these companies are not in Moncton for grants or natural resources. They are there because they need Moncton's *people*.

"People want to see the community prosper through private business, and they project that very sincerely," the city's industrial commissioner told me. "With its mix of French and English, Moncton is a mini Canada, like New Brunswick itself. It's come to terms with its cultural and linguistic diversity, and it's been able to turn what's often perceived as a liability into an asset. The university's been a major factor in that. We work very closely with the university. We're talking with them all the time."

The commissioner's name was Peter Belliveau. His parents were Ned and Gertrude.

On our second day in Shediac we planned to go for lunch with the Belliveaus and then visit Sue Calhoun and Gilles Thériault, whom I knew well by reputation but had never met. It was a lovely day, warm and sunny, an ideal day for the beach—and the beach was right there, in front of the Belliveaus' house. We were all ready for lunch—clean clothes, clean shoes, clean minds— when the wind suddenly puffed up hard from the southwest. *Silversark* swung broadside, and then, instead of swinging back as the strain came on the anchor rode, she just kept going.

We scrambled on deck. *Silversark* was drifting sideways through the shallow water. *Both* her anchors were dragging.

I scampered forward and paid out more line. The plow was snatching fitfully at the bottom, but the nylon rode on the Danforth was completely slack. I pulled it in, hand over hand: the anchor came out of the water in a huge ball of eelgrass and slimy black mud. I thrust my leg out over the bow and scraped it clean with my foot, then heaved it to windward as far as I could. When the boat had drifted a little more, I snubbed the line hard, and the anchor dug itself in.

How could we have dragged not one but two anchors—and

with lots of scope on both of them? The Danforth had fouled itself with weed, but what about the plow? Then I remembered the consistency of the muck I had scraped off. The bottom was a soupy black goo. Trying to make an anchor hold in that slop would be like trying to make a fish-hook catch in jelly.

Could I leave *Silversark* thus tenuously anchored? True, if she went adrift she would not destroy herself on the rocks: there were no rocks. But she might do a lot of damage to another boat, and she could well fetch up on the beach, lying ignominiously on her side waiting for the tide to pick her up again.

I would not be comfortable ashore with the boat on so precarious a mooring, and the wind was not going down, either. It was whistling in the rigging now, making *Silversark* pluck and twitch at her anchors. I went below, called Gertrude Belliveau, explained, apologized and cancelled the lunch.

Lulu was furious. All that misery—drifting in calms, headwinds, cold and rain—and now, the first time Mark could swim, the first time we had dressed up to go out—now, on this beautiful breezy day, we were condemned to stay on the boat!

Mark waited till the emotional temperature cooled, then asked for the inflatable canoe. I nodded gruffly, and he paddled ashore. He was back in minutes with a young man named Jason in an outboard motorboat. He had arranged for us to use a vacant mooring, and Jason would tow us to it.

Competent kid. We rowed ashore in time to meet Sue Calhoun.

"I was nine at the time of the Escuminac disaster," says Gilles Thériault. "It had a great effect on me. I decided right then that if I could do something for fishermen, I would."

Gilles is fortyish, balding, bespectacled, sitting in the warm sunlight. Sue sets out snacks on the picnic table, while their small daughter, Raphaëlle, helps to entertain the guests. The house on Shediac Harbour is a year old, stylish and bright, with chocolate-brown siding and polished hardwood floors. Birch trees hang over the sun-deck. Sue—an investigative journalist by profession—was the general contractor during its construction, as Lulu was on our renovations, and the two are soon talking about the experience.

"Tradesmen would come in and say, *Like to see the boss*," Sue remembers. "So I'd invite them to sit down, and then I'd wait. After a few minutes they'd startle, and then say, *Oh! Is it you?*"

"Someone had left an old book on construction in our house," Lulu grinned. "I'd read it at night, and I'd go down to the job in the morning and say, *We need a new header over that window, and the cripple's got to come out so we can get at the plate.* They were so impressed when I used the right terms that they never realized how little else I knew at first. But eventually I did know."

Gilles's father, Norbert Thériault, was in Louis Robichaud's cabinet, and his brother Camille is in Frank McKenna's. I met Norbert when I lived in Fredericton, twenty years ago. A tall, elegant, silver-haired man, he was one of Robichaud's most astute and powerful ministers. Like Robichaud, Norbert Thériault now sits in the Senate. But Gilles has spent most of his working life as an underpaid, overworked union organizer, criss-crossing the Maritimes in a succession of worn-out cars, reviled as a communist by the labour movement, fighting to gain collective bargaining rights for inshore fishermen. And it all began with Escuminac.

Certain events enter into the collective memory: the Springhill Mine disaster, the sinking of the ferry *Caribou*, the Halifax explosion, the Escuminac disaster. Escuminac is a tiny fishing village at the mouth of Miramichi Bay. One June day in 1959, its drift-net fleet went out for salmon. A major storm roared into the bay. Twenty-two boats went down, carrying 35 men to their deaths. The loss traumatized the whole province. People still date things by it: "That would have happened, let's see, the year after the Escuminac disaster."

Later, as a teenager, Gilles worked out on a salmon boat which met a similar storm. The fishermen rode it out. Gilles spent a terrifying night below deck, wondering whether he would ever get ashore. When the fleet came in the next morning, everyone in the community was on the wharf. His parents had spent the night in the church, praying for their son.

Gilles arrived at the Université de Moncton in 1968, part of the first generation of Acadians to receive a secular education in their own language. It was an exciting time. The headlines were about civil rights, Vietnam, the Beatles, LSD, *la révolution tranquille* in Quebec. A wave of student revolt was sweeping the world. In

Moncton the revolt took three directions: Acadian nationalism, socialism and activism.

With a population nearly 40% French, Moncton was still an English city, named for the British colonel who had directed the expulsion of the local Acadians. The mayor, Leonard Jones, was openly anti-French, and City Hall was English only. The students expressed their view of Jones by marching to his home and depositing a pig's head on his doorstep. Nor were they much more pleased with the docile Acadian leadership of the day.

"One of the strongest criticisms of the elite was that the approach that they had taken was paternalistic, that it had never included empowering the grass roots," Gilles said later. "So the next most logical step was to attempt to give power to those who had none." By 1977, he was executive director of the Maritime Fishermen's Union, organizing the inshore fishermen of the Maritimes and trying to obtain collective bargaining for them.

Maritime inshore fishermen are notoriously anarchistic and parochial. They are direct, wry, adaptable and competent, but they fish different species, with different gear, at different seasons. Some are anglophone, some Acadian. They are scattered along the ragged coastline of three provinces, and their lives have made them fiercely independent, competitive, argumentative and suspicious of structures and authorities. The MFU was always strongest in Acadian New Brunswick, where it eventually did win bargaining rights in 1982, but it made valiant efforts in the other two provinces, and in many measurable ways it improved the fishermen's conditions even without proper legislation. Sue told the story in her book on the MFU, *A Word to Say*. In the spreading fisheries crisis of the 1990s, the union's role may become even more critical.

After ten years, Gilles left the union, to be replaced by Mike Belliveau. He became an independent fisheries consultant, working on Canadian and international projects. He must be doing well at it: there is the new house, with its new furniture, and there are two new cars in the driveway. It is a pleasant change from a job which, in his last year, paid him all of $14,000.

Sue and I had been reporting on the fishery for years, and the the four of us talked about mutual friends in the fishery, about the future of the union and the industry. The crisis in the fishery is among the forces propelling the Urgent Conversation. For

years we had backed the fishermen, fighting for the rural life-
style, arguing for the social programs which have given fishing
communities an unprecedented level of stability and dignity.
Now we found ourselves confronting a reality very different from
anything we had imagined: a world in which fishing had become
so efficient that the fish had all but disappeared. By the 1990s,
unemployment insurance was no longer an insurance scheme: it
was a faintly disguised form of welfare, a squalid game of cha-
rades played by the chronically unemployed and the government. What else can you call it when the acknowledged purpose
of government make-work projects is merely to employ people
for ten weeks so they can qualify for forty-two weeks of unemployment insurance? We looked at one another uneasily, each
wondering whether to say what we now believed.

"I think the fishery *does* need a drastic reorganization," Gilles
said. "I'd rather have fewer fishermen and a few fish plants all
working steadily and earning good money than the 10-42 UIC
pattern we see now, where the *function* of the plant is almost to
qualify the workers for unemployment insurance."

"That's right," I said. "Are we really doing people a favour by
playing these games with their lives?"

"I was on the Great Northern Peninsula in Newfoundland
recently," Sue said. "The pattern there is that the guy who's
capable of filling in forms becomes chairman of the industrial
development association. Then they get a grant and they do
something, it doesn't much matter what—but if they don't have
a grant they won't do anything. I was in one community where
they had run out of money. They had all the materials to build a
community hall, but nobody would do it without a grant to pay
their wages, even though all of them were *already* on UIC."

"Same thing in the fishery," said Gilles. "Fishermen can't get
steady crews: the guys will work ten weeks, get enough stamps to
go on UIC, and then they don't want to work any more."

He paused for a moment, then summed it up.

"I think we've created a monster."

It was a disturbing conversation. Here we were, four people of
the left, talking like prosperous, conservative middle-aged professionals. Well, we *were* relatively prosperous middle-aged professionals. But had we become conservative? Or had we simply
learned something about paternalism and dependency? Maybe

what people need is not total security but merely disaster insurance; maybe we abort personal growth when we eliminate risk and danger.

A good many left-wing theories have become tattered, but the values endure—a heritage of caring and fairness, a sense that society is not a dogfight but a compact among free people for the benefit of all. But the other ideas are all up for review. The Urgent Conversation requires an uncomfortable level of honesty and presents us with a disquieting need for fresh thinking.

Perhaps those are among the risks that middle-aged left-wing professionals will have to take.

THE
COLOSSUS
OF
BOUCTOUCHE

We left Shediac under grey skies at ten in the morning, hurrying across the wide harbour before a businesslike westerly. We waved to a crowd of people fishing off the wharf as we hardened up off Pointe du Chêne and sliced through the narrow channel out into Shediac Bay.

The weather was cold and damp again, and the wind was fair for home. It was tempting simply to ease the sheets and run for Cape Breton. Instead we hung on, plunging and bucking to windward in the chop as we passed the fishing hamlet of Cap de Caissie. We wanted a good offing before we tacked for Bouctouche, and we stood well out to seaward, crossing paths with one lobster boat after another. This was slow, tiresome sailing.

The harbour of Bouctouche, 18 miles away, is the estuary of the Buctouche River—the river has the English spelling, the

town has the French one—but we would have to sail up Buctouche Bay, following the course of the river's narrow channel
through the submerged mud banks. The final approach would
be through a narrow, winding channel marked by stakes planted
in the mud on either side—the sort of place we could go only with
an ideal breeze. And this breeze was far from ideal.

I went below, turned on the phone and called Rhéal Savoie,
the stocky, sandy-haired executive director of Kent County's
industrial development corporation. Did he know a fisherman or
someone who might tow us the last couple of miles?

"Sure!" said Rhéal. "I'll get the industrial commissioner. He
keeps a speedboat in Cocagne."

"Well, look, I don't want to wreck his working day—"

"Jean-Guy? He'd love to get out of the office. And you're
gonna write about Bouctouche, so it's business. Call me when
you get into Buctouche Bay."

The sky cleared as we tacked, and the wind went more northerly. Now we could lay a course direct to Bouctouche. Suddenly
the boat was clipping along over a blue and summery sea. Mark
had been seized with an idea for a hydroplane design; he constructed it out of a plastic pop bottle, using tape and string, and
tried it over the side.

We passed the outer buoy for Cocagne Harbour, another stop
on the Grand Prix hydroplane circuit. Cocagne had a marina, but
a low bridge barred it to sailboats. And there was that classical
strain in Acadian culture again, for in mediaeval romance the
name Cocagne—or Cockaigne, in English—was a mythical land
of idle luxury. In Cocagne the rivers ran with wine, the houses
and streets were built of cake and pastry, roast geese wandered
about inviting people to eat them, and buttered larks fell from
the sky like manna.

By now we could see the tall lighthouse at the end of Buctouche Dune, proud as a pencil, white against the summer haze.
It was my turn to make lunch, but we were coming up on the
lighthouse very fast.

"Where's the entrance?" Lulu asked.

"To the right of the lighthouse."

"Right? Are you sure?"

"I'll check."

I was wrong. The entrance was to the left of the lighthouse, and a long sandspit ran seaward from the dune. To avoid the sandspit, we had to alter course at once.

"Whoops," I said, coming on deck. "Ease sheets. Bear away. Bring her about 20 degrees to port."

"I thought so," said Lulu.

With the sails broad off, *Silversark* sprinted ahead. No time for lunch now. In minutes we were at the red buoy off the dune which marks the narrow entrance to the narrow bay, heading into the even narrower channel.

We sailed into the channel and the wind died.

Whaaat—?

Now we faced an hour of miserable sailing. Up went the sails and then down again, as shrieking blasts of wind followed total calm. Sandbanks waited for us on both sides, demanding that we tack almost as soon as the boat began to move again. The wind came now from this side, now from that, determined to catch the sails aback. I called Rhéal again, but he was out of the office. We might have help getting up the staked channel, but we might not. Mark stayed at the sounder; I went forward, watching the sandbars and scanning for buoys.

In a perverse way it was enjoyable, using our skills to claw our way along under blue skies and white fluffy clouds. To port were low bluffs surmounted by houses and cottages, with small boats anchored close inshore; to starboard was the Bouctouche Dune, a six-mile barrier beach, grassy and windswept, separating the bay from the Strait. It was new country, wide and open, with long feather-shaped sandbars and slow, meandering rivers.

Up ahead was a big white building that looked like a convent, though it lacked an adjacent church. At the entrance to the staked channel, we were still far from shore. Down at the mouth of the bay we saw a tiny white dot: a speedboat, moving fast. Rhéal and Jean-Guy? The wind had baffled around again; we could sail the first leg of the staked channel, anyway.

We turned into the approach channel just before the speedboat came roaring up. Sure enough, there was the broad, cheerful smile of Rhéal, and a warm grin from the tall, dark-haired young man at the wheel.

"That's the *industrial commissioner?*" I said quietly. I had expected someone grey-haired and pin-stripy; Jean-Guy Dube looked more like a young Yves Montand.

"It's easy to imagine *him* attracting industry," said Lulu. "Or anything else."

We sailed a little longer, chatting between the boats, till the channel twisted and the wind came foul. While Rhéal was fastening the tow line, Jean-Guy drifted out of the channel: his depth sounder immediately peep-peep-peeped, full of electronic anxiety, while his propeller churned up silt. So the channel really *was* that narrow.

The quay at Bouctouche is an active place, though there are hardly any boats there. It lies just below a bridge, in front of the massive church, at the downriver end of the main street. With the two boats secured, we gathered in *Silversark*'s cockpit. Mark had noticed fishing gear on Jean-Guy's boat, and soon the two of them were deep in conversation about fishing.

"Jean-Dixie!" said Rhéal, looking up at the wharf. A prosperous-looking young man in a white shirt and tie was gazing down at us. Jean-Dixie Belliveau. He and Jean-Guy planned to go to Shediac by boat, but Jean-Dixie had a car to sell first.

"So, Mark," said Jean-Guy. "I've got some time, let's go fishing." In minutes, the speedboat was skimming out of the bay, bound for the mackerel grounds at the seaward end of the Dune. Lulu and I walked uptown to scout out the village.

The main street of Bouctouche is named Irving Boulevard.

K.C. Irving, allegedly the eighth-wealthiest person on earth, began with gas pumps and a Ford dealership at his father's general store on this very street. The Irving presence is palpable in Bouctouche, as elsewhere in New Brunswick. Irving Boulevard boasts two Irving gas stations, a Kent Building Supplies store, storage tanks on the harbour, a prefabricated-home factory, an impressive arboretum and the carillon that tolls from St. John the Baptist Church. The Irvings even own the Dune.

Drugstore, fast-food restaurants, post office, Rhéal Savoie's office, Chrysler Dodge dealership—

"Don! Lulu!" cried Jean-Dixie, waving to us from the car lot. "Jean-Guy just phoned on the cellular. It was rough out there, so he took the boat to Cocagne. He'll drive Mark back later."

We bought ice-cream cones and looked over the schedule for the Fête Nationale des Acadiens: *jeux traditionnels, musique acadienne, service de nourriture, tintamarre, soirée traditionelle,* and a concert by Les Méchants Maquereaux. Traditional games, music, food, concert—but what was a *tintamarre*? We asked the ice-cream vendor. She didn't know.

Back at the boat I looked up to see a tanned, fair-haired man in a muscle shirt standing astride a mountain bike, looking at the boat. Roger Daigle had an ambition to own a sailboat, but it seemed impossible.

"Build one," I said. "We built *Silversark*."

"I wouldn't know how to begin."

"Get some good books," I said. "Ask for advice. You can learn it. There were hundreds of ships built on this river in the old days. *All* those guys can't have been smarter than you. Come on aboard and I'll show you how this one's constructed."

Roger beckoned to his wife, Oliva, waiting atop the low hill in the adjacent park. She walked her bike down the hill and came below. We showed them the ribs and stringers that defined the boat's shape, the planking bent over that structure, the laminated deck beams, the compact galley. Yes, it had been a lot of work, and it had taken a long time—but then again, we had often been needlessly fussy. Overall, boat building had been one of the most satisfying things we had ever done—and the effort had yielded a boat that fit like a well-tailored suit.

As the sun went down, they rose to leave. Were we finding everything we needed in Bouctouche? Was there anything they could do for us? Well, we had found everything but a laundromat and—

"There isn't one," said Roger. "But it's no problem. You can do your laundry at our house. Just call whenever you're ready."

Moments later Jean-Dixie hailed us and came aboard.

"Where did you get that name?" I asked.

Jean-Dixie laughed. His father had bought a building for a furniture store, and a Dixie Lee chicken franchise came with it; Jean-Dixie had put himself through university serving chicken. Then he had worked two years for the Irvings, declining his father's invitation to take over the franchise. After he took his MBA, his father lured him home by buying the car dealership and making Jean-Dixie a partner.

"It's tough to compete with Moncton," he said. "But we sell 400 cars a year, and 30% go to Moncton. People here are careful, you know, they don't spend lavishly. Bouctouche is a good place to live. Moncton's only 35 minutes away, but I don't even go to

Moncton, I stay here. I love Bouctouche. Listen, while you're
here, if you need a car you just come and tell me. I'll lend you a
used car off the lot."

Jean-Guy and Mark arrived with four fresh mackerel. Rhéal
dropped by with his wife, Murielle, who had once been Jean-
Dixie's teacher. We sat together for an hour and talked about
Bouctouche, about education and human growth, about power
and politics. We talked a lot about business. Jean-Guy is the
industrial commissioner, after all, and Rhéal manages the local
development corporation. Rhéal and I had met through the
Urgent Conversation, at the Baddeck Symposium, and I was
curious about the reported entrepreneurial revolution among the
Acadians.

But of course Bouctouche is not entirely unfamiliar with successful businessmen.

K.C. Irving was in Bouctouche while we were there, spending
the last summer of his life in a house on the same site as his
father's. He was legally resident in Bermuda, but he spent nearly
half the year in New Brunswick, much of it in the serene river-
side village where he was born. He died that December.

In his 93 years, Kenneth Colin Irving had amassed perhaps
the greatest fortune ever built in Canada. The empire is privately held, secretive, tightly controlled by Irving's sons and
grandchildren. It includes pulp mills and newspapers, bus lines
and frozen-food plants, timberlands and building supply
chains. The Irvings own Canada's largest oil refinery and largest shipyard, as well as 3,000 service stations and a fleet of ships
larger than the Canadian navy. Irving companies command
assets worth about $7 billion, and in the summer of 1992 K.C.
Irving still walked up the main street some evenings to watch
the cash being counted when the local Irving station closed for
the night.

Why does it seem almost *easier* to make an immense fortune
than a decent living in the Maritimes—as witness the Killams,
Beaverbrooks, Jodreys, Sobeys, McCains and others? I have
been an amateur Irvingologist for more than a quarter of a century; I excoriated his New Brunswick newspaper monopoly
before a Senate committee in 1969, and later tried to buy the

Fredericton *Daily Gleaner* from him. My associates and I concluded that entrepreneurs like Irving are not only determined, courageous, intelligent and so on; they are also highly creative people. They discern possibilities, imagine their fulfillment and create structures to embody them. The creative impulse may be what drives them. In some respects entrepreneurs resemble artists: obsessive, disciplined, talented, manipulative, certain of the inherent value of their work and dedicated to the point of ruthlessness.

New Brunswickers view the Irving colossus with a mixture of fear and pride. It's nice to see a local boy doing well in a wide and treacherous world, and Irving generated jobs. But great wealth brings great power and frees you from many restraints. The most disagreeable feature of life in New Brunswick is the ubiquitous power of the Irving interests. A family which commands more than 40% of the economy is almost beyond the reach of competition or control.

Like Dobermans, such fierce competitors have their uses, but they should never be mistaken for domesticated animals. The Irvings are pitiless players who press their advantages with unholy single-mindedness. K.C. was not unique; John DeMont, author of the prizewinning *Citizens Irving*, portrays K.C.'s father, J.D. Irving, as having "a stranglehold over local commerce . . . as strong as the sway his more famous son would one day hold over an entire province." Old J.D. was into a dozen enterprises, including silver foxes. For a decade or more, day-to-day control of today's empire has been in the hands of K.C.'s sons, Arthur, James and Jack, now in their sixties. The new wave, in their 30s and 40s, appear to be just as single-minded, just as aggressive.

Voices in the Bouctouche air:

In the old days, a man owed the Irvings $200, and he died. The Irvings came to the funeral and asked if they had a son who could come with them and pay off the debt. The boy was 12, and he worked for the Irvings for years.

If you worked for the Irvings, you were expected to shop at the Irving store. If you didn't, you got a note in your pay envelope saying someone in your family had been seen shopping elsewhere, and please try to improve. If you didn't, you were simply fired.

They never hesitated to fire someone like that. They didn't explain. You never knew why. They'd just tell you your services were no longer required, and that was it.

I don't know what they want with the Dune. Six miles of sandbar, and they're in court to prove that they own it.

They don't want the Dune. But they'll use it as a bargaining chip. They'll give it to the government in return for something they do want.

He didn't exactly start with nothing. When he started his oil business back in the 1920s, his father and a friend loaned him $100,000 to get started. Can you imagine how much money that was, back then? Pretty good start for a young fellow.

My father worked for the Irvings for years. We were a big family. He earned 85 cents an hour.

The Irvings move into any business very aggressively. They want to be dominant. They set the standard for truck stops and convenience stores here and then moved into Maine and raised the standard there.

K.C. Irving is still a Ford dealer, you know. He still has a dealer number.

People are very cautious in business here. They don't take on debt. They keep their overheads down. That way, they can't get into trouble and give the Irvings a chance to pick up their businesses. That's why a relatively low percentage of local businesses are Irving-owned.

I met one of the grandchildren once at some social occasion. I said, What's it really like to be an Irving? He said, It's damned hard work.

They used to drive very plain cars, but Arthur Irving drives a Lincoln now, and some of the others drive Porsches and Jaguars.

They're very private. They have a big place on the beach north of town, and they'll come in and out of there and you never see them. They're very private.

The common thread in everything K.C. Irving did is, it was based in New Brunswick. When he got the oil business going, he didn't expand it into the States. He expanded into other businesses in New Brunswick. And of course the more he expanded here, the more dominant he became here, and the more he could do anything he wanted here. He wouldn't have had that kind of power if he'd been running an oil company spread across New England.

People don't talk that much about the Irvings. But you always know they're there.

We stayed several days in Bouctouche, liking it more all the time. Images: a tractor rolling across the bridge by the boat, its engine rapping, towing a wagon full of vast wheels of hay. An old man, bald, sweeping the shingles of his house with a broom. Neat yards, tidy parks, freshly painted houses. Giggles and laughter in the night, the Latin beat of youthful mating behaviour along the main street and down on the quay. A tiny model lighthouse in a backyard above the bridge, flashing bravely in the dawn when I wake early and go for a walk. Herons spaced out along the sandbanks, patiently waiting for tiny fish.

Bouctouche men are *obsessed* with angling: every evening the wharf is crowded with men and boys with their rods, patient as herons, waiting for the fish to strike. I wake up at three in the morning, restless, and go on deck to check the lines—and three boys are standing on the bridge, fishing. One night there is a thumping and banging on deck, and the boat suddenly rocks. I scuttle out of the delta berth and fling the hatch open, ready to repel boarders. On the afterdeck is an unkempt middle-aged man, full of beer and apologies. His casting was inaccurate, and his fishing line has wound around our backstay. I check my watch: it is four-thirty in the morning. *Ah, bien,* I say, *bonne pêche,* and crawl back under the eiderdown.

Acadian New Brunswick—unlike France and Quebec—has a lovely, accommodating attitude to language. If you try to speak French, people encourage you, no matter how foul your accent, how contorted your grammar. If you're forced back to English, *pas d'problème.* They can do that, too.

So French becomes a pleasure, not an obstacle. You get used to speaking it. One night a Quebec couple pull up on the quay in a small motor home, a carpenter and his wife. They speak almost no English, but we talk for 45 minutes all the same. They loved Cape Breton, its mountains, its whales. They want to know how we find our way over the sea in a boat. They're in their 60s, but ageing is not a matter of the calendar, it's *à l'intérieur.* They wonder why Maritime houses are all made of wood, not of *brique.*

C'est culturelle, je pense, I say. *On a beaucoup de bois icitte, c'est le matérial normal pour toutes usages—pour les bateaux, pour les maisons, pour le chauffage, pour tout.* Poor French, no doubt, and poorly pronounced, but they know my opinion, and we've had a good time.

One afternoon Rhéal took us for a long tour of the local economy. In Cocagne he showed us a Victorian red-brick building built by the late E.P. Melanson.

"He's the guy who came up with the idea of putting lobsters in cans, and he made millions," said Rhéal. "He had a tunnel built from his house to the factory. The United Maritime Fishermen had it later, but they went bankrupt. Then a fellow came here, Raoul LeBlanc—a Kent County guy, but he had been living in the States. He had nothing to start with, but he started making some trips to Montreal, buying furniture and bringing it back to sell. Now he's one of the biggest furniture retailers in Atlantic Canada, and he's building furniture himself. He's got 30 people working for him.

"Next door here is Enspeco. It belongs to Alvin Brun. He's developed a machine that recovers freon gas from fridges and freezers. It weighs about 50 pounds and costs under $3,000. The ones they had before were huge, and they cost three or four times as much. Over there is Muffie's. They make muffin dough—you wouldn't believe how much muffin dough is consumed every day in the Maritimes."

As we drove inland from Cocagne, Rhéal talked about the problems of dependency and chronic unemployment. The unemployment rate was high—possibly 20% in summer, and much higher in winter, not counting those who have given up and are living on welfare. The total payout of UIC and welfare in Kent County is in the neighbourhood of $90 million a year.

Yet the actual number of people involved was relatively small. With just 12,000 people in the Kent County work force, 20% unemployment is a shortfall of only 2,400 jobs. One big plant would absorb most of them—but that had been tried in the early 80s, when Mitel built a factory to produce electronic switches for telephone networks. Mitel, however, had been badly gored in the last recession, and the big factory sat deserted in a field, surrounded by baled hay.

For Rhéal, development is not just economics; it is politics and morality. On the Big Cove reserve a few miles away, four young people had recently committed suicide, and more had tried. Drugs and alcohol were major problems—and not just for the Mi'kmaqs.

"That's demoralization," said Rhéal. "The best way to ruin a man is to pay him for doing nothing. That's my main worry, the way dependency is destroying our initiative. Kids who were illiterate 40 years ago *had* to go to work. Today kids quit at Grade 8 and they tell Murielle that they know the first year will be tough because they'll have to work for 20 weeks to get UIC, but after that it's only ten weeks a year. They live at home with their parents and watch television. They don't have any will to work."

He stopped the car in front of small plant. Around the plant was a whole cluster of small apartment buildings.

"This is Atlantic Roofers, it belongs to Arthur Allain. Fifteen years ago he couldn't borrow $5,000—today he's got 200 employees and he's probably got a pretty impressive line of credit. He built those apartment buildings to *break* that 10/42 habit. Give people some responsibilities, give them a chance to own a home, then they'll *want* to keep working."

Rhéal is passionate on the subject of education: every decent job today involves computers, manuals, training. There are no jobs for the illiterate and unskilled.

"I have a client, a printer, who's getting into a whole new process, printing in colour, and one of his key people was balking. I said, Can he read and write? They were sure he could, but he couldn't. That's why he was balking.

"Years ago you never thought of education. I quit school in Grade 10. I was going to go to the States and make a lot of money forever. Well, I did that. I worked in construction in Boston for a few months, and I could see that wasn't for me. So I came back and finished high school and decided to go to university.

"My father said, Look, I have six more kids, and I can't help you. If you can find the money yourself, good, then go. Murielle and I waited two and a half years before we got married. I was still in university, and we lived in an apartment that was smaller than your boat. After a couple of years my father said, Well, when are you going to build your house? That was a terrifying thought, $16,000, but you couldn't build it today for $100,000."

The tour went on. A boat-building shop with a revolutionary technique which allowed different fiberglass hulls to be built from the same moulds. A fish plant employing 300 and exporting most of its product to the United States. Little shops making buoys and laths for lobster traps. The 30-unit Habitant Motel, which began when Elzear Thibeau bought a small diner. He intended to turn it into a house, but the clientele wouldn't go away, so he expanded it and built an elaborate new home from the proceeds of a thriving business. A game ranch, still in development, but already selling deer and buffalo meat locally. A peat-moss mining operation. A fish-processing coop researching new products.

"They want to make seafood dishes here and sell them to Marriott Hotels and Pizza Hut. If five percent of Pizza Hut's pizzas were seafood, that would be 160 million servings a year. That's enough to support sixty people a shift, three shifts a day.

"I've got a terrific job," Rhéal reflected, relaxing in *Silversark*'s cockpit. "Most of these people have been on my board. So I get to work with all these terrific people, and I'm always learning."

There aren't many development officers like Rhéal—shrewd, energetic, utterly committed to human growth. He's comfortable in a Halifax office tower or on one of the endless sandy beaches of Kent County. He's happy in French or English, at a desk in a business suit or astride a big motorcycle. Unlike many of his counterparts, he knows the frustrations of the entrepreneur first-hand: he operates a little lumber-export business himself, shipping a carload of cedar to the United States every other week.

"I wrote my business plan and everything worked out the way I planned it—at least all the things that I could plan for," he said. "But every load I shipped the first few years, that was the *last* one. It was a learning experience for me, and it was a teaching experience for the people I advise.

"Working with the Americans, that was a learning experience, too. They wouldn't do business unless I went down and saw them. They said, *You can't understand our requirements unless you see our operation.* Up here, the way people work, if you say you'll have the load ready Friday, it doesn't really matter if you get it Tuesday or next Friday. But the Americans say, *Look, we agreed on the amount, the quality, the price, the delivery. Now we expect to get what we agreed. And if you don't do what you said, then we're going somewhere else.*

"So then you have to deal with your own suppliers. I deal with three small mills, because cedar is not something the big mills want to saw. The bark comes off in long strips, and if you have a de-barker it all balls up on it. It makes a very fine dust. If you've got an enclosed mill, it chokes everybody in the plant. These small sawmill guys, they're very independent, they don't like anyone telling them what to do, but you've got to say to them, *Look, if you agreed Friday, then no excuses, it's Friday and that's it.*

"Now I've got the whole thing running pretty well the way I want it, but it took a long time." He stood up. "You have a good time tomorrow. And one of these days, Murielle and me, we're gonna come on the motorcycle and visit you."

We shook hands and he drove away. We would not see him again this trip. He was going fishing on the Restigouche with the Minister of Fisheries—Camille Thériault, Gilles's brother.

"You know," said Lulu, "this is more like home than anyplace else we've ever been."

"It is," I said. "It's unfamiliar, but they never make you feel like a stranger. This is what it was like when I moved to D'Escousse. That's why I stayed."

TINTAMARRE,

WITH

MISCHIEVOUS

MACKERELS

"I think if Acadia disappears, I disappear," said Michel Blanchard, a cohort of the students who put the pig's head on Leonard Jones's doorstep. "You see people that were taken from their culture, that had to live in a language that was foreign to them. Maybe they were a leader where they came from, but now they babble and jabber and they don' make sense any more. I've lived in Quebec. It's not the same there, *I'm* not the same there. So to fight for *la survivance de l'Acadie*, that's fighting for *me* to survive. You understand?"

Michel said that to me 20 years ago, and I've never forgotten it. At the time he was a community activist working in the Bathurst and Caraquet area, very keen on information systems—radio, video, computers. I asked whether he was concerned about privacy in this flood of information.

"Privacy?" he cried. "*Privacy!* I'm an Acadian, I don't know what that *is!*"

After two decades in an Acadian village, I now understand that, too. The Acadians have lived together so closely, for so long, that secrets are barely possible. Families have characteristics handed down through the generations. Often the families have nicknames; our own island has les Boudreaus Oiseaux, les Bonins Pot-a-clous, les Petitpas Castor—the Bird Boudreaus, the Nailpot Bonins, the Beaver Petitpas—and many others. Their characteristics are catalogued and known, and offered as a sufficient explanation of behaviour. One family is known for its generosity, another for its emotional volatility, a third for its religious devotion.

"Them Landrys, they're all like that."

Privacy? One might conceal an isolated action—an end run past a by-law, a casual amour—but one's character and anteced-ents are completely known. Acadians seem to read one another's genetic codes directly, as some birds directly sense the earth's magnetic field.

In an Acadian village, you live your life openly and candidly: there's no alternative. That may sound invasive and frightening, but in the end it's a relief. You are who you are: if you're not comfortable with yourself, the problem is not the lack of privacy. Eventually this openness becomes second nature; it makes urban life seem kaleidoscopic and treacherous, preparing a face to meet the faces that you meet. In the polite jungles of Ottawa I some-times feel like an extraterrestrial.

Besides—perhaps because they know one another so well—the Acadians are the most tolerant people I've ever known. They lived here for a century almost without government, making decisions by a consensus of the heads of families. To this day, they are democrats to their backbones. Unlike the English, they learned from the Indians, allied themselves with them and inter-married with them—and the Mi'kmaqs, too, are an easygoing and forgiving people. In my experience, Acadians rarely judge others harshly, or attempt to change them; they just steer around idiosyncrasies the way one steers around capes and sandbars.

"Ask her after dinner. She's always cranky in the mornings."

"You can always trust him wit' money, that one—if he owes it, he pays it. Don't leave 'im alone wit' your daughter, though."

The Acadians have bullies and fools, of course, but they remain a great people—tough, clever, merry, durable, with the souls of poets and storytellers and the hands of artisans. A priest who had served a dozen Acadian parishes told me his charges had drawn him out of his Scottish reserve, softened the harshness of his judgment, taught him to laugh at folly.

"In my next lifetime, I'm going to be born an Acadian," he said.

"So am I," I said.

This was once a culture inaccessible to others, but Antonine Maillet has changed that forever. Maillet is a Bouctouche native who lives in Montreal during the winter but spends her summers writing in a lighthouse-inspired summer home on the beach. Her most famous work is probably *La Sagouine*, 16 monologues spoken by an Acadian scrub woman, a pungent female Charlie Farquharson. *La Sagouine* must have been presented in every Acadian village in the Maritimes, its monologues brilliantly performed by Viola Léger. It has toured nationally and internationally and been adapted for television. The French-language edition sold more than 85,000 copies.

La Sagouine's fame prompted Bouctouche to build a $4.2 million theme park based on her. Le Pays de la Sagouine includes a restaurant, gift shops and an outdoor theatre on the riverbank. A long pier-like bridge leads out to Ile aux Puces— Flea Island, so named for a mysterious island of hay which suddenly appears offshore in another of Maillet's twenty-odd books. Clustered around a central square on Ile aux Puces are a fish shed, a lighthouse, a blacksmith's shop and the homes of the leading characters, notably La Sainte and La Sagouine herself. There's also a fictional tavern which serves real beer, and a performance space demarked by a handful of tall pilings. Grey shingles, bright red and blue paint, weathered plank decks: this is frankly an Acadia of the imagination—but then Acadia is a country of the mind in any case. This is the Acadia Maillet distilled from the town across the river, reflected back to the town through the magic of language.

There's a good crowd milling around, eating ice cream and drinking beer around the central square, and then a familiar

figure shuffles through the crowd. She wears an old dress and a
head scarf, and she carries a bucket and mop: La Sagouine, Viola
Léger herself, giving one of her two daily performances. She
starts talking with the audience, joking with the children. She's
everyone's funny old aunt. Little by little she glides into her
monologue. This time she's remembering the census—

> See, when they're incensin, they gotta cense every-
> body, includin chickens 'n pigs. But us, we ain't got a
> chicken coop 'r a pigsty, so they went right along 'n
> censed the cats.

And "the censors" want to know answers to questions no sane
person would ever think of asking: how much flour you use in a
year, how many shingles on your roof and what your father was
doing before he died. (*"—Fore dyin?"* replies La Sagouine's
husband, Gapi. *"My father stretched out both his legs 'n went:
heug!"*) They ask the names of all your children—not easy for the
town philanderer—and they want a lady of easy virtue to say how
she makes her living.

And—hardest of all, perhaps—they ask your nationality. But,
says La Sagouine, what are we? We live in America, but we're not
Americans; Americans work in factories and come to Bouc-
touche in the summer wearing white trousers, and they're rich.
Canadians? Well, not exactly: Canadians speak English.
French? No, French people live in France. French Canadians?
No, French Canadians live in Quebec.

> Fer the love of Christ, where do we live?
> . . . In Acadie, we was told, 'n we're supposed to be
> Acadjens. So, that's the way we decided to answer the
> question 'bout nationality: Acadjens we says to them.
> Now then, we can be sure of one thing, we're the only
> ones to have that name.

But Acadian is not a recognized nationality. In the end, "we told
'em to give us the nationality they wanned. So, I think they put
us down with the Injuns."

It is an accomplished performance, not a word or gesture
out of place. I wanted to meet Viola Léger, who had performed
in a television drama of mine, so we went backstage after the

show. She is a little bit of a woman, bright-eyed, bird-like and thoughtful.

"I've benefited from La Sagouine, but I've paid a price for it professionally," she said. "I'm now completely identified with the character."

It's a great character to be identified with, though.

"Yes. It's mysterious, but I respect that mystery," she said. "You get an idea, you follow it up, see where it leads. Things grow. It will last, I'm sure of that. After 21 years I'm sure. If it wasn't real, it would last maybe two or three years. But 21 years!"

We didn't stay long. She had another show to do. La Sagouine is 72, and Viola is not yet 60, but the daily routine is gruelling. You can see why when you watch her on stage: her focus, her intensity. And she was building a house in Bouctouche at the same time, another exhausting project.

The issue of the census leads La Sagouine to consider the Expulsion of 1755, and the possibility that political and economic forces may uproot the Acadians once again. That concern may illuminate the Acadians' passionate commitment to entrepreneurship. Economists and pundits periodically declare that the Maritimes can prosper only if they depopulate and urbanize. But the Acadians aren't moving. If they're going to prosper, they're going to prosper *here*.

Near the end of her census monologue, La Sagouine says this:

> If a time comes when a person can no longer name his
> religion, his race, his country, his land, 'n when he
> can no longer name the language he's speakin, well,
> maybe that person no longer knows what kind of a
> person he really is. Maybe he don't know not'n any
> more.

Michel Blanchard: *If Acadia disappears, I disappear.* And it was to questions of history, language, mythology—identity, in short—that Maillet addressed herself in her later books. The ones I've read (many remain to be translated) inhabit a terrain where folklore, mythology and epic poetry intersect with fiction. Maillet's Ph.D. thesis was *Rabelais and the Folk Traditions of Acadia*, and her mature work seamlessly fuses Rabelaisian gusto, history and Acadian folklore. Legends come true, historical events move into the realm of legend, familiar places mutate into landscapes of myth, other worlds are never far away. Acadian sailors ride whales through the northern ocean and spy ships of fire and ships of ice.

Her masterwork may be the book which won her France's top literary award, the Prix Goncourt: *Pélagie-la-Charette* (1979). Published in English under the flabby title *Pélagie: The Return to a Homeland*, it is the story of Pélagie LeBlanc, who leads a mismatched handful of Acadian refugees home from the American South after the Expulsion. Maillet's women are always wonderful—passionate and realistic, vivid and frank—and Pélagie is the perfection of the type. The ragtag cavalcade following Pélagie's ox cart—her *charette*—includes her three sons and her daughter, along with the club-footed herbalist, Celina, and the ancient seer, Belonie. Along the way she picks up a giant and a dwarf, a black slave, a beautiful mute and Acadian families from all along the coast—Bourgeois, Thibodeaus, Cormiers, Boudreaus, Landrys, Babineaus, Dugas . . . yes, and Belliveaus and Terrios, too. A people, a nation, they accrete around Pélagie and her cart. Behind them creaks a second cart, which only old Belonie can hear: the Cart of Death, jet-black, with no doors, drawn by six sleek black horses—and that cart takes some Acadians, too, but the losses are balanced by births and recruits. And the trek continues. *Hue-ho the oxen!* cries Pélagie. *North is up that way!*

The cart takes ten years to reach Acadia—ten years!—travelling through swamps and slave markets across a continent aflame with war and revolution. Even in translation Maillet's language crackles with life. The sun "leapt up from the horizon and struck the sky like a gong." Pélagie feels "beseiged by spring from the nape of her neck to the nick of her ankles." At a wedding party we see "clubfoot Celina, red with fermented dandelion, drunk on gooseberries and stew, high on tenderness and fraternity, tapping the club of her clubfoot on the planks."

A century later, the children of Pélagie's exiles recognize that "like the wheel of a cart, like the helm of a ship, the new Acadie had spread the spokes of its compass points to the four corners of the country without knowing it. Playing blindman's buff with Destiny, Acadie had, in the long run, reopened all its fields and replanted roots everywhere."

Yes, indeed. And the Acadians' strength is a resource which
survives even in Acadian villages which have all but lost their
language: what Maillet calls "the joyful and fantastical philosophy of [their] race."

Hue-ho the oxen! North is up that way!

The Acadians did, in fact, hold a reunion in 1884, almost exactly
a century after Pélagie's return, at Miscouche, Prince Edward
Island. There they adopted a flag—the original is in the museum
of the Université de Moncton—and designated the feast-day of
Notre Dame de l'Assomption, August 15, as their national holiday.

The morning of the *fête nationale* a car drove up beside *Silversark*, and a man got out and said, "Good morning. You're from
Isle Madame, and I've come to tell you you're coming to my
place for supper this evening." His name was Bill Boucher. His
father had joined the Royal Bank in his native Arichat and ultimately been transferred to Bouctouche, where he entered the
employ of J.D. Irving, K.C.'s father. The Bouchers had been in
Bouctouche ever since; Bill, indeed, had served as mayor. But
Bill retained a special fondness for his ancestral island, where he
had spent many youthful summers; his great-uncle, it turned
out, was the Father Boucher who had been parish priest in
D'Escousse for 50 years—the priest who had baptized Lulu.

"Is there anything you need?" Bill asked.

We were "dressing ship" that day, flying signal flags fore and
aft from the masthead to the deck, and hoisting to the cross-trees
the courtesy flags of the jurisdictions we had visited, namely
Prince Edward Island and Acadia.

"It seems to me we should have a New Brunswick flag, too,
but I haven't been able to find one," I said.

"Hop in the car," said Bill. "We'll go get one."

"Listen," I said, as we drove uptown, "what's a *tintamarre?*"

"A parade where people walk along together and make a lot of
noise, any way they can. Hell of a racket. Old Acadian custom.
Everyone can join in."

"Even visitors?"

"Sure, if you feel like it."

We checked all the stores. No New Brunswick flags anywhere.

Bill knew everybody, and ripped off greetings in French or English as required. At Kent Building Supplies the manager hurried over and offered to remove the New Brunswick flag from the roof, to the amusement of a smiling man in his 60s whom Bill had greeted as Jim. But the flag on the roof would have covered our whole boat. And Jim, I later discovered, was James K. Irving, the eldest of K.C.'s sons.

"The New Brunswick flag isn't very popular around here," Bill said. "It's seen as a Loyalist flag, a Saint John Valley flag. We may not be able to find one."

In the Irving station, where the bus stops, I checked out the schedules. Mark's Ontario cousins were in D'Escousse, and he was going home for a week while Lulu and I sailed on.

"If I saw a New Brunswick flag on someone's lawn I'd just take it," said Bill, looking around as we drove back down the river. "We'd give it back later on."

At the Musée de Kent, a stately building which was once a convent, Bill hailed a dapper, moustachioed man. Aldéo Saulnier was a village councillor.

"I'll get one for you somehow," said Aldéo. "Don't worry about it. I'll deliver it to the boat."

He did, too, but it was also too large. We concluded that the world was telling us just to fly the Acadian flag. Fair enough. Then Roger Daigle stopped by to see if there was anything we needed. Yes, we said, people would like us better if we had a shower. We extracted Mark from the crowd of kids on the wharf and climbed in Roger's four-by-four.

The Daigles had two children, Réjean and Mireille, aged (nearly) 14 and (nearly) 16. Réjean had developed a brain tumour a few years earlier, which could have been terminal, and had been through months of chemotherapy at Halifax's Izaak Walton Killam Hospital for Children. When a team eventually operated, the surgeon reported that he could peel off the tumour with his fingers—the only one he'd ever seen where such a thing was possible. And Réjean had recovered completely.

"It was a bit of a miracle," said Roger. "We're very lucky."

Mark, Mireille and Réjean vanished into teenage concerns. Lulu and I vanished into steaming hot water. When we came out, Oliva looked at my shirt and wrinkled her nose.

"Let me iron that shirt for you." The shirt did need ironing: it had been stuffed in a locker for days. But I didn't want to impose. The Daigles had been very generous, and they had offered to deliver Mark to the bus in Moncton tomorrow. Already the kids were plotting to have him stay overnight, as well.

"He can sleep in my bed," said Mireille.

I looked at this stunning young woman.

. . .!—as Antonine Maillet would say.

"I'm going to the Bryan Adams concert in Shediac," Mireille said hastily. "I'm staying with a friend overnight. I won't be here."

Ah.

Before Oliva could seize my shirt, Lulu and I escaped to the Musée de Kent, where the *fête nationale* had begun in a flurry of hot Acadian music. It had begun to rain, and despite all protests Roger wheeled around for home and came back with a beach umbrella. There had been face-painting earlier in the afternoon, and half the kids seemed to have the Acadian flag across their eyes and noses. But the music was over, and we went into the museum for food: *poutine à la tron*, pastry stuffed with apples; *fricôt*, the Acadian stew; *poutine rapé*, a deep-dish pie made of pork and grated potatoes.

Outside again, I asked an older couple about the *tintamarre*. They directed us to the man "à la barbe blanche." The man with the white beard was Jean-Clovis Collette; he had an Acadian flag on his face, too, with the gold star over his left eye.

"You want to be in the *tintamarre*?" he said. "That's great! Have you got an Acadian flag to wave? No? I'll get you a couple."

Someone behind us commented on my "beau chapeau." In a moment we were giving Tilley's brag tags to two couples, Legers and Gallants from Moncton. They had noticed the boat, and were delighted to see it dressed: "C'est le 15 aôut—on se fête!" Jean-Clovis came running back with two small Acadian flags. We wove them into our hatbands and walked back to the Daigles's.

"I'm going to iron that shirt," said Oliva. "Give it to me."

"I'm living on a boat," I protested. "Don't trouble—"

"If you're living on a boat, okay, but you're not on the boat now and I *do* have an iron."

Pélagie's sister, *bien sûr*. I handed over the shirt.

Roger drove us back down Irving Boulevard, stopping at the boat to pick up the foghorn and emergency whistles. The *tinta-*

marre was halfway down the main street—police cars and fire engines wailing, people ringing bells and hammering with spoons on frying pans. We caught up with Jean-Clovis.

"Ah, there you are!" He grinned. "You know Aldéo Saulnier? Come and meet the mayor. This is André Goguen." The mayor was a youthful sandy-haired man with Acadian flags flying from both hip pockets. He was beating on a No Parking sign with a wrench. A teacher by trade, Goguen surprised everyone by getting elected, raising taxes, and getting re-elected handily. But people felt they were getting value for their tax dollars. He is said to be genuinely independent, a member of no clique. So he can take difficult decisions without being accused of favouritism.

"I've heard good things about you," I said.

"You've been talking to my wife." He grinned. "But it's nice of you to say so. Where are you from?"

Aldéo was carrying a big piece of metal—a pizza pan or something similar. He threw it ahead of him, and it clattered noisily on the ground. We talked whenever the din faded a little. The *tintamarre,* said Goguen, is a people's parade: you don't have to play an instrument or wear a uniform or belong to an organization to take part. Anyone can take part.

As the *tintamarre* passed, people stood on their lawns, clapping and waving flags. Mark let fly a blast from the foghorn. Mireille and Réjean laughed. Sirens whooped, horns honked, bells rang, whistles shrilled, pots and pans clanged. Jean-Clovis pointed at the RCMP cruiser, lights flashing, draped in Acadian flags.

"*At last!*" bellowed Jean-Clovis. "*We have our own national police force!*"

At length the parade turned into the Musée de Kent. The noise died away, and the crowd gathered around a flagpole. As the Acadian flag rose up the pole, a choir sang:

> *Salut, étoile de la mer*
> *auguste mère de Dieu*
> *qui toujours demeuras vièrge,*
> *heureuse porte du ciel . . .*

When we met Roger at the museum, Mark, Réjean and Mireille sprang their plan on us. They would watch movies together this evening, and Mireille would sleep at her friend's house. Next day they would bring Mark down to say goodbye and put him on the bus in Moncton that afternoon. We could have dinner with the Bouchers and go to the evening concert without any worries about Mark.

Bien, I said, but the movies should be in French.

"In English!" said Mireille.

"En français!" I said. *"Pour Mark!"*

"No, in English, in English!"

"Well, do what you will—you know what I think."

They piled into Roger's four-by-four and drove away—to rent movies, I am certain, in English.

"What do you think of Mireille?" murmured Lulu.

"Whoof!" I said. "A knock-out. And self-confident and charming, as well. Some people have it all."

"Are you worried about Mark?"

"About Mark? I'm almost worried about *me.*"

But Mark's heart survived, apparently intact. I should have checked his pulse.

We heard music coming from the museum balcony. When we went to listen, Bill and Pauline Boucher appeared. The band was Des Froliceurs. The lead singer was a tiny woman dressed all in black. Her name was Nicole Poirier, and she looked about as tall as a yardstick, but she was pure, concentrated energy, belting out tunes which sounded like Quebec-flavoured country and western. Standing under the trees, I fell into conversation with an older man named Ozzie LeBlanc.

"Ah, you're from the boat," he said. "You know the people in the other boat, the one that came in today?"

"The big power cruiser," I said. *Legend*, out of Shediac. "I haven't met them, but we saw the boat in Summerside."

"He's a big drug dealer from Moncton," said Ozzie. That got my attention, but it turned out the man was in pharmaceuticals.

The Bouchers' house stands on a bluff above Buctouche Bay—a comfortable home dating back to 1806, full of art by Acadian painters like Claude Roussel and Ronald à Gonzague, our neighbour in Isle Madame. Bill has other treasures, like the chart of Buctouche Bay made by Captain Bayfield, RN, in 1839. Pauline Boucher had laid out lobster, shrimp, steamed mussels, potato salad, fresh bread, green salad and white wine. We made short and grateful work of it.

Bill wanted to talk about Isle Madame; nobody could ever understand why he loved the place, so when I began to publish articles about it he took to showing them to people and saying, *See? See? I'm not the only one.*

Pauline is a nurse, from Saint John. She's learned to speak French, but she only speaks it in the house, and with children, "not with an adult who can really speak it well." Did she also find the Acadians here very relaxed about language—unlike some Acadians in Nova Scotia, who can be very touchy about their linguistic rights?

"Oh, yes, we've been through all that, too," she said. "But that's insecurity. It's behind us now"—in large part because of the Université de Moncton, which has "made it okay to be French, and professional, and prosperous."

The final event of the *fête* was a concert in an enormous particoloured tent at Le Pays de la Sagouine. When the four of us made our way inside, the place was literally hopping: hundreds of people pulsing up and down in time with the music, slapping their thighs, waving flags. Les Méchants Maquereaux played the crowd like an instrument—half a dozen musicians led by a chunky, curly-haired extrovert named Roland Gauvin. His co-star was Johnny Comeau, an enraptured fiddler with a beatific smile.

They played a driving blend of rock, country and traditional Acadian music. A lot of the songs were topical, and well beyond the limits of my French; one saucy number about unemployment insurance delighted the crowd, and Gauvin explained that whenever he sings it, unemployment goes up somewhere: now it's at ten percent even in Toronto. The tent shook with laughter. And from time to time he paused between numbers, and chanted:

"Maaaaaaaaquereaux!"

The crowd called back:

"MAAAAAAAAQUEREAUX!"

Gauvin smiled, and sang:

"J'ai dit *maaaaaaaaaquereaux!*"

The crowd responded, even louder:

"**MAAAAAAAAQUEREAUX!**"

At one point he said, I want them to hear it in Montreal!

"MAAAAAAAAQUEREAUX!"

No, that wouldn't have reached past Edmundston. Again!
"MAAAAAAAAQUEREAUX!"
La ville de Québec, peut-être. Encore!
"MAAAAAAAAQUEREAUX!"
Bon! Bon! And off into another song.

For me, the high point of the evening was *Alouette*—but *Alouette* done as you never heard it before, in a minor key with a distinctly Russian flavour.

> *Alouette-ski! Gentille Aloue-e-tt-ski.*
> *Alouette-ski! Je t' plumerai. HAI!*

And so through the whole tune:

> *Je te plumerai la tête-ski . . .*
> *. . . et les yeux-o-vitch*
> *. . . et le nez-ski*
> *. . . et le bouche-ka*
> *. . . et le perestroika*

But that did it. *Le perestroika!* Gauvin gazed soberly out at the crowd and pointed just below and behind his ear. *Le perestroika*, he confided, was a little section of skin just in there. Now then, all together:

> *Alouette-ski! Gentille Aloue-e-tt-ski,*
> *Alouette-ski!*
> *Je-te-plu-me-RAI!*
> **HAI!**

A

STAR TO

STEER

HER BY

"**H**ave a good sail!" cried Bill Boucher, casting off the tow-rope while Pauline snapped a photo. The Buctouche Dune lay to port, with its proud, lonely lighthouse. The grey water lay ahead. Beyond the haze was the western tip of Prince Edward Island.

We had been up early, lifting the anchor laid out as a precaution across the stream (fouled by a clump of oysters and clams), cleaning the dinghy and loading it aboard. We said our farewells to Roger, Réjean and Mark, and then Bill and Pauline motored up in their outboard-powered fishing boat. With just enough wind to fill the sails, we cast off and ghosted away. A hundred yards from the wharf I looked over the starboard side.

"Lulu," I said, "those weeds are going by awfully slowly. In

fact they aren't going by at all." *Silversark*'s keel had slipped into
the mud so gently we hadn't noticed. We were firmly aground.

"That's a lesson to me," said Lulu. "Don't shave the edge of
this channel. Those stakes must be planted right in the mud
bank, are they?"

"Yep."

Bill and Pauline towed us free, and kept on not just to the end
of the staked channel, but clear out of the bay, saving us hours of
slow sailing. We waved again as their boat grew smaller. It was a
bright morning with thin, high overcast. Outside the bay, the
low coast stretched away to the north for miles. I remembered
standing on one of those broad sandy beaches with Rhéal a few
days earlier, looking into the distance.

"That beach extends for more than 20 miles," Rhéal said.
"And it's empty. There isn't even a road along it."

The lighthouse on the Dune melted to a white pencil and then
to a spot. The southwesterly breeze slowly increased. Little by
little, the small seas grew. The coast of the Island emerged: a
smudge, a thick line, a strip of red dotted with white buildings, a
husky lighthouse with black and white horizontal stripes.

West Point.

We were eager to see this corner of PEI: Roger Daigle had
given it an enthusiastic review.

"The people are insanely friendly," he said. "You want to go
somewhere, they say, *Take my trailer*. But I don't have a hitch on
my car. *Then take my truck, take the whole rig. Go ahead, I won't be
needing it. Enjoy yourself*. You'll love it over there."

But as we sailed towards it, the lighthouse drifted to starboard.
By now the sky was heavy and dark, and the wind was stronger.
A current had to be pulling us past the harbour, so we bore away
to the eastward. We picked up the outer buoy, then came hard on
the wind. West Point is another artificial harbour with a narrow,
oblique entrance, which can't be seen from seaward. I peered
through the binoculars, looking for clues.

There were range beacons, and we were able to stay on the
range. We dropped the genny and sailed closer, then dropped the
jumbo a few yards from the tumbled rock breakwater. The
entrance opened up right beside us. Lulu swung the tiller, and
Silversark forged through the entrance. Instant decision: in this
little basin, where to go? *There, beside that fishing boat*. I called to

Lulu and pointed. She nodded. We were moving fast: was she holding onto the mainsail a little too long? Lulu swung the helm again and luffed up, sails aquiver.

"Drop the main!"

I let go the halyard, and the big red sail collapsed. With a dock line in my hand, I stepped over the rail onto the fishing boat and made fast. Perfect.

A man clambered down from the wharf onto the fishing boat. He was Ralph Bulger, a fish buyer, and he pointed out a spot where we could lie right alongside. We took long lines from the boat and worked *Silversark* over to the new berth, scrambling across the decks of boats and flicking the long dock lines over their exhaust stacks and radar scanners. I jumped from a boat's wheelhouse to the wharf.

"I'm too old for that," grunted Ralph, heading for a ladder.

"No older than I am," I said.

"Too drunk, then." He grinned. But his gait was steady. Some difference in you, Cameron, I thought to myself: five weeks on the boat, and you're skipping up and down the faces of wharves like a monkey.

Two women and a girl were sitting in a new Saturn: Karol Bernard, Audrey MacDonald and Holly Doucette. While I went ashore to ask the fishermen about the water depths outside the harbour, Lulu invited all four aboard. When I got back, Ralph was saying, "No engine at all? What do you do when the wind dies?"

"Read a good book," said Lulu.

"Swear a lot," I said.

"You wouldn't catch me out there in a boat without an engine," said Ralph.

"What do you do when the engine dies?" I asked.

"That's why you buy a diesel."

The little store near the wharf closed at five o'clock, Karol said. I checked my watch: it was five o'clock. Scrambling on the wharf, we ran for the store. The owners saw us coming, and stayed open while we picked up scallops and pork chops.

Our new friends had pointed out a nearby provincial campsite, and urged us to visit the lighthouse, now converted to an inn, museum and restaurant. We put some towels and clean clothes in a bag and headed off across the sandy ground. Sure enough, the

campsite had showers, and we helped ourselves. Fresh and
clean, we walked on towards the lighthouse. The sky was darker
yet, and it began to sprinkle rain.

The lighthouse is the tallest in PEI, and the first one built after
Confederation. During its 87 years of manual operation, it had
only two lighthouse keepers; when it was automated, the community development corporation took it over under the leadership of Carol Livingstone. We never met her, but she and her
project have been featured in textbooks on entrepreneurship.
The new management built a gift shop and a restaurant on the
side of the lighthouse. The tower itself was converted to a
museum and a nine-room inn, complete with a bar, antique
furnishings and whirlpool baths. In front is a supervised beach,
and behind the inn are "fairy paths" through the dwarf dune
forest.

We had no intention of eating out, but when we saw the
comfortable dining room we weakened. It was almost full. We
checked the prices on the menu and surrendered. The food was
good and the service efficient. West Point Lighthouse was a find.

"I'd like to spend a honeymoon weekend here," said Lulu.

"So would I."

When we left, it was drizzling. We walked along a red sandy
road between stunted cedar trees. Whenever a car came by, the
driver smiled and waved.

"*Damn!*" said Lulu suddenly. "Damn, damn, *damn!* I meant
to buy fresh veg in Bouctouche and in all the excitement I forgot.
I don't know how long it's going to take us to get to the Magdalens, and I wanted plenty of vegetables aboard."

"We might be stopping in Tignish."

"I know, but—damn!"

We walked along for a few moments, and a red pick-up truck
pulled up beside us. Ralph and Karol were in the cab.

"We've been looking for you," they said. "We've got some
garden vegetables for you."

We looked at each other. Who Had Been Listening To Us?
Ralph and Karol had brought beets, green and yellow beans,
onions, lettuce, new potatoes and green peas. The cornucopia
overflowed the galley table. We were speechless with gratitude.

"So we won't get scurvy on the way to the Magdalens," said
Lulu. "I was worried about that."

"Roger was right," I said. "They *are* insanely friendly." They
had asked whether we knew Farley Mowat; when we said yes,
they asked us to say hello: they had enjoyed his visit. But Farley
would have sailed in here a quarter of a century earlier, on his way
to Expo 67 in *Happy Adventure*. Weeks later, I passed along their
greetings, and Farley shook his head. He had not stopped at
West Point in 1967: he sailed in aboard his father's boat, *Scotch
Bonnet*, in 1953. His father had corresponded with West Point
friends till the end of his life.

While Lulu stowed away the vegetables, I went on the wharf to
plug in the battery charger and fill the kerosene lamps. Sand was
everywhere, piling up in little drifts on the wharf, crunching
underfoot on our deck.

"I expected wind and rain," said Lulu, wrinkling her nose,
"but not an Arabian sandstorm."

Tomorrow to Tignish—or the Magdalens, as the case might
be. It might be a boisterous voyage. The rain was splattering
down, and the wind was whistling as I blew out the light.

"We're coming back here, aren't we?" I said.

"Yufff," said Lulu. She was already asleep.

At five o'clock in the morning there was not a breath of wind.

At six o'clock in the morning there was not a breath of wind.

At seven o'clock in the morning there was not a breath of
wind.

Wait a minute. This is a tall wharf.

I got out of the berth and pulled on my clothes. Up on the
wharf, a nice little west wind was ruffling the Strait. We had been
too sheltered to feel it. Half an hour later we were sailing through
the gap in the breakwater, driving for the fairway buoy.

You do not want to know about the next seven hours, during
which we averaged one knot in the general direction of the West
Reef buoy, seven miles away, where we could turn down the
western shore of the Island. Light winds, foul current, no wind,
head wind. According to my calculation we should have had the
tide with us from nine o'clock on. Instead, it headed us until
noon. By then we were well out in the Strait, but still more than
six miles from the buoy. We couldn't even see it.

A horsehead seal raised his massive head out of the water.

Aeolus and Neptune chuckled. The tide changed. A steady
south wind filled in. The sea was flat as piss on a plate, as the
fishermen say. Heeling slightly, *Silversark* slipped gently westward.

We reached the buoy at five past three, and turned north-
northeast down the coast. The new course brought the wind
behind us, and I poled out the genny on one side and vanged the
main on the other, "readin' both pages." Now it was magic,
hushed sailing, unlike anything we had ever enjoyed before: dead
calm water, the wind pressing on the sails like a steady weight,
the boat riding level under her widespread red and white wings.
Yet we were doing more than four knots, skating swiftly past the
distant shoreline. High clouds sailed by, casting fleeting stains on
a clear sky.

Lulu went below and found the cabin sole as steady as if the
boat were in her cradle. She lit the stove to cook supper, a thing
she can rarely manage at sea, sautéeing scallops and boiling new
potatoes, green and yellow beans, spinach. We ate off our laps in
the cockpit, enjoying the summer evening, the little vessel's
smooth, rapid flight, the solitary gannet coasting high above us.

The West Point fishermen had predicted that the lobster traps
would be close inshore, since the water was warm and the lobsters were moulting, but we passed through plenty of them four
or five miles out, with their vivid little flags made of vinyl-siding
off-cuts. We had no need to go closer: we were not stopping.
There are a few shallow boat basins along this coast, but the
Sailing Directions, dour as usual, say "they are entered through
narrow, nearly drying channels in the sandy beaches, which shift
in heavy weather and sometimes are completely blocked." Two
feet of water in Howard's Cove. Three feet in Miminegash. Four
in Skinner's Pond, home of the Island's own Stompin' Tom
Connors.

We passed Miminegash at sundown, fixing our position from
its range lights. The sun dropped into the sea, huge and red.
Standing on the main deck, I could see the last fiery strip of its
rim a full half minute after Lulu, in the cockpit.

"Red sky at night, sailor's delight."

We picked up the North Cape light before dark, while I was
taking down the genny and setting the jib, lashing the pole to the
shrouds, making all snug before nightfall. I went below for a nap,

but found myself on deck again by eleven. The wind had been building, and *Silversark* was hurrying along in the dark, quite close to the land now, the lighthouse painting our sails and faces with yellow light every five seconds. Off the starboard bow Prince Edward Island was fading away to a north-pointing arrowhead. The Gulf lay open before us, stretching out to Quebec, Cape Breton, Newfoundland.

Yet far ahead were bright lights, like the headlights of cars— and again the creative self-doubt of the navigator descended on me: could I have misunderstood something, misjudged our position? Impossible, I thought, quickly scanning the evidence—but still . . . And then the lights moved, revealing themselves as the working deck lights of offshore draggers.

The North Cape buoy was a mile and a half north of the land's end. *Silversark* charged down on it, pushed by a rising wind and rolling sea that would feel much stronger when we stopped running and turned east for the Magdalens.

"We're not going into Tignish," said Lulu. Not a question.

"No."

We rounded the buoy in the rushing wind and racing seas. *Silversark* laid her ear in the water and leaped forward, going like a racehorse, tugging hard on the tiller. This was exciting sailing— too exciting, really, for a single person on watch in the darkness. While Lulu steered, I lowered the mainsail and raised the jumbo. *Silversark* loped along comfortably under the two headsails, and the helm was as docile as a sleepy old cat.

"Don, nobody knows we're out here. Shouldn't we have filed a float plan?"

"Probably."

"Should I call the Coast Guard and file one now?"

"If you can reach them, sure."

She picked up the VHF and called. Charlottetown Coast Guard Radio came back, crystal clear, no doubt from the tall radio mast we had descried beside the North Cape lighthouse.

It was eleven-thirty: my three-hour watch was to begin at midnight. I took the helm. Steer 108 magnetic. Lulu made me coffee and went below, leaving the ship swinging along under the three-quarter moon. I looked around, feeling small and happy in the soft black night. The glow of the compass light, the silvered peaks of the waves, the tricolour masthead light weaving against the black sky. The flash of North Cape light dimming slowly astern, and the necklace of lights from the north shore of the Island, sweeping off into darkness in the southeast. Cool, lonely, beautiful.

Some of those lights would be Tignish, a devoutly co-operative Acadian village. The supermarket-cum-hardware, the gas station, the funeral parlour, the clinic, the fuel-oil service, the insurance agent, the fish plant, the financial centre: co-ops, every one. The Island's most successful fishing co-ops are all in Acadian communities; co-op organization resonates powerfully with the joyful and fantastical Acadian philosophy.

Interesting place, Tignish. The Church of St. Simon and St. Jude has a magnificent pipe organ with a Tracker action, installed in 1882. I haven't a clue why it should be there, but great European organists come to Tignish specifically to give recitals on it. And Tignish produced two stockbrokers whose careers almost constitute a morality play.

Len Gaudet quit school early, found work as an errand boy in a Toronto brokerage office and by the 1980s had risen to become chairman of the august firm Osler, Inc. He had a five-million-dollar house and a million-dollar art collection, and he was transported to work in a chauffeur-driven limousine equipped with three mobile phones. Rod MacInnis joined a chartered bank and after several transfers moved to MacLeod Young Weir. The two had known one another as boys; they met again on Bay Street.

But Gaudet was a stickhandler whose firm imploded in 1987, leaving a $60 million crater behind it. Gaudet himself went bankrupt and is facing criminal charges.

A decade before that, Rod MacInnis found himself facing high blood pressure—nothing terrible, but enough to worry his doctor, who recommended a change in life-style. Don't be silly, said MacInnis, I lead a healthy life, jogging, golf, squash—

"What did your father do?" asked the doctor.

"My father was a fisherman."

"That's what you should do. You aren't attuned to this life."

He went back to Tignish for a holiday. His father kept pressing him to buy a farm which had once been in the family and which he had repurchased. Rod bought it, mainly to placate his father. And then he was trapped on the Island by a ferry strike, and something clicked.

He moved home in 1975, took over his father's lobster license, got some silver foxes from Lloyd Lockerby, put in 125 acres of blueberries and thrived for 15 years. When the Star of the Sea Fisheries Co-op got into trouble recently—with $15 million in annual sales, it is a mainstay of the town—the members asked Rod to manage it. He is there now, working long hours and enjoying himself hugely. When Len Gaudet comes home in the summers, he sometimes hints that Rod should join him in the big deals he's got cooking. Rod thinks about his blood pressure, which is normal, and just shakes his head.

I would love to go to Tignish again, but not on this trip. I have seen Tignish Run, the harbour entrance: 150 feet wide, steel-clad on both sides, a quarter of a mile long. If we could enter in daylight, in light weather, perhaps—but not at night, and in a breeze.

I had only had a few minutes' sleep before North Cape. Lifting my eyes from the compass, I fixed my gaze on a star, trying to hold the bright spot in the sky just to windward of the headstay. Bob and weave, bob and weave: the dance of the star was almost hypnotic. A tall ship, and a star to steer her by. Full and by. In the sweet by and by. Romantic old Masefield. But that's a gift, to be romantic. A man's reach should exceed his grasp, or what's a heaven for?

Or old Tennyson's Ulysses. This grey spirit yearning in desire to follow knowledge like a sinking star...Imagine being an Acadian, a seaman, and your parents name you Ulysse. Now strive, *jeune homme*, live up to that. The kids don't memorize poetry any more, what a shame...The wind's song and the white sails shaking...shaking...Oh, hell, they *are* shaking. Bring her back on course. Which star was I steering by, anyway? What was the course? 108, for 82 miles. Eighty-two miles across the sea, Santa Catalina is waitin'...*Flap! Bang!* Damn, the sails again.

Wake up. Pinch yourself, that helps. Slap your face. Maybe if I sang...and Bobby clappin' hands, we finely sang up every song I ever knew. Sing it out, lad. Go on. Every song you ever knew. Sea chanteys. Shenandoah. Too slow. The Walloping Window Blind, my father loved that. No, Stan Rogers. On a night like this. Rise again! Rise again! Though your heart it be broken and life about to end...That big bald man drinking Glenlivet in

Banff and railing against rapists. How long after that did he die?
Four months? A decade back now. But he'll never die . . . The
Rankin Family. . . . thought she saw a picture but it really was
the sunnnn— and we knew the paaarty was oh-ohver.

Flap! Bang. Done it again. 108, 108, and which star—

"Don, are you all right?"

"Uh, yeah. Fine."

"You're falling asleep. I'm coming on deck."

Splendid woman, that. Everyone should have such a friend.

Lulu came on deck with a coffee for each of us. I read the log.
We had covered ten miles, not bad under small sail. We could still
see the distant flash of North Cape, the ever-fainter lights of the
Island. I went below and fell instantly asleep.

When I woke, the sails were luffing; Lulu was falling asleep. I
was dog tired. I made coffee and came on deck. It was daybreak,
grey seas striding northeast under grey skies. The log said we had
done 18.1 miles since North Cape, but the spinner in the end of
the line was covered with weed, so it was probably under-
recording. I went forward, raised the main and changed the jib
for the genny. It seemed an unbelievable effort.

But it had to be done. The wind had dropped, and *Silversark*
was shuffling along at three knots.

"We're going to have to get the main on her," said Lulu,
sipping her coffee. "Be careful. There's a bat in the sail somewhere. . . . "

That day remains a confusing collage of grey skies, grey seas,
heavy showers of rain, light winds and a very weary crew. At one
point I slept on the cabin sole in my oilskins, with my head on a
sail bag, too tired to bother undressing.

There was nothing to give place and definition: just the grey
disk of sea under the grey bowl of sky, and our only friend the
compass. We slept when we could, snacked when we could. The
boat rolled, creeping slowly eastward. The sails slatted. The
rigging creaked—or was it the bat, hidden away somewhere,
peeping? We searched, found nothing, decided it was the rigging. At four o'clock we were completely becalmed, but the sea,
at least, was flattening out. The Loran and the log agreed that we
were nearing the Magdalens, though the mist and rain shrouded

everything. But when we picked up the CBC news, it came from Montreal.

The forecast had been calling for moderate southwesterlies backing to the south and then veering back to southwest—but the wind, when it came, was a light breeze from the northeast, right on the nose. I remembered Roger Daigle: "They can't tell us what the weather was *yesterday*, never mind tomorrow." We tacked to the north, moving steadily for the first time in hours.

Ohh—wwwwoe! Ohh—wwwoe!

A groaner. A whistle buoy somewhere out there in the mist. I checked the Loran, the chart, the *Sailing Directions.* It could only be Le Corps Mort, an island just west of the main Magdalen group, which from some angles resembles a recumbent human form. The lugubrious *Sailing Directions* thought it a nasty bit of goods: "A reef extends 1 mile SE of its east end. Soundings give little warning of approach to the island, since the depths are fairly even until close to the island." We were still some distance off, but we prudently tacked to the southeast, beating mechanically into the light wind. Our Loran fixes looked like the tracks of a drunken chicken.

It was a lonely place, this grey and heaving world: no friendly whales, no curious seals, no busy dolphins. And if there were no mammals, did that mean there were no fish? The Atlantic cod fishery had collapsed: how healthy was the Gulf?

A human memory is not a long time to measure environmental change, but twenty years earlier I had talked with old people in the upper Gulf, around Bathurst and Campbellton, who told me they remembered herring roe coming ashore on the beaches so thick that a horse would mire in it. Then the seiners had come to the Maritimes from British Columbia, and soon the herring roe was only a thin pink tinge on the pebbles. So what had the Gulf been like a century ago, two centuries ago? If we saw a dozen whales we were thrilled—and we had not seen many more than that in the course of a whole summer. But how many had there been in the days of Cartier and Cabot?

The human race, says John McPhee, "by and large has retained the essence of its animal sense of time. People think in five generations—two ahead, two behind—with heavy concentration on the one in the middle. Possibly that is tragic and possibly there is no choice."

Farley Mowat's *Sea of Slaughter*—perhaps his *magnum opus*, the landmark book he was born to write—is an attempt to reach beyond that five-generation span. Mowat's goal is to describe the European impact on the birds, fish and animals of the Gulf and its adjoining coasts and waters from Labrador to Cape Cod. Mowat is Darwin in reverse: his subject is not the *origin* of species, but their *elimination*—an elimination so complete that few of us are even aware such creatures ever existed in this region. And Mowat is not concerned only with the elimination of individual species: he is describing "a mass decline in both the volume and diversity of non-human life," which is still going on. It is a terrifying story.

One can make allowances for the mistiness of the historical record, for the hype of promoters selling the New World to European potentates and settlers, even for Mowat's fierce sympathies. None of these caveats matters very much. The evidence is incontrovertible: when Europeans came to this country, the land, sky and water simply teemed with life, and they are not teeming now. Mowat ploughed through ancient logs and diaries, reports to the rulers of Europe, books and articles, talked to ageing fishermen and mariners, and they all tell the same story: clouds of birds that darkened the sky, fish so thick they "stayed the passage" of Cabot's ships, oysters the size of shoes in bays where no oysters grow now, rocky islands carpeted with the eggs of now-extinct birds, seven-foot codfish weighing 200 pounds. Here is Mowat's picture of Northumberland Strait as it may have looked to the Portuguese navigator Joao Fagundes in 1519:

> The Strait surges with billions of herring and mack-
> erel schooling so tightly as to form almost solid
> masses of living flesh. Seabirds wheel and dive into
> this stew in dense formations. Feeding cod rise up
> from the bottom in such mighty phalanxes that their
> assaults upon the baitfish make the surface roil as if
> from an underwater eruption. Grey seals in their
> thousands watch, dark-eyed, as the ship slips past.
> Pods of whales, both great and small, cruise in such
> numbers that the caravel sometimes has to give way
> before them.

Again and again, Mowat tells the same savage story: killing for profit, killing for sport, killing to remove a nuisance, killing for "management," killing for the sheer pleasure of killing—a slaughter that ends only when too few animals survive to make the butchery worthwhile. Feathers for hats and pillows, furs for clothing, mammal blubber for oil, fish roe for Japanese gourmets. Carcasses for bait, for mink feed, for fertilizer, for pig swill. Always the story has the same ending: for some mysterious reason, the creatures become too scarce to be worth pursuing. Perhaps the climate has changed, or food has become scarce, but the great populations of the past have somehow migrated elsewhere. One might think another explanation would have occurred to people like the "sportsman" who shot more than 69,000 snipe in 20 years of hunting.

With commercial species, the end was even sorrier. As the animals became rare, the law of supply and demand raised their value, even to scientists who wanted specimens for mounting, and the last individuals were hunted down relentlessly until every single one had vanished. Gone forever, extinct: eastern grizzly, woodland caribou, great auk, Atlantic grey whale, Eskimo curlew, Labrador duck, passenger pigeon, heath hen, sea mink, eastern buffalo.

And other species which survive elsewhere, often tenuously, have vanished from what was once the Sea of Whales, a sea of life: the basking shark, the long-billed curlew, the trumpeter swan, the oystercatcher, the white ibis, the "arctic" white fox, the wolverine, the cougar, the grey wolf, the white sea bear, which is now known as the polar bear.

Another whole list of species is near extinction: the bowhead whale, grey seal, piping plover, harlequin duck, golden eagle, peregrine falcon, forest marten, lynx. Others remain only as rumps and relic populations: the sturgeon, sea turtle, black right whale (so named because it was the right whale to kill), gannet, puffin, sea otter. The grey seal, the horsehead we saw near West Point, was believed extinct for generations until a few individuals suddenly reappeared in 1949.

Walrus—walrus!—once bred in hundreds of thousands clear down to Cape Cod. Their name remains, but people have forgotten what it means. They were called "sea cows"—as in Seacow Head, Seacow Pond, Cow Bay. They once swarmed in PEI, on

Sable Island, in the Magdalens. Before I read Mowat, I never knew there had been a walrus rookery near my home on Isle Madame.

One of Mowat's sources remembered white belugas "as many as the whitecaps on the St. Lawrence."

I looked around me at this grey, heaving world. Sea of slaughter, all right. The whitecaps remained, but—a few gulls and terns excepted—we did not see a single living thing between Prince Edward Island and the Magdalens.

After dark, while Lulu slept, the mist was suddenly wiped away—and there were the lights of the Magdalens ten miles off, exactly where they were supposed to be, dominated by the triple flash of the lighthouse in Ile du Havre Aubert. Half an hour later came a sudden gust of wind. As Lulu came on deck, the lights vanished and the world went very dark, as though someone had dropped a black velvet cloth on us. Rain between us and the coast—and soon the rain came sweeping over us, thundering on the deck and gushing off the sails. When we emerged from the murk we were much closer to the coast.

We sailed on, gradually working our way north and east. The Magdalens form a 40-mile curve like a boomerang, open to the east; we had to traverse the whole south coast before turning to enter Baie de Plaisance, within the curve. Grumpy and exhausted, I handed over to Lulu at two in the morning. We were still tacking to windward.

"What course?"

"Just work her north and east."

I caught three blessed hours of solid sleep. When I woke, *Silversark* was approaching Entry Island. Lulu had had a lovely sail, and I had made an egregious error; I had failed to give her precise directions, and *Silversark* had loped north until Lulu had heard the breakers. When she smelt woodsmoke and the warm, vegetative fragrance of the land, she had tacked east.

Lloyd Bourinot used to talk about "sniffing the coast," but I had never seen it done before. Down-east skippers, groping through the fog, used every piece of evidence to confirm their position—the character of the seaweed, the directions the birds flew, the smells of fish plants and spruce woods, of smokestacks and hayfields and guano. If you smelt chocolate in Halifax Harbour, you were near the Moir's factory on Duke Street.

So Lulu had sniffed the coast, like Miller and Aimé and Honoré Terrio before her, the Acadian skippers who were her father's immediate ancestors.

I feasted my eyes on the Magdalens—a vivid landscape of high red sandstone hills, each one swathed in green and linked to its neighbour by not one but two low-lying tombolos, strips of sand with beaches enclosing a lagoon. A one-mile distance between islands thus adds up to four miles of beach—which is how a 40-mile chain of islands can have 150 miles of beaches. Buildings lay sprinkled across the hills. With 15,000 inhabitants, the Magdalens are densely settled. Entry Island, the least populated, has fewer than 200 people, all English-speaking. It is the only inhabited island not connected to the chain by a beach.

I had been wanting to sail here for years. I had been here only once, briefly, in midwinter, by helicopter. More than once I had set sail for the Magdalens, only to be thwarted by time constraints or weather. During the night I had entertained fantasies of another rebuff: a gale or an irresistible current springing up while we were within sight of the islands, an intractable force that would drive us back to PEI.

Well, we were not there yet, though we were close enough to see pick-up trucks moving along the shore roads. The doleful *Sailing Directions* describes La Passe, the channel between Entry Island and its neighbours, as narrow and shallow, and recommends against its use without local knowledge. And the wind, now robust, was against us. We set a course to clear the island, charged past its south face—and stopped cold. Becalmed.

Becalmed!

Our patience snapped.

We swore at the wind, at the boat, at the fates, at each other. We argued about the utility and futility of rowing. We unshipped the oars, shipped them, tacked the sails, tacked them back and cursed. A puff of breeze came up, carried us a quarter of a mile and faded away again.

"We're *never* making another trip in this goddam boat without an engine!" cried Lulu.

"All right! All right!"

"It's *still* ten miles across the bay to Cap aux Meules!"

"I *know*, Lulu!"

A long line of fishing boats emerged from main islands, hazy in the distance, moving towards us side by side—open boats like Walter Largaud's, away back in my childhood, with wheel-houses at their sterns. They ambled past us and on out to sea, jigging for mackerel, waving as they went. We discovered we were sailing, reaching into Baie de Plaisance before a light but steady southwesterly breeze.

I was on the foredeck when I heard a sharp cry from Lulu.

"The bat! *The bat flew away!*"

I wheeled just in time to see a black shape fluttering against the pale sky, like a tattered oak leaf in full flight.

"It just flew out from under the dinghy and took off," said Lulu, her voice full of joy. "It's all right."

Now it was my turn for a delightful sail. The sun came out, and the sky cleared. While Lulu napped on the deck, *Silversark* ran on into the bay, pushed along by a low ground swell rolling in from Newfoundland. Picking up a rhythm from the seas, I found myself humming. *Heel, toe and away we go! Heel, toe and away we go!* Lulu woke up, and we draped our wet clothing on the lifelines, turning the ship into a floating clothes rack.

The islands slowly revealed themselves: a tall, cone-shaped hill at Havre aux Maisons, a ridge in the south which must be Ile du Havre Aubert, more islands indistinct in the distance to the north. We took in the clothes. A big church, oil tanks, a building that looked like a hospital.

And then the familiar challenge and excitement of a new harbour, converging on the fairway buoy with fishing boats, a big steel trawler and a catamaran. The artificial harbour at Cap aux Meules was made of concrete structures tumbled together. They looked like gigantic versions of a child's jacks.

Down with the genny, then the main. *Silversark* glided into the road-like entrance. Smiling fishermen. Big draggers tied up around the basin. Utilitarian metal fish plants. A brick Coast Guard building. Quebec flags flying everywhere, the white fleur-de-lis quartered on azure. We spotted an empty berth behind an opulent white schooner, the only other yacht in the basin. Down with the main. Lulu laid the ship alongside, and I stepped ashore and moored her.

Back in the cockpit, we hugged. We had been 54 hours at sea.

THE

ACADIAN

ATOLL

In the Musée de la Mer, in Havre Aubert, is a barrel with a metal sail bearing the words WINTER MAGDALEN MAIL. It commemorates an episode in 1910, when the telegraph cable broke down. The Magdalens are locked in by ice from Christmas to April—even today's icebreaking ferry only operates ten months of the year—and in 1910 the telegraph line was the sole winter connection to the outside world. When it failed, Madelinots clubbed together and on February 2 put their outgoing mail and the postage in a puncheon. They set it adrift, assuming it would eventually find someone on the mainland.

It did. In April it found one Murdoch MacIsaac in Port Hastings, where the Canso Causeway is now. He sent on the letters as requested, and duly claimed his $30 reward.

The story of the Magdalens is a story of communication. Two of the islands—Grosse Ile and Entry Island—are English-speaking, with numerous inhabitants who even now speak little or no French. Small wonder: until the 1950s there were no roads along the tombolo beaches. To visit a neighbouring island you went by boat, or took your chances driving along the sand at low tide. The next island, however near, was a long way away.

We were sitting aboard *Silversark* one afternoon with Gus d'Entremont, who works in telecommunications with the Coast Guard in Cap-aux-Meules, when a fishing boat came roaring into the harbour, aiming for the berth behind us. He was going far too fast. We rushed on deck to fend off, shouting *"Attention!"* and *"Donnez-moi vos lignes!"* and any other snatches of French which might express alarm and solicitude. But the skipper handled the boat as deftly as a sports car. Gus laughed.

"You don't have to speak French to them," he said. "They're English."

"How do you know?"

"They've got red hair."

"Red hair?"

Gus explained. The anglophone islands were settled by the Scots and the Irish, and there are only 1000 of them even now. By some arcane Mendelian calculus, red hair has become a dominant characteristic, after two centuries of intermarriage. Gus was right, too: we met plenty of redheads in the Magdalens, and all of them spoke English.

All over the Magdalens are trucks, buildings, containers labelled CTMA. This stands for Co-operative de Transport Maritime et Aerien. The cooperative was incorporated in 1945 to ensure proper communication with the mainland. It raised $85,000 by local subscription and bought *Maid of Clare*, a 104-foot wooden coaster. The Musée de la Mer displays photos of her and of all her successors. Until recent decades, the islands were closely allied to the Maritimes, albeit controlled by Québec. Planes flew to Charlottetown and Halifax, and coastal freighters sailed to those two cities and to Pictou. Now the planes and freighters go directly to Montreal; only the car ferry *Lucy Maud Montgomery* ties the islands to the Maritimes via Souris, PEI.

Very definitely, this is Québec. Cap-aux-Meules is well-sprinkled with provincial government offices. Corner grocery stores carry a nice range of beer and wine. Supermarkets strive to persuade you that food is a pleasure. This is the summer of the constitutional marathon, and in the fall we will see TV footage of Jacques Parizeau in Cap-aux-Meules campaigning for the *Non* side. Québec usually seems far away; it is odd to see Parizeau striving for independence just 40 miles from Cape Breton. The Magdalens have a distinctly French sense of style: waitresses in black leather miniskirts, saucy fishing vessels, bold modern buildings. Where the islands are ugly—chiefly in Cap-aux-Meules, the industrial and administrative centre—they are ugly in a very French way, with stark, slab-sided buildings deposited almost at random along a dusty, treeless main road.

It was not really practical to sail from island to island, so we took a short cut and rented a car from the amiable Jean-Francois LeBlanc. I told him we would be happy with anything—a Trabant, a Tatra, a 1948 Skoda. He rented us a well-used Escort. It drove just like a 1948 Skoda.

We drove to Havre Aubert to see Father Frederic Landry, director of the Musée de la Mer, whose press publishes his six books on the islands. White and modern, the museum sits on Cap Gridley, overlooking a beach known as La Grave, a historic district once favoured by shipchandlers and storekeepers. The museum has a fine collection of model ships and artifacts of the fishery and some really excellent displays of fishing techniques. It also has relics of the islands' hundreds of shipwrecks, and examples of the Magdalens' own coinage, issued in 1815 by the proprietor of the islands, Isaac Coffin. Below, on La Grave, is an aquarium and a line of craft boutiques in little shingled buildings which look like gear sheds. These, too, are part of the Musée complex, a tiny incubator for micro-business.

A short, square man with a formal manner, Father Landry has an encyclopaedic knowledge of his native islands. They were part of the huge grant awarded to Nicolas Denys in 1635, and they had various seigneurs during the French era. In 1763 they were transferred to the British. Colonel Jeffrey Amherst, as the local commander, conferred fishing rights on Richard Gridley, who gratefully gave the name Amherst Island to Ile du Havre Aubert.

"Next year, July 28, 1993, is the bicentennial of the parish and the legal system," said Father Landry. "A group of 223 Acadians came here in 1793 from St. Pierre and Miquelon with their priest, Father Allain, in reaction against the liberal ideas of the French Revolution. A smaller group, 115 people, went to Cape Breton at the same time—to Arichat, as a matter of fact."

In 1798 the British Crown awarded the islands to one Captain Isaac Coffin—much to the dismay of several hundred Acadians who had lived there for a generation. Coffin's family collected rents for 160 years, until the Québec government took over the proprietorship in 1958. As a result, most Madelinots are still renting: according to one recent estimate, the Québec government still owns 70% of the "privately held" land as well as the Crown lands.

As in PEI, land tenure became an open sore. By 1828, the Madelinots numbered more than 1,000, and were petitioning for lands elsewhere. In 1848, a group of them settled on the west coast of Newfoundland, in the Port-au-Port peninsula and around St. George's Bay. Between 1854 and 1872, another group moved to the north shore of the Gulf, opposite Anticosti Island.

"One of those settlements is Natashquan, where there are Vigneaults and Landrys from the Magdalens," said Father Landry. "Gilles Vigneault, the *chansonnier*, comes from there. He's from one of those families."

The Gulf might as well be called the Acadian Sea. The Acadians are on every side of it—and right in the middle, too.

We went to the Café de la Grave for lunch, and liked it so much we came back another evening for supper. The café is located in a one-time general store established in 1865 by a Jerseyman named John Phillip Savage. It became a café in 1980, but it retains many of the antique shelves and furnishings. The menu gives its history and invites visitors to take the time to reflect on the past, to dream, to talk—and, of course, to savour the food. *Ici vous êtes chez-vous . . . chez-nous.* Books and magazines are strewn around, along with a wood-block game which works rather like a two-dimensional Rubik's Cube. Clients obviously take the invitation seriously. People were unhurriedly reading and writing, gossiping and debating over bottomless cups of coffee.

When we came back for the second time, we were evidently *habitués*; we were greeted as old friends. The *croque monsieur* and salmon aspic were splendid. When the café filled up, an older

couple asked if they could use the two empty chairs at our table.
Criss-crossing between fragmentary French and elementary
English, we learned that Roland Arseneau was a retired skipper
who had sailed coal schooners from Sydney and knew Leonard
Pertus, the skipper who taught me to sail; Corinne Painchaud
was a widow who ran a bed-and-breakfast nearby. I handed
Roland the wood-block puzzle, and he slapped the pieces back
and forth, solving it in three minutes.

A waiter seated himself at the piano and played "The Skater's
Waltz" and "Annie Laurie," and then, at some hidden signal,
swung into a Gilles Vigneault song, which has become the birth-
day tune of Québec. The whole restaurant joined in.

> Bien cher Clarisse
> C'est votre tour pour laisser
> Parler d'amour.

Clarisse was a beautiful black girl at an adjoining table who
laughed and hid her face in pleasure and embarrassment. She
was the only black person in the room. My mind spun back 30
years to a black American friend in London, remarking on
French colour-blindness: "If you stay in Paris for a week," she
said, "you almost forget that you're ... different."

We were driving out of Havre Aubert when Lulu suddenly
cried, "Stop!" She had spotted the atelier of Les Artisans du
Sable, the sand crafters whose work she recalled from a Halifax
craft show. Inside was Albert Cummings, a lean greyhound of a
man presiding over a unique showroom full of sand-castles,
vases, clocks, bowls, lamps and sculptures of fish and seals—
whimsical and elegant, all made of sand. Along one wall are vials
of sand from all over the world, sent by friends and patrons. But
Les Artisans' stock-in-trade is the beige sand of the Magdalens,
and a local black "magic sand" made of hematite, which contains iron and makes elegant patterns under the influence of
magnetism.

Cummings and two partners spent several years and a good
deal of money—Cummings had mortgaged his home—to pay the
Québec Centre of Industrial Research for developing a patented
resin. They mix the resin with the sand, and for half an hour the
mixture remains a liquid, which can be poured into moulds, like
jelly. For the next three days the mixture is semi-soft; it can be

worked with woodworking tools—blunt files, hand saws and so forth. Then it hardens like rock.

"You should have been here a week ago," said Albert. "For the sand-castle competition. We've sponsored it for six years. Look." He pulled out some photographs. The sand-castles were amazing: turrets, archways, onion domes, gables, crenellated battlements. The contest occupies a full day, from eight o'clock to four, and the prizes run as high as $400.

I asked him about the "sonorous sands" I'd read about in Celtic folklore—sand that hums, squeaks and drones when you walk through it, kick it, draw a finger through it.

"Ah, yes, we have that in the Magdalens," Albert said, springing to a wall covered with photos of magnified sand grains. He pointed at a picture. "The grains must be almost round, and of a particular size. They have it in Prince Edward Island, too, and in Cape Breton, the Hebrides, a few other places."

We lusted for their lamps, with parchment-like shades dusted with sand, but we had no space to carry one. We bought a small vase instead.

"Here," said Albert, "take some of these. A gift." He reached over and pulled down five stylish window envelopes. "These are magic seeds. Plant them and you'll grow what you like." The "beach seeds" were sand grains, the "sea seeds" looked like salt crystals, the "island seeds" were tiny shells.

"Oh, and you should have these, too. We made them for trade shows and craft markets, but we don't do those any more." He reached under the counter and pulled out two tiny vials of terracotta sand, each with a label.

The labels said, "A Gift from Sandy Claus."

We drove on towards Cap-aux-Meules.

"You know," I said, "Les Artisans haven't just developed a new product, they've developed a whole new *métier*. It's like pottery. Other artists could do other things with it. It's like the Gougeon Brothers with epoxy boat building—they could sell the resin, sell books on it, run seminars . . ."

"You're in the Urgent Conversation again."

"Of course."

"What's that?" said Lulu. "A sailing school!"

Centre Nautique de l'Istorlet, said the sign, pointing down a side road towards Le Bassin, one of the smaller lagoons. We had been told to look up Allain Arseneau and Rita Castonguay, who ran a sailing school in the Magdalens.

The school is a bunk house and a classroom-cum-office on flat sandy ground beside the lagoon. On the shore was a whole fleet of tiny boats—Optimist prams, Lasers, sail boards—with kids at the helm and small outboard runabouts mother-henning them, shouting encouragement and instructions. The Magdalen lagoons are an ideal place for dinghy sailing and wind surfing. The Gulf breezes blow steadily over anything from 40 to 200 miles of open water, but the lagoons are calm: the beaches stop the seas. You see small, brilliantly coloured sails all over the lagoons, shooting along at speeds that would do credit to a runabout.

Allain Arseneau casually presided over this midget navy. A fit-looking curly-haired man of 45 or so, he is a professional sailor. He and Rita and their daughter keep a CS 36 down south and spend four months chartering in Florida and the Bahamas during the winter, returning to operate the sailing school in the summer. Rita also has a part-time teaching job in the local school system. They have several times sailed their own boats from the Maritimes to the Caribbean and done the same trip delivering yachts for others. But after capsizing a 35-footer in the Gulf Stream, Allain is reluctant to do more deliveries.

"It's too dangerous," he explains. "Everyone wants their boats taken south now, at this time of the year, in the hurricane season. The last time I had to sail it alone, with a kitchen timer set to wake me up every 15 minutes."

He led us into a shed to show us his latest creation, a tiny plywood dory designed by Phil Bolger. One of the Magdalens' summer events is an instant boat race: contestants have to build a boat from scratch in three hours, using no more than $75 in materials—and then race it. Allain had used a stitch-and-glue technique, and the glue had set up too quickly, so he couldn't bend the sides out to make the boat broader. As a result he capsized several times during the race.

"But I finished." He shrugged. "And I've lowered the seat now, so it's not so unstable. Maybe the kids here will use it."

I made some quick observation about boat building. Allain didn't catch it.

"I'm sorry, I don't understand English very well," he said. "I speak it fairly well, but I know what I'm going to say, you see? So I can prepare. But I don't know what the other person is going to say, so I can't prepare."

"Allain," I said, "you . . . have . . . perfectly . . . explained . . . the . . . state . . . of . . . my . . . French."

We drove along the south shore of the island to Cap du Sud, to the lighthouse which had been our destination for 82 lonely miles, and then followed the back roads to the top of the island's highest hill, the site of the islands' CBC transmitter. The view was spectacular: the stunted forest dropping away below us, the shallow trajectories of the attenuated beaches curving away to the hazy hills of Ile du Cap-aux-Meules, the houses sprayed about the landscape in what a surveyor quaintly describes as the *morcellement anarchique du territoire*—the anarchic subdivision of the land.

We eased the Skoda down the mountain again, and rumbled along the beach to the western shore of Ile du Cap-aux-Meules to see La Belle Anse, the Beautiful Cove, where wind and water have carved the red sandstone cliffs into dramatic arches and pinnacles which even the Madelinots consider exceptional. The road passes through L'Etang du Nord, on the outer face of the great curve of the islands, a spacious artificial harbour guarded by an offshore bluff and a ruined ship, stranded and rusting. Overlooking the harbour is a powerful sculpture by Roger Langevin of seven husky fishermen pulling together on a rope.

L'Etang du Nord is the home of Ernest Bouffard, the port manager of Cap-aux-Meules—"the ambassador of the Magdalens," according to friends in Nova Scotia. One wild night in 1963 Ernest's father thought he saw lights offshore. In the morning he got up to look and saw a ship on the beach. She was the *Corfu Castle*, with 24 men aboard, all of whom were saved. It was the last major shipwreck on the islands.

Ernest had been aboard *Silversark* our first morning in the islands, and he had told us about *dolosse*, blow-outs and wind surfers. Visiting wind surfers find it hard to grasp that the Gulf of St. Lawrence is not a lake. Ernest once came up with a wind surfer eight miles out, scooting off towards Newfoundland.

"He really didn't realize there was no limit to this lake," said Ernest. "I convinced him to come back with me."

Blow-outs occur when the dune grasses are disturbed, leaving the sand free to blow away. The big problem currently is recreational tricyles and four-wheelers. One unfortunate Madelinot had been using a particular route constantly and had thus killed off the grass. One morning he came with a friend, scooting along and shot off the sand into a 50-foot gulch which was not there the previous day. He was killed instantly.

Ecologically, the Magdalens are like a big ship, or a scale model of the earth. On these small, heavily populated islands, the environmental limits are very clear. The islands have no rivers, for instance, so all their fresh water comes from aquifers under each island. All those people—the number doubles in the tourist season—stress the aquifers. If they are diminished beyond a certain point, salt water will seep in and make the water undrinkable.

By the same token, the garbage does not just go away; the Madelinots have to live with it, and have a strong motivation to minimize it. The vegetation is fragile—a local ecotourism company is wittily named Frag'Iles—and the only local source of energy is the wind. We passed the abandoned wind-test site outside Havre aux Maisons, with its inactive turbines still describing black arcs on the sky; the problem is that the wind does not blow exactly when you want it and sometimes blows too hard. If the turbines could survive the gales, and if the energy could be accumulated, stored and metered out later, then wind power could provide much of the Magdalens' requirements. But those problems remain to be solved.

Dolosse (which is plural for *dolos*) are the strange, ungainly concrete structures which rim Cap-aux-Meules Harbour. They were developed by an engineer named Eric Merrifield in East London, South Africa. They look like the letter H with one leg turned at right angles to the other the way an anchor stock stands at right angles to the crown. Merrifield got the idea from the knucklebones of goats and sheep, which since the 1830s had been used by Afrikaaner children as toys, like jacks. Instead of resisting the ocean's force, Merrifield's *dolosse* absorbed and dissipated it. The first *dolosse* breakwater in North America was the one at Cap-aux-Meules, installed in 1971. The sea shook it down the first winter, and it has never budged since. Today *dolosse* are used all over the Magdalens.

We saw them again at Old Harry, on Ile de la Grande Entree, at the other end of the chain. Old Harry is an anglophone community, close to Grosse Ile, and yes, it was full of redheaded children playing around the one-room schoolhouse, which has been turned into a museum. The harbour is so small—and, one assumes, so rough in an easterly gale—that the fishing boats are hauled ashore after each fishing trip, using a power winch and a cable running down the slipway.

At Grande Entree itself, we watched from the shore as a freighter carrying salt from the mine at Grosse Ile felt its way out through the shallow lagoon towards the open sea, accompanied by a bustling, noisy little pilot boat. At the end of the wharf was a big blue dragger, exactly the same as the ones which towered over *Silversark* in Cap-aux-Meules Harbour, but speckled with white barnacles. The *Nadine* is a *cause célèbre* in the Magdalens. She was fishing off the islands on December 16, 1990, when someone left a manhole cover loose on her deck. When she filled and sank, eight men drowned. She was a $3 million ship, and a consortium raised her 18 months later—but they had spent $1.5 million, and nobody wanted the ship. When we were there, a deadly hush prevailed. Everyone was waiting for the report on an official inquiry; the captain, who survived, had vowed to tell all, once the report was issued; lawsuits had been threatened, but none had been filed. Meanwhile the *Nadine* lay at the wharf in Grande Entree, a ghost ship attended only by her ghostly crew.

We took a walk along the sea cliffs, through a bonsai forest sculpted by the wind, along paths marked *Privé: Piétons bienvenue*: only pedestrians were welcome. The owner of the land had planted signs urging *pietons* to stay on the path and pointing out the damage done by careless four-wheelers. Down on the shore we climbed along the sandstone rocks, peering into grottoes and squinting through sea-cut arches. And then we headed back towards Cap-aux-Meules, looking for Leonard Clark. We found him in Old Harry, in a bungalow on a side road, a big man with a shock of unruly white hair over a mind full of knowledge.

In the late 1920s and early 30s, when Leonard Clark was growing up, the Magdalens were still locked in solitude every winter by the ice. Isolated both from the mainland and from the other islands, people passed the time in visiting, telling stories around the kitchen table. The oldest people there had been born in the 1830s and had known the first settlers when they, in turn, were old. Tales were told of shipwrecks, walrus hunting, sealing voyages, tragic deaths and heroic rescues. Little Leonard Clark huddled under the table, listening. When Leonard talks about life in the Magdalens just after the British conquest of the Gulf, he is giving eye-witness reports at third hand.

His own father made a notable rescue early in this century. Two men had set out one January day in an open boat, carrying mail to Entry Island. The boat stalled in the slush, and a north wind carried them out to sea. They drifted so close to the Cape Breton coast that they could see people in horses and buggies going along the shore. Then the gale swung around to the southeast and blew them back to the Magdalens.

Leonard's father had been looking for them from the beach and came back with the gloomy conclusion that "nothing can live in the Gulf today." When he heard the men had been sighted at the edge of the bord ice a quarter mile from shore, he borrowed a dory and two 1,200-foot coils of rope and called for a volunteer. Against the protests of 100 people, the two made their way out from Grande Entree harbour to the mail boat. Following the local doctor's instructions, he gave the two men each a spoonful of brandy. "That's a damned small drink," croaked one, lying on the bottom of the boat.

Leonard's father then went overboard with two dory oars and the end of a coil of rope. Supporting himself on the oars, he crawled and wriggled across the slushy ice to the shore. The people on the beach pulled the two boats in across the ice. The feat had taken Leonard's father eight hours in the freezing tempest, and it won him a Canadian Humane Society medal.

The story's sad sequel took place in 1986, six years to the day before our visit, when Leonard's son Aaron saw some tourists swimming in an area with a dangerous undertow. Aaron called to them, and one panicked. Aaron organized a human chain.

Though he was not a strong swimmer, he insisted on being at the end, holding hands with a sister. A wave broke the chain, and Aaron was lost. His body was never found. He, too, was decorated for his valour. His posthumous medals hang in his parents' living room.

"It's as well you came today," said Leonard quietly. "I don't do too much on this day."

Leonard is a self-trained scholar, an authority on the history of the Magdalens. When he began his researches, the Magdalens were known to be the site of more than 300 shipwrecks. He went tracking down shipwreck reports in archives, shipping registers, local newspaper accounts, diaries, making four research trips to Europe during the 1980s, almost entirely at his own expense. He has now identified at least 700 wrecks. The true total may be more than 1,000. The Magdalens lie almost astride the great trade route from Europe to the St. Lawrence; as the centre of a rich fishery, as well, they were always surrounded by ships, and until the mid-19th century there were no lighthouses.

"The deadly triangle of the Gulf lies between Cape Anguille, Cape North and Brion Island," says Clark—between the tips of Newfoundland and Cape Breton, and the largest off-lying island of the Magdalen chain. "Most of the wrecks were from the vast armada of lumber ships crossing the Gulf in the mid-19th century. They tried to make two trips to Europe each year, which put them in the ice every spring. One captain in the 1830s reports that three ships sank within a mile of him in an hour, and he saw another sink three leagues away with 700 passengers. There was no requirement for crew lists until 1869, so we have no real idea how many may have drowned."

As at Sable Island, the wrecks are swallowed by the sand and then disgorged briefly when the beach shifts. The day after we visited him, Leonard was going out on the sands with a pair of archaelogists to look at a wreck which had been carbon-dated to the 17th century. He thought he knew which ship it was: it had gone ashore around 1650. Some shipwrecks had comic aspects: in 1937 the crew of a rum runner ran her ashore deliberately, to collect the insurance. The Madelinots converged on it, chopped a hole in her bilge and fished out 5,000 cases of liquor with their boat-hooks, passing them back to their comrades.

"They were the happiest chain gang in the history of the Gulf of St. Lawrence," says Leonard. "My brother was out there. He came back late, and it didn't take an Einstein to figure out how he'd spent his day. The nearest RCMP detachment was in Charlottetown, and they got here a day later. The Mounties found one case of booze, that's all. The rest were hidden so well even a bloodhound couldn't find them. They tried to arrest one Acadian who stuttered, but only when he was drunk. The nearest jail was in Amherst Island, so they let him go for the time being. When they came looking for him, he'd given a false name and he wasn't drunk and didn't stutter, so nobody was ever arrested."

In his research, Leonard has a signal advantage, having lived on the site for nearly 70 years. Cartier's journals mention a spot where there were three hills. No such place now exists, but Leonard remembers that the third hill was razed to build a road. He knows exactly where the shoreline has shifted. Once, researching shipwrecks in a British library, he learned that Britain's greatest authority was actually in the room, working with some American scholars. Clark asked for a meeting, and was told he could have ten minutes at one o'clock. The expert, a retired admiral, was researching a British warship lost in the Magdalens in 1741. When he found out who Clark was, he spent the whole afternoon with him. He also gave Clark an introduction to the National Maritime Museum. The museum was only open five days a week but, said the director, "if you want to work on Saturday, Mr. Clark, just come to the side door and knock three times."

Leonard smiles, pleased at this small recognition of his work. Britain has a tradition of independent scholarship, but Canada does not. Leonard was a fisherman before he joined the RCAF during World War II and became a fisherman again after 16 years in the air force. He later ran a successful vegetable business until his greenhouses burned down. Through it all, history has been his consuming passion, but Canadian support for research is almost entirely restricted to scholars in universities, museums and similar institutions. We literally do not know what to do with researchers like Helen Creighton, Ron Caplan and Leonard Clark. Leonard has published an elegant shipwreck map, based on research which cost him $26,000. It has thus far recouped about $9,000. In his entire career he has received just two small grants with a combined value of $8,000. When he was 62, he went to visit his daughter at the University of New Brunswick and wound up enrolling, too. The next two years were some of the happiest days of his life, but blood clots in his legs forced him to quit in the middle of his third year.

Clark is now writing a history of the Magdalens, and he has turned his attention to their aboriginal people. The conventional wisdom says there were no aboriginal people in the Magdalens, but Leonard is not so sure. After the last ice age, 11,000 years ago, sea level was much lower than now, and the Magdalens may not have been islands. Fluted spearheads from the Paleo-Indians have been found in Debert, Nova Scotia, dating from about 8,000 years ago, and Leonard has found semi-fluted spearheads in the Magdalens. The salt miners have uncovered remnants of large trees, and draggers regularly bring up walrus remains from a point south of Entry Island—perhaps the site of an island later covered by the rising sea. The Mi'kmaqs, "the saltwater people," are known to have ranged far out to sea in huge canoes.

"Haldimand, the British surveyor, was here in 1765," Leonard says. "He reported that the people wore almost no clothes and lived on seafood and shellfish. Is it reasonable to suppose that he was referring to the Acadians who had arrived just two years earlier?"

Haldimand also reported on the "sea cow fishery," the walrus hunt. By then the walrus had already been completely destroyed in Sable Island, the Nova Scotia coast, Prince Edward Island, Anticosti Island, the Mingan Islands, Newfoundland and the St. Lawrence River. They survived—briefly—in the Magdalens.

"They were hunted here from 1590 to 1777," Leonard said. "Probably 200,000 were killed, maybe more. The hide was the thickest known, it made jackets that were proof against arrows. The tusks were ivory, and the blubber was rendered for oil.

"The walrus would haul themselves out on an *échourie*, a flat surface that sloped down into the sea. When one came ashore, he'd tap the one ahead with his tusks, and the whole herd would move up the *échourie*. They could move pretty fast when they had to. Haldimand says their flippers worked like suction cups. He claims he saw one using its tusks to scale a cliff 60 feet high.

"They had good ears and noses, but they couldn't see much beyond 20 yards. The hunters came up behind them when the wind was blowing seaward. They'd take long poles and tap the last one's hindquarters again and again, and they'd move the whole herd uphill. Then they'd slaughter them with muskets at point-blank range. I've got a whole collection of flattened musket balls. As a kid I used to dig them up to make BBs."

By 1798—eight generations ago—all the walrus south of Labrador had been killed.

Every single one.

AURORA

We intended to leave the Magdalens on Sunday, but the amiable northwest wind blew steadily all day Saturday, plucking at our sleeves and our consciences, disturbing our last lunch at the Café de la Grave and pressing against the port bow of the Skoda. The five o'clock forecast predicted clear skies and moderate northwest winds until noon Sunday, with southerlies thereafter. A fair breeze now . . . a hard buck later . . . 70 miles to the fishermen's basin in Souris, PEI . . .

Let's go, let's go!

The battery was low, and we would need the navigation lights. I set up the charger while Lulu put a chicken in the pressure cooker. Nestled among the hulking draggers at the grubby concrete wharf, *Silversark* looked like a toy boat among giants. I phoned Jean-Francois and told him to pick up the Skoda. As the sun went down, the tanbark sails went up, and *Silversark* stole out to sea.

I called the Coast Guard to file a float plan and was greeted with a veritable catechism. *Name of vessel? Master? Hull colour? Anchors? Life jackets? Radios? Emergency beacon? Engines?* "None," I said. Long pause. Estimated time of arrival? I can't estimate that, I said; I don't know what wind we'll have. *Twelve hours? Eighteen hours?* I don't know.

Beyond the lee of the land, the wind filled in, carrying us smoothly over the quiet water. The light faded as we ate the chicken, watching the sickle curve of the islands stretching out around us, a rim of lights where the pale blue and yellow sky plunged into the already dark sea. Ten miles to cross Baie de Plaisance to La Passe: two hours' good sailing, with luck. This time we had a fair wind—and if the car ferry *Lucy Maud Montgomery* could negotiate La Passe, so could we.

Two hours later we entered the channel, rocking from one green flashing buoy to the next, leaving Havre Aubert far to starboard and keeping Entry Island close to port. By midnight we were sailing fast in the open Gulf. The moon rose, full and brilliant, silvering the complex dance of bright waves and dark troughs. Lulu went below. In the high, open night, far off to port, a single moving light marked a fishing vessel. Our masthead light made tracings on the sky, red and green and white. The dark triangles of sailcloth erased and revealed the hard bright stars. The lights of the Magdalens dipped below the waves astern and went out, one after another. The boat and I raced on, doing a solid five knots and better.

When I called Lulu at three o'clock, all that remained were a few street lights and the reassuring flash of the Entry Island lighthouse. We had coffee, and I went gratefully below, already feeling the disorientation of broken sleep. I wriggled into the quarter berth

"Don. I'm sorry to wake you, but you really should see this."

Wake me? Good God, I had hardly closed my eyes. Stinging protests rose to my lips as I clambered on deck.

"Look," said Lulu, waving an arm overhead.

Behind the barely visible lights of the Magdalens, streamers of light blazed into the sky. The whole northern horizon was lit with flickering streaks of pale green.

"Look over there," said Lulu.

To the northwest, over Havre Aubert, a fountain of light pulsed into the night, surging and falling. Another fountain played in the northeast, beyond Entry Island. And now sheets of scudding green light, thin and ethereal as low cirrus clouds, came racing out of the north and over the boat, dissolving into shards and disappearing as they reached the southern darkness. New streamers arced into the sky from the whole northern quadrant of the horizon, meeting in a Gothic arch right over the swinging tricolour at our masthead: the greatest light show on earth, playing with the spar of our vessel.

Weariness overwhelmed me after half an hour, though Lulu watched the lights until daylight. I swung myself below and wriggled back into the quarter berth, lulled by the sound of water rushing past the hull. Under the flickering green lights, *Silversark* hurried on towards Prince Edward Island, a charmed boat bowling noisily over a charmed sea.

When Lulu woke me it was already daylight, and we had the East Point lighthouse in view. The wind had eased, and the speed was down to three knots. We raised the genny, but the wind dropped steadily through the morning. By noon we were still six miles from the lighthouse, and the wind was gone.

Not again!

Yes, again.

One-two-three o'clock, four o'clock, rock. And roll. And rock. *Silversark* tossed about in the leftover sea. Hour by hour we watched the waves fade away to nothing. And still no wind.

During the night, far off, *Lucy Maud Montgomery* had passed us heading north. On Lulu's watch she had passed again, heading south. Now we saw her once more, miles away over the calm water, coming back up the coast from Souris. As she passed between us and the land, we saw another vessel, far smaller, leaving a plume of diesel smoke in the still air and making the characteristic racket of a GM 6-71. We looked at each other. Could it be—?

"The Coast Guard!"

"Looking for us!"

I grabbed the VHF and called. Sure enough, the sound and smoke were coming from the Souris Coast Guard lifeboat.

"Charlottetown called and said you were past your ETA," said the lifeboat skipper. "And *Lucy Maud* reported you out here early this morning, so we thought we'd take a look."

"I didn't *give* an ETA," I snapped. "Charlottetown must have made one up. I told Cap aux Meules it depended on the wind—and any fool can see there hasn't been a breath of wind all day."

"Well, as long as you're all right—"

"We're fine. Thank you. We appreciate your concern."

I snapped the radio off.

"Don!" said Lulu, genuinely shocked. "You didn't have to be rude to them."

"I had a very good mother," I said. "She fretted about me all the time. She died in 1981. I don't need the bloody Coast Guard trying to replace her."

"Okay, okay, but it's not *this* man's fault."

"All right," I said. "I'll apologize to him in Souris. But I'm not filing any more float plans. We chose to come out here for pleasure, in a boat without an engine. It's up to us to take care of ourselves."

"But we might have been in trouble."

"Then we should fix the problem or suffer the consequences. If we're in distress, we make a distress signal. But why on earth should the Government of Canada pay to send out a three-man rescue vessel when we're just bored and tired and frustrated?"

The lifeboat shrank on the southern horizon. *Lucy Maud* shrank on the northern horizon. Little puffs of wind came and went. We crept in towards the coast, looking for shallow water to anchor in. We phoned John and Darla Rousseau. Mark had arrived at their place. We told them we'd be in Souris sometime soon.

Just before dark we heard what sounded like rain. But the sky was cloudless. A few yards away the surface of the water was ruffled as if by wind. *Silversark* drifted closer. Soon the ruffled water was all around us: thousands of tiny silver minnows feeding on the surface, and hundreds of sleek, dark mackerel feeding on them. The tumult must have covered an acre.

At ten o'clock the breeze came in from south of southwest—almost on the nose. Soon we were close-hauled on a course converging with the coast. By midnight the breeze was strong, and we were near the shore. The coast bellies out between East Point and Souris, and we could see the triple-flashing light at

Knight Point over the saddle of a headland. We tacked offshore for half an hour and then fetched the Morse A fairway buoy on one long tack. And now the harbour ritual: checking and rechecking the chart and the *Pilot*, identifying lights, calculating angles, readying fenders. We jogged in slowly under the jumbo alone.

Suddenly a spotlight came on behind us, washing our little vessel with light. It was the Coast Guard again, keeping station off our starboard quarter. What was he doing, and why didn't he pass us? Did he think we were carrying hashish, or Tamils, or out-of-province seed potatoes, or what? At the end of the breakwater, Lulu swung *Silversark* to starboard, ghosting towards the entrance to the boat basin. Did she want the main up, for manoeuvrability? She shook her head and bore away into the basin. The lifeboat came in behind us, and under the lights of the harbour we could see a fishing vessel lashed alongside her. Lulu jibed, hauled in the jumbo sheet and sailed to an empty berth.

"Drop the jumbo," she said. I did, and stepped ashore as she brought the boat gently up against the wharf.

"You're good, Lulu."

"Getting to know this boat." She smiled.

We walked over to see the Coast Guard. The boat they were towing had lost its transmission on Fisherman's Bank, 20 miles south. I asked them to close off the float plan, and apologized for being so abrupt on the VHF. They smiled. They had other things on their mind. It was two o'clock in the morning.

Souris has a fine harbour—two or three wharves, several fishermen's basins, a big berth for the *Lucy Maud*—but we saw little of it. Darla picked us up and took us home. We retrieved the car and had a quick reunion with Mark, who seemed to have grown still taller. But he was enjoying John Andrew and Ariana, Darla's and John's children, so we left them together.

Overheard when Mark and John Andrew were making sandcastles:

MARK: I can't believe I'm doing this.

JOHN ANDREW: Why not, Mark?

MARK: Because this is a kid's game. I'm not a kid any more.

JOHN ANDREW: You're a kid till you're 20. Unless you're Jewish. In that case you're a man at 13.

Having retrieved our car, we set out to find the sonorous sands of Celtic folklore. Basin Head Beach, near Souris, is at the mouth of a tiny river whose entrance is almost completely blocked by a sandbar. Despite this, a fishing boat was moored in the river. A collection of weathered buildings on the bank is the Basin Head Fisheries Museum. A steeply arched cast-iron bridge connects the armoured sides of the estuary.

We crossed the footbridge and sat down on the edge of the dune to eat a sandwich. This is a popular spot, with a couple of hundred people enjoying the sea and the sand while kids swung out on a rope suspended from the bridge and dropped like stones into the river. We walked down the beach. A few hundred yards along, it was almost deserted—and then we heard it, coming from our walking feet:

Chirp. Squawk. Chirp. Squawk. Chirp. Squawk. Chirp. Squawk.

Sonorous sands—or "singing sands," as they are called locally.

We scuffed the sand, drew our heels through it, walked softly and heavily. We played with the sand like kids, listening. Each movement drew a slightly different sound.

So the old Celtic folk-tales were right, after all.

We stopped for coffee in Souris at the Uptown Restaurant, a Chinese café on the main street. There seems to be one Chinese family in every little Maritime town, and they always own a restaurant. The Uptown's menu offered "bumbleberry pie"—a surprising and delicious combination of apple, raspberry, blueberry and rhubarb. The decor featured an aquarium with a fifteen-inch-long silver fish in it—a sinuous, aggressive-looking creature with a delicate fin rippling along the full length of its spine.

"It's a silver arowana," said the petite waitress. "The name means 'silver dragon.' It originates in Malaysia, but I bought it in Toronto last November. It was three inches long then. If I don't put it in a bigger aquarium it won't get any bigger than that, but if I do, it will grow bigger."

"Do you think that would work with kids?" Lulu asked.

The waitress looked at Lulu. The two women were about the same size.

"With our genes, probably not."

Back at the Rousseaus, we picked up John Andrew and Mark and brought them back to Souris. We were sailing in the morning.

I did not feel like sailing in the morning. I was still tired from the long run in from the Magdalens. The weather was hazy and muggy. Murray Harbour, our nominal destination, was 25 miles away—six hours' sailing in average conditions. But the forecast called for southwesterlies, then variables, and then southeasterlies. That sounded to me like a perfect prognosis for another miserable wallow in calms and head winds.

The wind was little more than a zephyr. As we drifted out of the harbour we met an overloaded herring boat coming in, loaded far below its marks, torpid and unsteady. Herring are a scaly, slippery little fish, which slither around like a liquid in the hold. This free-surface effect destabilizes the boat by accentuating any change in its trim. That—plus the inevitable voracity of a fisherman in a good school of fish—makes herring so dangerous that some fishermen's wives will not allow their husbands to fish them. This boat had its catch in boxes to reduce the free-surface effect—but it looked precarious all the same.

We rowed a few strokes to get past the herring boat and hobbled slowly seaward on the feeble breeze, making wide, shallow tacks outside the harbour. John Andrew toured the boat with Mark, pronounced every feature "cool," and fell seasick. He took a Gravol, squirmed into a quarter berth and slept for three hours.

This end of the Island is hilly and wooded, indented by numerous bays, drained by several small rivers and flecked with islands. The wind slowly built, and we tacked in and out of Rollo Bay and Bay Fortune, an idyllic little estuary much favoured as a summer home by wealthy Americans. We crept past Eglington Bay and picked up more wind in Howe Bay. A couple of hard puffs persuaded me to lower the genny and go with the three red working sails. In Boughton Bay the wind steadied from the southwest, and suddenly we were slicing along on a close reach, just clearing the end of Boughton Island and opening the broad expanse of Cardigan Bay, fed by three rivers, with the fishing harbour of Georgetown on a point between them.

John Andrew took the helm for a few minutes, enjoying the tremble of the tiller. He and Mark had been watching an ecology commercial on television: it became the refrain of the day.

"No garbage on a boat, b'y. Throw it overboard."

"Where does it go, Da?"

"Awaaayyyy . . ."

It was mid-afternoon, and I had long since decided that we should stop at Georgetown, another cluster of lovely old houses on an 18th-century grid of streets by the waterfront. The Irvings had taken over the local shipyard, and it was said to be booming. Good news, if true. Despite its imposing stone courthouse and stately churches, Georgetown looks like a town whose people quit before finishing it—but Homefree Productions runs a repertory theatre in the King's Playhouse all summer long, and I could have been interested in an evening of theatre.

On the other hand, the wind had become alluring. Blowing steadily off the land, it was giving us a brisk close reach in flat water. Should we waste a fair wind, only ten or twelve miles from Murray Harbour? Lulu was napping, but Mark and John Andrew had their sea-legs and were having a good time together.

"Lulu," I called, "we've got a good breeze. I'm going on to Murray Harbour."

"All *right!*"

She came on deck, grinning. By now we had picked up a favourable tide, and *Silversark* was hoofing it. As we closed the outer shore of Panmure Island, the Loran was showing five to six knots. Mark took the helm as we approached the buoy at Graham Point, and now the Loran was giving us more than six knots. John Andrew braced himself below, reading it out:

"It says 6.5 . . . 6.7 . . . 6.6 . . . 6.5 . . .

Would we touch seven? We had never done that before.

"John Andrew, I'm going to come so close to that buoy you'll be able to touch it!" called Mark, the wind blowing his hair to leeward, a huge grin on his face. John Andrew hesitated, torn.

"Go on deck," I said. "I'll watch the speed."

"Not too close, Mark," said Lulu. "Not at this speed."

I gazed at the Loran: 6.7 … 6.8 … 6.7 … 6.9!

"Six point nine!" I called. And then, as we rocketed past the buoy, *"Seven! Seven!"*

We were approaching Murray Harbour obliquely, and now the wind slackened, though the current still bore us onward. To starboard was the long sand spit of Poverty Beach, crowded with gulls and cormorants. The water was shallow—30 feet or less, and sometimes as little as ten. John Andrew went to the sounder, Lulu to the helm and Mark to the cross trees. Mark picked up the harbour's features, one by one, and I checked them off against the chart: the lighthouse on Oldstore Point, the houses, the fairway buoy, the channel markers. I could see Johnny Williams's boat shop on the hill.

"Wind is gone," I said.

"Where'd it go, Da?" said John Andrew.

"Awaaayyyy … " came the chorus from the masthead.

The broad shallow basin of Murray Harbour is the shared estuary of five small rivers, almost closed by Poverty Beach. The main fishermen's basin is Beach Point, just inside the narrow gap in the beach. A mile farther in, the estuary of the South River opens to port, navigable until it reaches the village of Murray Harbour. A mile and a half farther on, the channel between the shore and the islands passes the Fox River—too shallow to be useful—and divides. To port is the Murray River. The channel to starboard opens into the Mink and Greek rivers—favourite gunkholes of Island sailors—and a wide sheet of water enclosed by Poverty Beach and the Murray islands.

It had been 18 years since I sailed in here on *Hirondelle*, but it looked the same: idyllic, almost dreamy, the dark green islands floating on the water, the sinuous waterways curling into the low forested hills, a perfect setting for an Arthur Ransome novel. If I were exiled from Cape Breton, I thought, I would look for a house in Murray Harbour. On that first visit I had met Johnny Williams. This time I could only visit his grave. But this would always be his harbour.

We had seen enough of rock-rimmed fishermen's basins for now; I wanted to moor in the village of Murray Harbour, if we could get there. But could we? *Silversark* had just enough wind now to keep the sails asleep, and it was chiefly the current which carried us onward. We eased through the entrance, wavering this way and that as the whirlpools shoved us sideways, greeting a line of fishing boats both overtaking us and meeting us.

"Lot of mosquitoes up here," Mark said.

"Here, too," said Lulu, swatting herself.

A boatload of happy people slowed down and circled behind us.

"Heading for the Harbour?" called the skipper.

"Yeah, if we can."

"Watch the buoy where the channel forks. Don't hug it too close. There's an unmarked sandbank in there."

He waved and headed out.

The boom swung over, and the mainsail filled. A little draft of easterly wind, just for us, perfect to take us in.

I looked at Lulu. Lulu looked at me.

"Thank you, Johnny," said Lulu.

THE

BONNIE LASS

O' BON

ACCORD

You may recall the term "constitution," though most Canadians seem willing to forget it. While we had been disporting ourselves in the Gulf, enjoying Canada, phalanxes of politicians and officials had been flying around attempting to rearrange it. One such official was my brother David, who was now in PEI working on what became known as the Charlottetown Accord, and we kept the cellular phones busy trying to arrange a meeting.

In the meantime, we went to Beach Point to pay our respects to the Williams family.

In 1974, when I sailed into Murray Harbour in my schooner (with a dead engine), the wind had almost died, and Ernie Williams had towed me in behind his garish power boat, *Pink Pullet*. That evening, his father Johnny had sailed a 30-foot ketch out to meet me. He had built the boat himself, and he handled it like a daysailer, tacking and jibing around my schooner as he chatted.

Later that evening he flashed his headlights under the range lights at Machon's Point, and I rowed ashore for a tour of the community. At the time there were no auto-safety inspections in PEI. Johnny was driving a terrible old red Anglia, and every time he made a right turn, the left front door fell off. Johnny would stop, back up, retrieve the door and slap it into place, talking all the while about the community, the fishing industry, the boats he had built and the boats he wanted to build.

He built the first trimaran in the Maritimes, a boat fast enough to throw a rooster tail up behind it in the right wind. He built fishing boats for a living and yachts for pleasure, and he had the restlessness of mind which marks an artist. He was planning to build a 45-foot motorsailer for his retirement, and he did. *Lily* was a sweet and tranquil vessel, with her dark green hull, buff decks and white spars. She didn't sail well to windward, but that's why she had a big Perkins diesel. She was strip planked like all his boats, and she had an interior so spacious that Johnny didn't bother building his furniture in: he simply toted two couches below and let it go at that.

I got to know him fairly well over the years. He and Annie never allowed their children to fight: brothers and sisters, they said, should help one another. In later life, that was a strength for all of them. When Charley became a dentist, for instance, Johnny and his sons held a building bee, and in a few days erected an office with an apartment above it. He served a term in the legislature, but I can't recall that we ever talked politics. I saw a lifesaving award on his living room wall—he had jumped overboard to save someone, back in the 1940s—but I can't recall that he ever talked about that, either.

He was an undistinguished but enthusiastic fiddler, and we both admired the Scottish compositions of J. Scott Skinner. Once, when I was visiting him, I mentioned a particularly haunting melody called "The Bonnie Lass o' Bon Accord," which I had just encountered in a new LP by John Allan Cameron. Johnny smiled and dug through his record collection till he found an ancient LP of Skinner playing his own compositions. He put the record on the stereo, and the melody flooded the room. He passed me the record jacket. On the back was a blurry photograph of the young woman for whom Skinner had written the tune, the Bonnie Lass o' Bon Accord herself.

Johnny loved speed under sail, but he understood cruising in the same way as the Water Rat: the purpose of a cruising boat was to go places and meet people, to learn and explore and have fun. After *Lily* was launched, Johnny would sail to Cape Breton every year or two, stopping at D'Escousse for a day or so before heading into the Bras d'Or Lakes, usually accompanied by a quiet friend named Vic Brooks. I began building *Silversark* long before he laid the keel for *Lily*, and I launched her long after. Johnny would come up to the shop and offer suggestions and assistance; several bits of *Silversark*'s hardware are gifts from Johnny.

The last time he came to D'Escousse, *Silversark* had been launched and Johnny came sailing with us. We were still wary of the boat; we had never built one before, after all. Johnny took the helm, put her through her paces and said she was just fine. His approval gave an enormous boost to our confidence in her—and all our later experience told us he was right.

And then, one year, *Lily* came sailing into D'Escousse and Johnny was not aboard. Ernie was sailing his father's boat, as he has ever since. Johnny had died of cancer the previous winter.

This trip we went up to the house to visit Annie, who keeps herself busy crocheting, knitting, quilting, hooking rugs. She's in a dozen organizations, and can't stand cards or bingo; she'd "as soon have a poke in the eye with a sharp stick" as go to a bingo game. Her daughter Lily lives in Beach Point, and so does her son Kenny, who now builds boats in Johnny's old shop.

We went down to the shop and were shocked. A new fishing boat stood just outside the shop, long and slender, with clear spruce planking and a cedar ceiling. The man beside it smiled and said hello, and he looked and sounded uncannily like Johnny. Sometime during the past 20 years, Kenny Williams had grown 20 years older. He was building the boat for his son-in-law. When I remarked on its quality, the son-in-law smiled and said that Johnny was good, but he thought Kenny was better.

Johnny is buried in a tiny cemetery a few yards away, overlooking the harbour entrance. His simple stone slab lies flat in the ground, among the graves of several generations of Williamses. He lies within the triangle of land marked off by his home, his boat shop and the wharf: the triangle of his life.

The Charlottetown conference was still going on, but David could free himself for dinner—and maybe for the evening, if they made good progress in the afternoon. While the premiers went for a barbecue at Joe Ghiz's home, David and two colleagues came to Murray River. We had a drink in the cockpit. David has an agreeably rumpled academic demeanour, but his colleagues were fast-track civil servants in sharp suits and brilliant shoes. Just getting aboard was an encounter with a new reality. They were grateful to be there: they felt they were possibly the only people in the entire conference to gain even a glimpse of the real, unofficial Prince Edward Island. They had been living for months in a strange artificial world, a form of virtual reality: office-to-cab-to-plane-to-cab-to-conference-centre-to-cab-to-plane-again. Where were you? *I don't know: someone said Winnipeg.*

And now, for a few minutes, they were sitting in a boat in an Island river, with rum in their hands, the smell of fish in their nostrils, the cry of gulls in their ears, red sandbars, green and white birch trees and a whole sensuous world going on all around them. Michael Mendelson had an uncle in Glace Bay and had some experience of the Maritimes, but for Stephen Bornstein it was all brand new.

"I didn't know the water was warm enough for swimming down here," he said. "And the beaches are amazing. They rival the ones in Cape Cod!"

The conference was going to reconvene that evening after all, so we hurried across the bridge to Brehaut's Restaurant—a warm, homey little place with a take-out and café downstairs and a dining room up. The conference was going fairly well, they said: an agreement seemed to be within reach, chiefly because all the players had looked into the abyss represented by failure and had drawn back from it. They ate in a serious, businesslike way, dropped money on the table, leaped back in their car and roared off to Charlottetown.

Lulu and I looked at each other. It had been faintly like a visit from a flying saucer. When I paid the waitress, I mentioned that our friends were involved in the constitutional conference.

"I kinda thought so," she said. "They didn't seem like people from around here."

In Buddhist thought, says E.F. Schumacher, work has three functions: to give a person "a chance to utilize and develop his faculties; to enable him to overcome his egocentredness by joining with other people in a common task; and to bring forth the goods and services needed for a becoming existence." In the 1970s, many young idealists seeped into eastern PEI with some such possibility in view, and the society they found there made them feel they had come to the right place. Like Farley Mowat, they saw the Western attitude towards other people and the natural world as ultimately suicidal, and they were determined that their lives, at least, would not add to the problem. They were interested in things like organic gardening, owner-built housing, crafts, horse logging, wood heat and communal living. They dissented not only with their voices, but with their lives.

John Rousseau and Darla Thompson were just such a couple. I had known them 20 years earlier, when they were students at the University of New Brunswick and I taught there. Over the years, they worked at fishing, tree planting, subsistence farming, blacksmithing, construction. They built three houses: one burned, one was lost in the collapse of a partnership, and the third gradually evolved into a comfortable, environmentally friendly homestead with a marvellous view over miles of woodland to the waters of Northumberland Strait. John became an expert renovator of chimneys, for which there is an adequate market in a community which still heats with wood.

There is a sanity about their lives which always impresses me. John told me one autumn that he faced the winter with equanimity; he would not have much work, but they had no regular bills except for telephone and electric power. The freezer was stuffed with chickens and vegetables they had raised; the woodshed was full of wood; they had plenty of preserves in the larder and homemade beer in the cellar; he had some good books to read and some satisfying work to do on the house over the winter.

Every autumn, the Rousseaus and their circle get together for

Thanksgiving dinner. We joined them one year. They played touch football with their kids, went for a long walk in the vivid hardwood forest, ate well, made music. After 20 years, the people of the 1960s were still different from their neighbours. Wry, self-aware, ironic, well-travelled, they had unusual skills and understandings from their university years. And now, in their 40s, they were applying those skills again, having paid their dues to their own value system. Mike Nicholson had become a counsellor in Montague, Don Harris was doing computer-based research at the university, Darla was teaching full-time. But they were still living in the houses they had built, and in many ways their lives closely resembled the traditional lives of their communities: close families, close friends, hard work, practical common sense. Yesterday's hippies had become an instrument through which rural life could adapt to a new age of knowledge-based enterprise and global trade.

With that thought in mind, I took John's advice and went to visit Greg Keith, who holds 13 acres of aquaculture leases in the Brudenell River, not far from Georgetown. The leases run 20 years, though the Minister of Fisheries and Oceans can cancel them on 90 days' notice. Nearby is an exclusive riverfront resort and a small island, which is actually a pioneer cemetery. Greg is a fortyish man who could pass equally easily for a chicken farmer or an anthropologist. He had just come back from the Canadian Aquaculture Producers Council, preparing for consultations with no fewer than 19 federal departments.

"I didn't know there *were* that many," he said, shoving his boxy, industrial-strength fiberglass boat off the beach.

The process of mussel farming starts in the spring, when Greg puts out two hundred feet of rope supported by 100 buoys. Each buoy has an eight-foot piece of old lobster line attached to it. Mussel spat are free-swimming, looking for a place to lodge, and the lobster line is perfect.

By October, the seed mussels are an inch long. Greg raises the lobster lines and takes them to the wharf, where he transfers masses of young mussels into a monofilament nylon mesh tube— a "sock"—about eight feet long. The socks go back in the water, and there they stay for 15 to 24 months. By that point the mussels should be at least two inches in length, which is market size.

"You're always running two crops," says Greg, lifting up

socks and inspecting the mussels. "You've always got seed mussels and markets growing at the same time." It sounds simple, but a whole set of environmental variables can affect the growth of the mussels, and even their survival—water temperature, acidity, nutrients, pollution. Greg must also be constantly alert for predators—crabs, lobsters and particularly starfish, who can clean out a mussel bed completely.

"Small starfish can actually be helpful, though," he says. "They clean small mussels off the socks, where they tend to loosen and weaken the market mussels."

Market mussels are worth 45 cents a pound, delivered to the wharf—but the price hasn't risen since 1985. Greg Keith now harvests about 150,000 pounds a year—about $67,500 worth, which barely covers his costs. As with most businesses, the key to profit is to hold costs down while production goes up.

"I used to do all the work myself, hauling the socks by hand, but I finally bought some hydraulic equipment and hired some help. You have to. But labour is a big cost, and UIC is my greatest competitor. We have people needing medical attention and counselling because of the stress of working 14 weeks. They've never worked 14 weeks in their lives. Ten weeks is a year's work around here. With the best will in the world, I think we've created a huge problem with UIC."

Greg Keith is a marine biologist by profession, with a good deal of experience in Nova Scotia and Newfoundland as well as PEI. Back on the beach, he reflected on the difference between aquaculture and the traditional fishery.

"There's been some conflict between aquaculture operators and traditional fishermen, particularly on the mainland, and that's partly a matter of mind-set," he said. "The traditional fisherman is really a hunter. He goes back to the earliest forms of human organization. He goes out and catches the wild animal to feed the tribe. It's chancy and risky, but that's part of being a hunter. But people like me have a completely different outlook. I'm really not like a fisherman at all. I'm a cross between a farmer and a scientist. And that's at the root of those problems."

True enough. Back in Murray Harbour, the fishermen were bringing in boatloads of herring and groundfish—and now, in late August, some of them were getting some tuna. One boat brought in two tuna one day while we were there; one dressed out at 300 pounds, the other at 700. With prices running at $14 a pound and up, as one fisherman noted, it was "a pretty good day's pay. A day like that would pretty well make your summer."

I had noticed a big steel-mesh trap, like an enormous lobster trap, lying in the water on the slipway. As I passed, two men were wrestling it ashore. What was in it, silver and squirming?

"Eels, b'y. Want to buy some?"

"I don't think so. They're not a big favourite of mine."

"Boil 'em first and then bake 'em. Some good that way."

"Maybe so, but . . ."

"They're a delicacy, you know. Make your old joint stand right to attention. Add an inch to it."

A good selling proposition, unquestionably. But I didn't buy the eels.

The night before we left, a car drove up on the wharf and a smiling man with a grey beard came down to the boat, carrying a bottle of rum. It was Jim MacNeill, whom I'd been trying to reach for days. A native of the isle of Barra, MacNeill has been publishing a weekly newspaper in Montague, the *Eastern Graphic*, for 20 years, winning a bucket of awards and serving the eastern end of the Island with an independent-minded brand of journalism which is all too rare anywhere. With the success of the *Eastern Graphic*, MacNeill expanded: he now publishes the *West Prince Graphic*, to serve the western end of the Island, and also *Vacation Times*, *Island Farmer* and *Atlantic Fish Farming*.

Jim moved into aquaculture publishing in a very tentative way when he found that nobody else was publishing anything directed at this rapidly growing industry. *Atlantic Fish Farming* had quickly gone national and was threatening to become the tail that wagged the *Graphic* dog. Its success led MacNeill to organize a small regional trade show; when the trade show drew participants from as far away as the Pacific Northwest, MacNeill blinked. The national aquaculture organization was planning a convention in PEI for 1993, and they had asked MacNeill to organize the associated trade show. So now he was in trade shows.

"I must say I enjoy publishing a special issue for BC from Montague, PEI," he said, "especially when BC is ten years ahead of us in aquaculture. But you know, it's already a ten-million-dollar industry here on the Island, and it's a hundred million in New Brunswick—it's twice the size of the New Brunswick lobster fishery, although nobody seems to have noticed that. And of course the feds are very interested, because it's export-oriented and labour-intensive, and it has lots of opportunities for creating value-added products."

Jim was an ardent opponent of the fixed link and had written 46 articles against it in one six-week period.

"It's based on some very fishy arguments and even some downright lies," he said. "But it's one of the four or five great engineering projects *in the world*, and for a lot of these guys it's their chance at immortality. The environmental panel rejected it because it would retard the dissipation of the ice—and thus the spring—by one to two weeks. Once every ten years the ice stays till the end of May, and the bridge would hold it there until mid-June, with disastrous implications for agriculture, tourism and the fishery.

"There are all kinds of things—they make their wind-speed projections based on winds at the shore. But the thing will be the height of an electrical transmission tower, and the winds are much stronger that far above the ground. On top of that the ferry captains will tell you that the winds are ten to fifteen knots higher in the middle of the Strait. They don't seem to take these things seriously, but there are bridges in Britain which have to be closed completely now and then because the winds blow vehicles right off the bridge.

"And you know, the ferries aren't even a problem. It seems like a big deal to outsiders, but Islanders just live with it and work around it. We get some of our printing done in Amherst, Nova Scotia, and we never have any problem with the ferries, never."

We talked about mutual friends, and about the quality of life in Kings County. Inevitably, we talked about Johnny Williams. Jim had known him well. Indeed, he had owned one of Johnny's boats.

"Johnny had an almost scholarly interest in vessels and design and anything to do with boats," Jim said. "He wasn't just inter-

ested in his own problems, he was interested in the whole subject. That may be one of the marks of a great boat builder. He
reminded me of another fellow around here, a moonshiner, who
drops by the office two or three times a year with a sample of his
latest shine and wants my opinion on its quality. I asked him
something about the process one time, and he responded with a
history of distillation from the ancient Chinese to the present
day. He probably has a Grade Four education. Johnny was like
that. He really knew his subject. He loved it.''

"To Johnny," said Lulu, raising her glass. "He's been a presence in this whole voyage.''

STEERING

FOR THE

PALACE

Six in the morning. Just daylight, and barely a trace of wind. The little cutter glides out through the narrow inlet, drawn by the ebbing tide. The couple in the cockpit talk quietly, sipping their morning coffee. As the ship frees herself from the land, the breeze strengthens. In half an hour she reaches the fairway buoy. She lifts and swings on long, leftover rollers. At seven she passes the Cape Bear buoy and turns southeast for Cape George and the Strait of Canso.

The wind strengthens. This is the first time this crew has ever deliberately sailed when strong winds were forecast and small craft warnings were issued. Southwesterlies and westerlies, 20 to 25 knots. But the gale is going our way. Why not?

The wind rises steadily. We douse the jumbo and reef the main, douse the main and raise the jumbo to run under two

headsails, then douse the jumbo and roll towards Cape George
under the jib alone. Dark blue water and clear blue skies, and
steep choppy seas tipped with foaming white. The Island fading
rapidly astern, and the hump of Cape George slowly rising off the
starboard bow. Off to port, we can see high land faint against the
sky: the Cape Breton coast, the shoreline of home.

This is a noisy, surging passage. The wind moans in the
rigging, the bow wave roars as the little ship tramples down a sea.
With a hiss and a bang, whitecaps explode under the curve of the
bilge, driving spray up in the air and into the sails. The wind
dries it immediately, and the boom, the mast, the side of the
dinghy are soon encrusted with crystals of salt. The dinghy
lashings slacken under the constant movement. I creep forward
to tighten them, hanging on hard and keeping my lifeline
attached. The ship rolls to windward as the waves pass under her,
then back again to leeward as the next wave picks her up. A hatful
of water slops over the rail into the cockpit.

"Eee-ha!" shouts Lulu.

At ten-thirty I relieve her at the helm. It's a thrilling ride, the
red jib taut, the boat leaping forward. At this rate we'd make
Cape George at noon, the Canso Causeway at four o'clock. Math-
ematically, at least, we could make Isle Madame tonight. Down
below the Loran is giving 5.3, 5.8, 5.6, sometimes six knots—
just with the jib. Cape George looms up ahead. Prince Edward
Island is a faint blue memory astern on the horizon.

We run in under the lee of Cape George, the lighthouse high
on the cliffs above us, a fishing boat rolling viciously near the
shore. *Silversark*'s speed drops to an easy lope, a welcome respite
after an athletic morning. I grab some snack food and pass it
around—apples, crackers, juice.

The wind hits like a fist as we clear Cape George. We had a notion of picking up the Waylings in Ballantyne's Cove and sailing
home with them as crew, but there's no chance of that today, and
this is not a breeze to waste. *Silversark* puts her shoulder into it
again, trembling, roaring, tearing across St. George's Bay.

My job is to navigate and worry. Mark's job is to fight off
seasickness with Gravol and a snooze. Lulu's job is to point the
boat and go fast. I am below when a gust of wind drives the boat
down on her ear and makes her swing up to windward. Are we in
danger of broaching? Should the jib come down in favour of the

jumbo? I look out the hatch. In her white oilskins and Tilley hat, Lulu has both hands on the laminated tiller, hauling it right up to her chest, forcing the boat back on her downwind course. She looks down at my face in the companionway. I cock my head, questioning. A huge grin splits her face.

"Life doesn't get much better than this!" she cries.

My trick at the helm again. The sun is overhead, and the wind is stronger than ever. The sea is like boiling mercury, with the bay waves coming in from all directions to meet the main wave train, like secondary chords against the dominant. They peak, flatten, heap up together. Every now and then a big one smacks us hard, throwing dollops of spray over the glistening foredeck. The twin towers of the church at Havre Boucher detach themselves from the haze. I pick up the white spike of the North Canso lighthouse, the big white church at Creignish on the Cape Breton shore. Cape George is melting behind us. We can see right into the Strait of Canso now.

The sea diminishes in the shelter of Cape Jack and goes flat as we enter the Strait. The breeze falls off, though occasional angry puffs whirl around the headlands, ruffling the water and hurling us forward. I hoist the jumbo again. We can see the causeway, the bridge, the entrance to the canal. I call ahead to the lock master. We are going to come into that canal as though we had been shot from a gun. Let us not ricochet off those tall concrete walls, or smack our bow into the steel gates, or drive under the bridge. Talking on the radio, the lock master is remarkably calm. He will open the north gates as we pass the last transmission line and have a crew ready to catch our lines.

As we charge down on the canal I stand on the foredeck, tense as a hunting cat. Mark puts fenders down over the port side. We are flying along, but it seems to take forever to get there. I drop the jib under the transmission line, and we forge into the entrance under the jumbo. Too fast. Mark drops the jumbo and we throw our lines ashore. The lock crew snubs them up, and *Silversark* swings heavily against the high canal wall, heaving in the waves chasing in behind us. I glance astern: the north gates are already swinging closed. I note the time: four o'clock on the button.

We climb the steel ladder to the canal bank, stretch our legs, go to the washroom, rinse the salt off our faces. When we come out, the gates and the bridge are open. *Silversark* tosses restlessly to the wind in her rigging. You are not supposed to sail in canals, but there is no holding her back anyway. I raise the jumbo. Mark fends off. The lock crew tosses the lines aboard and we are gone again, the stern anchor scraping briefly on the concrete as we push off and get her moving.

Through the open gates and past the bridge with the lines of waiting cars, the curious faces looking down at us, the waves and shouts. The wind is howling down the Strait, blowing the brims of our hats flat against our heads, making the jumbo thunder and chatter. Mark and I are coiling lines, bringing the fenders back aboard. By the time we look up we are almost to Port Hawkesbury, and the wind seems stronger than ever.

A quick shouted conference. Too much wind, too late in the day? Stop overnight in Hawkesbury? No, sail on! Go for Arichat! We can almost see the Isle Madame archipelago. In a pinch we can anchor in Bear Cove or somewhere in Lennox Passage.

The wind eases quickly as we sail past Hawkesbury. By the time we pass Point Tupper we have full sail again in calm water— a lovely summer afternoon, picture-postcard cruising with occasional hard, squally puffs. As we clear the Strait at Eddy Point, the main body of the breeze reaches us once more, and we drop the main again, making a quick, lunging reach out into Chedabucto Bay under the two headsails.

The shores of home. Janvrin's Island: could we make out Betty Peterson's house on the hilltop? Steer wide of the rocks and shoals off Crichton Island, behind West Arichat. Look, the West Arichat church, and the ruff of houses along the crest of Bodet's Point where Lulu's grandparents lived, long before her birth.

The wind drops. Up with the mainsail. The sun is falling, and the land is stained by shadows. We'll enter Arichat Harbour through Crid Passage, a narrow, rock-encumbered gap at the end of Jerseyman's Island. The Jerseyman's Island lighthouse is a fixed red glow against the shore now, directly in front of the twin towers of Notre Dame de l'Assomption, the magnificent cathedral church built in 1838 when Cape Breton Island was the Diocese of Arichat. It's a natural range, leading us in clear of all the shoals. Just off the range is the bishop's palace, the only one in Cape Breton, later a hospital, now Ivo Winter's stately law office. When we get close, we'll steer for the palace, just shaving the island.

It's dark now. Mark is at the sounder again, calling out the depths. Plenty of water. The shore is bold right up to the island. The wind is coming back, a nice steady breeze. I stand at the bow, conning. *Steer for the palace, Lulu. Just like that.* The red light comes closer and starts mounting into the night sky. We are very close. There's the sound of the surf on the island beach, the momentary flashes of grey from the breakers. *Steady. Hold your course.* The red light is abeam, towering over the mast. *Make your turn now, nice and easy. Steer for the liquor store or the bank, somewhere down that way. Mark, let's get some sail off her, we're coming in too fast.*

A scramble in the dark to furl the main and jib. Fenders and dock lines ready. Where's the wharf? Mark goes below and gets the spotlight. It's a very dark night, no moon at all, the shore like black paint with white and amber pinpoints of light. We are quite close when we see the wharf and drop the jumbo. As we slip past the high pilings, we are going much too fast. I am ready to scramble with a line, but a man is standing on the dock. He catches the line and wraps it around a bollard. *Silversark* comes to an abrupt, wrenching halt, pitching and rolling against the dock.

No good. We'll have to work her around to the back of the wharf. I climb ashore, and suddenly there are men all around. The shift is just ending at Premium Seafoods, and the men have seen the boat come in. Here's Edgar Samson, Premium's bright young proprietor, and Aubrey Brushett, who's married to Lulu's cousin, and Arthur Boudreau, the father of a school friend of Mark's. A dozen hands to warp the little ship in beside Newman Skinner's big steel dragger. Acadian voices, and laughter in the dark: the voices of home.

2100: Secured, Arichat, I wrote in the log. Eighty-three miles in 15 hours, in round figures, including the transit of the lock. An average speed of more than 5.5 knots, most of it under the jib alone.

Not bad, little ship, little crew. Not bad at all.

As we walked ashore we could feel Isle Madame fitting itself around us like a glove. The first and last of our Acadian islands, the centre of the known and unknown universe.

We hitched a lift down the long waterfront street to Lulu's brother's home. Chris is a chef by trade, and he puttered around the stove, a perfect audience for three people babbling about a miraculous day. In a moment, excellent coffee appeared before us, followed a few minutes later by a glass of wine and then— wholly unexpectedly—a succulent plate of vermicelli with zucchini, tomatoes, onions, garlic and herbs.

"After a day like that you must be hungry," he said, lifting a glass of wine. "Cheers. Welcome home."

His wife Danick joined us for a snack, having settled the four kids. Someone knocked on the door: it was Everett and Ann Delorey, our neighbours from D'Escousse. Home, home, home.

Chris drove us back to the boat. Lulu and Mark went below; I took a turn on the wharf with my pipe, enjoying Arichat. It was the right place for our last stop. Jerseyman's Island had been the headquarters of the Jersey trading empire which once covered the gulf we had been exploring. In those days, Arichat was an important town, a town of judges and bishops, publishers and professors; St. Francis Xavier University was founded here, in 1853. This town once built big ships and traded with the world. Well, it could do something similar again: the people were no different, and perhaps things were opening up after a century of stagnation. That was the gist of the Urgent Conversation.

Isle Madame has its own cadre of savvy young entrepreneurs, and their numbers seem to be growing—Greg Boucher, our fuel-oil dealer, whose chain of Beaver service stations now stretches into New Brunswick; Herman Samson, who started in fiberglass boat building and is expanding into other ventures; Edgar Samson, who buys freezing equipment for his fish plant in Denmark and flies off to the Orient looking for new markets.

In the end the Urgent Conversation makes me optimistic, because it assumes that when we figure out what to do, we will be ready and able to do it. "Ready" implies self-confidence, which seems to be growing; "able" probably requires a flexible, dynamic and responsive educational and research structure, which may be much more difficult to achieve.

I was encouraged by the attitude we had seen everywhere: the sense that our crisis was also an opportunity, and that it would be solved not by some large outside agency like a government or a corporation, but by our own intelligence and imagination and courage. That is why a myth like *Pélagie-la-Charette* is so important, for it provides a model of struggle and success, a moral and political standard to attain.

One way or another the Maritimes would be all right; our restructuring was probably less wrenching than that of Ontario. The truly ominous issue was not regional and not economic: it was environmental. We had sailed a ravaged sea, and even the empty sea was only a symbol. The forests were being clear-cut, topsoil was eroding from Prince Edward Island, the pattering on our decks was acid rain. Is there an inherent conflict between the economy and the enviroment? Can we learn to care for the planet the way sailors care for their ship? If we fail the ship, the ship will fail us—and our record is far from reassuring.

It was appropriate that Chris had given us such a welcome at the finale of this Acadian voyage, for the family I had joined by marriage had long, deep roots in this dignified old dowager of a town. Rene Thériau, the ancestor who was captured in New Brunswick during the Grande Dérangement, had been imprisoned in Halifax, but had settled in Arichat by 1768. His descendants had been Isle Madame seamen and skippers for more than 200 years.

In this long chain of ancestors—a dozen generations, listed for Lulu just recently by Stephen White of the Centre d'Etudes Acadiennes at the Université de Moncton—one name stood out for us. Lulu's great-great-grandmother had been born here in Arichat on September 4, 1842. When we saw her name we both laughed aloud at the vibrant echo from Bouctouche.

Her name was Pélagie Thériault.

Hue-ho the oxen! North is up that way!

EPILOGUE:

CLOSING

THE

CIRCLE

Chris let go our lines at eight o'clock on the crisp and sunny morning of September 1, with five-year-old Aschaelle waving from the wharf. *Silversark* plunged out into the rollers coming in before a brisk southwesterly. We tacked down to the harbour's southern entrance and out past the bald, rocky point of Cape Auget, leaving Cerberus Rock and the wreckage of the tanker *Arrow* to starboard. Two decades ago, this water and these shores had been coated with Bunker C in the worst oil spill in Canadian history. Just yesterday a yacht bound for the Magdalens had split a plank on that same rock and limped into Arichat to be beached.

Outside the harbour we bore away for Green Island, past the entrance to Petit de Grat, Isle Madame's largest village and the one most conscious of its Acadian character. Rolling downwind in the sunlight, we fell in with a school of dolphins going up the strait, jumping and capering. Among them was a big silver fish with a wide tail, jumping high: a tuna, pursuing the same prey.

The wind eased as we slipped between Green Island and Isle Madame, and eased further as we passed Little Anse, a tiny village facing straight to the open Atlantic. Mark came forward with me to bend on the genny, but the wind piped up again as we cleared the tall, narrow island of Gros Nez at the mouth of Rocky Bay, which cuts deep into Isle Madame's east coast. Mark took the helm, sprawled in the sunlight as *Silversark* hissed along through the tiny waves.

This was holiday sailing—relaxed, warm, steady. The familiar landmarks of home were passing by, places rich with memories and associations: the Winter farm at the tip of Beak Point, the Mauger farm and the Samson farm at Cape La Ronde, the crumbling headland which once held a lighthouse and a light keeper's home. The keeper had been Lulu's great-uncle, and for a while her father had lived there with him. I could see St. Peter's, where Lulu's brother Terry lives. I looked around me at the stainless steel work he did for *Silversark*—the pushpit, the lifelines, the husky stanchion bases which other sailors often envy. Terry is a finikin about safety, and his work has always kept us safe.

A long reef smothered in breakers stretched out from Cap La Ronde, and Mark steered out to seaward, keeping clear. Inside Lennox Passage we strapped the sails in and made a long tack almost to River Bourgeois. There was the big silver roof of Farley Mowat's barn, the church at River Bourgeois, the beacon on bald green Ile Ouetique. We tacked close to the shore and fetched the outer buoy of D'Escousse Harbour with the next tack. And here we crossed our outbound track, closing the circle. We had touched four provinces in seven weeks. Almost absent-mindedly, we had circumnavigated Entry Island, Isle Madame and Prince Edward Island. We had seen old friends and made a lot of new ones. We had tested ourselves and our boat: when a larger challenge came along, we would be ready.

As we turned into the zig-zag channel we saw Chris's van streaking down the hill. Harbour drill again: dock lines ready, fenders over. Three quick tacks, and we were in the harbour, ghosting up to our own wharf under the jumbo. The big blue house on the shore had never looked better.

Friends and neighbours were waving. Chris took our lines, along with Ernie Gurney and Joey Kernick. The sails came down, and *Silversark* settled back on her mooring lines.

"Want a beer?" said Lulu. "I think we've earned a drink."

That evening, when Lulu and I were unloading the boat, I pulled a bag of gloves, hats and watch caps from under the settee. A khaki bag with brass grommets and a denim patch, it was more than 40 years old, and its fabric was almost rotten. On its side was written in black ink:

Don Cameron
3676 West 23rd Avenue
Vancouver 8, B.C.

"That old bag," said Lulu.

"Treat it with respect," I said. "That seabag can tell the future."

Acknowledgements

A book like this one rests on the generosity of dozens of people, many of whom are named in the book. In addition, I owe special thanks to the following:

- Novatel Communications and MTT Cellular, for making it possible for us to use an Avante cellular phone on the voyage. I would hate to do another coastal voyage without one. In addition to its uses as a ship-to-shore link, it saved hours of time trudging through villages in the rain, looking for pay phones.

- Leigh Robertson of Networx, the Halifax Sony distributor, who again loaned us a professional-quality video camera for the voyage. As both an *aide-memoire* and a promotional tool, videotape has proven invaluable.

- The Ontario Arts Council, which provided a small grant to buy me time to work on the manuscript.

- Alex Tilley and Tilley Endurables, who make the best voyaging clothing I know, and whose hats consistently attract the attention of people you really would like to meet.

- Graham MacKay and Mike Pearson of the Land Registration and Information Service, who produced—in an eyeblink, it seems—the map which appears at the front of the book.

- My sister-in-law Stevie Cameron, and Stephen White of the Centre d'Etudes Acadiennes at the Université de Moncton, for invaluable help in chasing down information.

Credits

Poem entitled "The Profile of Africa" by Maxine Tynes, which appears on page 88–89, is reprinted with permission of the author.

Lyrics from "Sweet Georgia Brown" by Maceo Pinkard, Ben Bernie, Kenneth Casey, Sr. reprinted on pages 118 and 133 by permission of Bienstock Publishing Company on behalf of Redwood Music Ltd. and © 1925 Warner Bros. Inc. (ASCAP) Renewed, All Rights Reserved.

Excerpt from poem by Leon Berrouard, which appears on pages 183–4, is reprinted with permission of the author.

Poetry excerpt which appears on page 184 is from "Dig Up My Heart," *Selected Poems* by Milton Acorn. Used by permission of the Canadian Publishers, McClelland & Stewart, Toronto.

Poem by John Smith, which appears on page 184, is reprinted with permission of the author.

Excerpts by Antonine Maillet which appear in the chapter entitled "*Tintamarre*, with Mischievous Mackerels" are from her work entitled *La Sagouine*. Every effort has been made to obtain permission from the applicable copyright holder. Such holder is asked to contact the publisher.

Quote from *Sea of Slaughter* by Farley Mowat which appears on page 238, is reprinted with permission of the author.

The accommodations plan of *Silversark* which appears on page xiii was prepared by David Montle.